WITH LIBERTY
AND JUSTICE
FOR ALL

WITH LIBERTY AND JUSTICE FOR ALL

A Life Spent Protecting the Right to Choose

KATE MICHELMAN

To Tracie —
With much appreciation —
Kate Michelman
January 2006

HUDSON
STREET
PRESS

HUDSON STREET PRESS
Published by Penguin Group
Penguin Group (USA) Inc., 375 Hudson Street, New York, New York 10014, U.S.A.
Penguin Group (Canada), 90 Eglinton Avenue East, Suite 700, Toronto, Ontario,
Canada M4P 2Y3 (a division of Pearson Penguin Canada Inc.)
Penguin Books Ltd., 80 Strand, London WC2R 0RL, England
Penguin Ireland, 25 St. Stephen's Green, Dublin 2, Ireland
(a division of Penguin Books Ltd.)
Penguin Group (Australia), 250 Camberwell Road, Camberwell, Victoria 3124, Australia
(a division of Pearson Australia Group Pty. Ltd.)
Penguin Books India Pvt. Ltd., 11 Community Centre, Panchsheel Park,
New Delhi – 110 017, India
Penguin Books (NZ), cnr Airborne and Rosedale Roads, Albany, Auckland 1310,
New Zealand (a division of Pearson New Zealand Ltd.)
Penguin Books (South Africa) (Pty.) Ltd., 24 Sturdee Avenue, Rosebank,
Johannesburg 2196, South Africa

Penguin Books Ltd., Registered Offices: 80 Strand, London WC2R 0RL, England

First published by Hudson Street Press, a member of Penguin Group (USA) Inc.

First Printing, December 2005

10 9 8 7 6 5 4 3 2 1

Copyright © Kate Michelman, 2005
All rights reserved

Photo credits: Photos 1–3 and 23 courtesy of Kate Michelman. Photos 4–9, 11–15, 21, and 22
copyright © NARAL Pro-Choice America. Photo 10 courtesy of Justin Lane, *New York
Times*. Photos 16–20 copyright © 2004 ImageLinkPhoto.com and G. Chesman.

REGISTERED TRADEMARK—MARCA REGISTRADA

HUDSON
STREET
PRESS

CIP data is available.
ISBN 1-59463-006-2

Printed in the United States of America
Set in Goudy

For Fred, Lisa, Tasha, and Anya

ACKNOWLEDGMENTS

THIS BOOK, LIKE MY CAREER, REFLECTS THE CONTRIBUTIONS of countless people to whom I can never adequately express my thanks.

I am especially grateful to Laureen Rowland, whose patience and support were exceeded only by the personal passion with which she has guided this project, and to Greg Weiner, whose sensibility and patience were both an inspiration and a pleasure. Many people helped with research or shared their own recollections, including Alex Baumgartner, Jo Blum, Donna Crane, Lauren Gaum, Allison Herwitt, Dawn Johnsen, Stephanie Kushner, Gloria Totten, and Marcy Wilder. Harrison Hickman and James Wagoner provided, as always, valuable advice and treasured friendship. There are many others without whom this book would not have been possible, including Flip Brophy, Renee Smith-Taylor, Ty Tisinger and Janna Paschal, as well as Candy Cox and her team at DDB Bass & Howes. I am especially grateful to NARAL Pro-Choice America, and its president Nancy Keenan, for supporting this project and allowing me to draw upon their always illuminating research, publications, and other materials. I would also like to thank all those whose support, large and small, has made my work possible. Above all, my gratitude to my family, for their support in this endeavor is, as in all matters, endless.

Chapter One

———

THE ROOM WAS STERILE, SPARSELY DECORATED—THE ONLY furniture, a rectangular table. A fluorescent light hung from the ceiling.

I sat on one side of the table, staring at four suited men who stared coldly back. One of them, clearly in charge of the proceedings, sat at the table's head.

The questions began.

Did I dress my children each morning?

Was I capable of feeding them?

What kind of sex life did my husband and I have?

Their interrogation, probing the most intimate details of my personal and family life, was humiliating, but not nearly as humiliating as its purpose. In order to make the choice I knew was best for me and my three small daughters, I had to be declared unfit to raise a child. In order to make one of the most morally significant decisions of my life, the government required that I convince these four strangers that I was mentally or emotionally unbalanced. My decision was to have an abortion in America in 1969—three years before *Roe v. Wade* recognized reproductive freedom as a constitutional right.

The interrogation before a state-mandated hospital review board was the most recent in a string of humiliations that had left me feeling as if my life had descended into chaos. A short time earlier, I was a busy, frazzled, happy young mother of three girls— Lisa, five; Tasha, four; and Anya, three. I had married my high-school sweetheart at age twenty. I was a practicing Catholic who accepted the Church's teaching that birth control was a sin. Like many other Catholic wives, I practiced the "natural" means of contraception—the rhythm method—and believed the claim that breast-feeding prevented pregnancy. I exploded every myth. We had three daughters in three years.

Following the birth of Anya, after a particularly difficult labor and delivery, a young doctor came to my hospital room to talk with me about birth control. He seemed uncomfortable as he tried to raise the issue without offending me. I smiled. "Doctor," I said, "you don't have to be delicate. I agree it's time!" I had thought long and hard about using birth control. I finally decided that, for my family, *not* using birth control was simply wrong and irresponsible.

My husband, James (not his real name), and I had recently moved to Pennsylvania, where he had accepted a position as an assistant professor. I was a homemaker. James's career took center stage in our life as a family. I hoped to eventually pursue a career in early childhood development, but my priority was raising our daughters and supporting James's career goals.

Like many women of my generation who made similar choices, I never questioned my role in our marriage. James and I were building a life together, and this sacrifice was what it took. Certainly having three children in three years caused the expected financial and emotional pressures, but, by and large, we were a typical, struggling young couple.

Then, one evening, James didn't come home.

I lay awake the entire night, worried and afraid. I was sure something terrible had happened. Desperate, I called the police and hospital to see whether there had been any accidents reported. There were none. Finally, early the next morning, James walked through the front door unharmed, and announced he was in love with another woman and wanted a divorce.

I was stunned. Waves of pain, fear, shock, anger, and an overwhelming sense of disbelief rocked my world. For hours, I implored him to seek counseling. We had shared too much together, I said. There was too much at stake for him to walk away.

James was immovable; he knew what he wanted to do and was not willing to reconsider. It was not a gradual separation, but a sudden, dramatic break. In an instant, my life changed from that of a typical young mother to complete turmoil. I was devastated, frightened. My self-esteem was destroyed; my identity crushed; my life shattered. I had been rejected by the person I loved. I had no money or job. Our family was disintegrating before my eyes, and I blamed myself.

But the real breaking point was still to come.

A few weeks later, I learned I was pregnant. I was devastated by the news. How could I possibly have another child? How could our family survive? James was gone and was not providing regular financial support. Our situation was desperate. I was now responsible for my daughters' every need—financial, emotional, and physical. There was no way I could care for another baby and still give my children what they deserved. Another child would turn a crisis into a catastrophe.

I felt I had nowhere to turn. One morning, in desperation, I swallowed a bottle of sleeping pills. My next-door neighbor stopped by to visit, discovered me unconscious, and called an ambulance. She saved my life and my family's. I awoke in the hospital, shocked by the reality of what I had done. Later that day, our family doctor stopped by to see me. I told him all that was happening to me and my family—James's leaving, my pregnancy, my worries about my three daughters, and my feeling that my life was no longer worth living. The doctor told me I might qualify for a "therapeutic abortion"—one performed in a hospital rather than a back alley—but that I would need the permission of a hospital review board. It was then that I began to seriously consider the possibility of an abortion.

Before that moment, I had felt so overwhelmed, so unable to go on, that I had not carefully explored my options for dealing with the pregnancy. I knew that I should not have another baby; what I did not know was what I could do about it. The Church's position on abortion was clear. As a married Catholic mother of three, abortion had never entered my mind as a choice I might face in my life.

When I did squarely confront abortion as a possibility, it was a very difficult decision. Personal, moral, and ethical questions pulled me in a number of different directions. Was it morally right to bring another child into my already struggling family? Would it be selfish of me to have an abortion? Would I be doing it just for me? I had to weigh the responsibility I felt for the developing life within me against the moral, material, and practical responsibilities of my daughters' well-being. Religious beliefs mingled with the only complete point of clarity in my thinking: It would be impossible to have another child. While the decision was difficult, in the end, the choice was clear.

I had two options. The first was the "therapeutic" abortion my doctor had mentioned, which, under state law, a hospital review board could approve if they determined I was mentally unstable or medically unfit to continue the pregnancy. The alternative was an illegal back-alley abortion, which terrified me. I had heard stories.

Back-alley abortion meant having a surgical procedure performed by someone of uncertain competence, often in unsafe and unsanitary conditions, probably without anesthesia.

The choice was straightforward. I opted to submit to the review board, sacrificing my dignity, although I obtained the phone number of an illegal abortionist as a last resort.

That decision led to the hospital conference room and the battery of humiliating questions. Each of us—the doctors on one side of the table and I on the other—played our respective roles. Even though I was caring for my daughters under the most difficult of conditions and making this very decision for their sake, I knew I could have the abortion only if the doctors decided I was unfit to raise a child. It did not occur to me then that being declared unfit to have another baby could have been used to take away the children I did have. Thankfully, I was never threatened with that possibility, but I learned later that other women were.

The purpose of the entire process was to find me incompetent and inadequate, and that was exactly how I felt as the meeting concluded. The doctors told me I would have to return the next week for another meeting at which they would deliver their decision. In the interim I felt completely helpless; these men held my fate and my family's in their hands. I worried terribly about what I would do if they turned me down.

At the second meeting, they peppered me with more questions. The fact that they had not been convinced by our first meeting made me anxious. Waiting had already been very difficult, but the clock on my pregnancy was also ticking. Physically or emotionally, there was no more time for delay.

After about forty-five minutes, one of the doctors addressed me: "We have considered your case carefully and have decided you may have the abortion."

I felt like a child who was obliged to ask a parent for permission, but, above all, I felt relief. A few days later, I arranged for a friend to look after my daughters and checked into the hospital. I felt sad, abandoned, and completely alone. I had not told anyone that I was having an abortion, not even the friend who was watching the girls. I knew that ending the pregnancy was the right thing to do, but I also knew that society condemned my choice.

A nurse took me to a room and handed me a hospital gown. A short time later, the nurse returned to the room, clipboard in hand. She looked over the paperwork it held.

"Are you divorced yet?" she asked.

"No," I replied. The divorce process had become complicated by the issue of financial support.

"We forgot to tell you about a requirement," she said, politely but matter-of-factly. "You must have your husband's written permission before you can have this procedure." I was furious that the hospital staff, having probed every minute detail of my personal life, had failed to mention this until I had already been admitted and prepared for the abortion. I was even more outraged at the prospect of humiliating myself by asking the man who had just abandoned my daughters and me for permission to do what was necessary to hold our family together.

"This is ridiculous! I don't even know where he is!" I said. But there was no point in protesting. State law required me to have his permission. The nurse handed me a form for James to sign.

I got up, put my clothes back on, and went home. A couple of days later, James and I arranged to meet. Seeing him under any circumstances, much less these, was difficult. I handed him the form, he signed it, and I left. Our meeting had all the warmth of a business transaction.

A few days later, I had the abortion. The experience of my family falling apart, submitting to the humiliation of the review board, and having to obtain James's permission stands out as one of the most traumatic of my life. But I have never, not once, questioned my choice to have that abortion. It was a difficult decision but I knew it was the right one for my family—the people I cherished above all else in the world. And it was their needs that were foremost in my mind when I made my choice. For my daughters and me, a new and better life was now possible.

I do not tell my story because it is unique. On the contrary, I share it because it is so common. Millions of women in varying circumstances suffered the indignities and dangers of illegal pre–*Roe v. Wade* abortions And yet, incredibly, America is on the brink of subjecting women to this tragic reality once more.

Roe v. Wade and a woman's right to choose are in grave danger—a case originally decided by a 7–2 margin in the Supreme Court is now hanging on by a bare majority, and a steady stream of court cases has gradually but seriously weakened *Roe*'s protections. Presented with the historic rarity of two simultaneous vacancies—including the Chief Justice's seat—President Bush has moved to shift the Court dramatically to the right. His appointments nearly ensure that *Roe*'s protections will be eviscerated. The Roberts Court may become as influential in history as the Warren Court—except for one critical distinction: The Warren Court expanded rights; the legacy of the Roberts Court may very well be curtailing them. Given the likelihood of more vacancies, *Roe* itself is in grave danger. Without *Roe*, women will once again live at the whim of politicians, their rights and choices ebbing and flowing with the tide of every election cycle in every state.

In a nationwide poll conducted by Greenberg Quinlan Rosner Research Inc. in early 2003, 80 percent of Americans agreed that the choice about whether or not to have an abortion should be made by a woman and her doctor, not by the government. Many people are tempted to believe that the right to choose could never be taken away. But President Bush has already signed the first federal ban on abortion, abandoned America's commitment to family planning around the world, propagated myths about abortion, and worked to restrict sex education. He has declared that all children should be welcome and protected, yet done nothing to address the grave crises of health care and child care that continue to seriously afflict our families.

Without *Roe* in place, the Center for Reproductive Rights estimates that twenty states would likely ban abortion altogether and another ten would enact severe restrictions. Tens of millions of women who live in those states are at risk—not just of a ban on abortion but also of losing access to birth control methods, such as the IUD and emergency contraception, that anti-choice legislators regard as abortifacients. Even if they are illegal and unsafe, history tells us these women will have abortions if they know that doing so is right for themselves and their families, jeopardizing their health and their lives.

Already, anti-choice legislators who control our national government and many of the statehouses are steadily chipping away at a woman's right to choose. Since 1995, state legislatures have enacted more than four hundred restrictions on reproductive rights. These restrictions do everything from imposing arbitrary waiting periods on women seeking abortions to harassing doctors who provide abortions with random and needless regulations.

This book is an urgent wake-up call to American women, and to all those who care about women's rights and personal privacy, to defend their freedom in what is surely, in President Kennedy's words, "its hour of maximum danger." It is a direct challenge to the right wing's caricature of women as amoral creatures who are incapable of exercising moral judgment or who choose abortion for casual reasons. Above all, it is a plea to every American to confront—not as a matter of hypothetical debate, but as a real, looming, imminent possibility—the consequences for our sisters, daughters, wives, friends, and mothers of being denied the right to make their own reproductive choices. In addition to a plea, it presents a possibility: a nation of people who have the means to make deliberate and informed choices about their sexual and reproductive lives, a nation where abortion is legal but far less necessary.

In the three decades since *Roe* was decided, an entire generation of American women has been born and grown up without the experience of illegal abortion. A twenty-seven-year-old woman today was not yet born when I, as a twenty-seven-year-old young mother, underwent an abortion in pre-*Roe* America. Many of these young women are inspired and passionate activists, but many others do not perceive a threat because they have never lived in a world that women my age experienced.

For too long, many Americans have clung to the belief that the debate about reproductive rights was an abstraction, that no matter what the politicians did, the courts would safeguard the right to choose. But while Americans were lulled into complacency by the belief that their right to make private medical choices was forever enshrined in the Constitution, the anti-choice movement quietly set about to destroy it. By electing three presidents—Ronald Reagan, George H. W. Bush, and George W. Bush—they have successfully packed the federal courts with anti-choice judges. From the Oval Office to local hospital boards, they have permeated the fabric of our social and political institutions with anti-choice decision-makers. A growing number of anti-choice pharmacists are refusing to dispense methods of contraception ranging from condoms to birth control pills. The more extreme elements of the anti-choice movement have terrorized abortion providers, clinics, and patients. One extremist has posted Web cams outside abortion clinics and broadcast pictures of women going in and out of them over the Internet. Another has posted an online hit list of medical professionals who provide abortions. Innocent health care providers have been killed simply because they provided women with the medical services they needed.

With the anti-choice political and legal infrastructure in place, with so many clinics literally terrorized out of existence so that abortion is often unavailable even where it is legal, the stage is set for an end to the right to choose and our right to personal privacy. Already, opponents of abortion have succeeded in taking away reproductive rights piece by piece so that, on the eve of *Roe*'s potential extinction, American women have fewer rights than their mothers did on the day the decision was handed down. The anti-choice movement needs only the last characters waiting in the wings: the one or two anti-choice justices whose votes will eviscerate or overturn *Roe*.

The right to choose is about more—far more—than the right to a safe and legal abortion, as important as that right is. Reproductive choice is fundamental and central to women's health, autonomy, and equality. Without the ability to control her reproductive life, from birth control to childbirth to abortion, a woman is unable to enjoy many of the rights our nation guarantees. She has no autonomy. She cannot pursue her dreams as she defines them. Whatever is important to her—whether her priority is to get an education, start a job, or tend to her family—could at any moment be derailed by a decision forced upon her by the government. She is a captive of her reproductive function for the totality of her fertile life, a span that can stretch anywhere from thirty to forty years. Her professional, personal, educational, and social lives are dominated by that fact. A woman who cannot control her reproductive life becomes defined by her capacity to reproduce rather than by the totality of her character and the contributions she offers society.

For women who are able to choose the timing and circumstances of their pregnancies, motherhood can be what it has been for me: a rich and fulfilling life of challenge, joy, and rewards. But for those who cannot, unintended pregnancy can be tragic—not just for mothers, but for their children as well. Women who become pregnant unintentionally make a wide range of choices for an equally wide range of reasons, but they share one common trait: They face an unexpected crisis. Their determination to be successful mothers is so innate and so strong that they will do what they believe they must, either to provide for their children or to avoid having children for whom they cannot adequately care. Some may call that statement a generalization. But after more than thirty years of working closely with women from all walks of life, I can attest to its authenticity.

And so we must ask: Without the choice of safe and legal abortion, what will women do? Both the experience of pre-*Roe* America and that of many nations around the world where abortion remains illegal today suggest that large numbers of women will resort to the so-called back alley. The back alley is not a relic of history. In countries where abortion is illegal, it is still a harrowing reality, a place where thousands upon thousands of women die every year. Some women will choose adoption, but the fact—a fact that is not likely to change—is that very few actually do.

The decision to have an abortion involves deeply held personal, moral, and ethical beliefs. But another fact is too often forgotten.

The decision to bear a child is an equally profound one. That we treasure children so much is precisely why we must give such careful thought to the circumstances under which we bring them into the world. Even with the best of intentions, we are less prepared to be parents than for almost any other job we undertake. As a society, we claim to value the choice to bear children, yet we provide tragically little of the meaningful, tangible support—such as health care, child care, and social services—required to ensure the best outcomes for families.

In a lifetime devoted to protecting a woman's right to choose, I have met countless women struggling with some of the most important decisions of their lives. Women like the heart patient in Louisiana who was denied Medicaid coverage for an abortion because doctors concluded she had only a 50/50 chance of her pregnancy killing her. This was not enough to overcome the federal prohibition on using Medicaid funds for abortion unless the woman's life is endangered. Or the navy wife who was unable to obtain an abortion in a military hospital even though she was diagnosed with a fast-metastasizing brain tumor and could not start radiation therapy while she was pregnant. As a child-development specialist, I have also worked with hundreds of women struggling heroically to raise their children under the most challenging of circumstances.

I write this book with these women and their children in mind. They have taught me many things over the years. But above all, they have confirmed what I have always known to be true: Women make choices about their reproductive lives thoughtfully and deliberately. They, far better than the government, know what is best for themselves and their families. And that raises the fundamental question at the heart of the controversy over abortion.

Who decides?

Who should make decisions about pregnancy and childbearing? Women or the government?

If we hope to preserve a fundamental, constitutional right that is dangerously imperiled, that is a question Americans must answer—and act upon—with conviction. If we do not act now, a freedom that shapes the course of our lives will be lost for generations of women.

I would have been proud to devote my career to the sole cause of fighting for women's right to control our own lives. But there is even more at stake. The issue is what kind of society we want to build. The debate over reproductive rights is a cauldron for over-heated rhetoric. Individual women and children are often forgotten in the shouting. But when the rhetoric is stripped away, a simple fact remains: Society begins in a single moment—the moment a woman decides to bear a child. How we prepare for that moment determines the kind of society we will become.

This is a book about one woman's choice—my choice—how I came to terms with it, how I came to believe reproductive rights were central to women's and children's well-being, and how we can continue to create and sustain the conditions in which women and children can flourish.

It is also a book about liberty and justice. The liberty to pursue our dreams, the freedom from government interference in the most personal aspects of our lives. And the justice of a society that values and supports every child and respects the rights of every person, no matter who they are, what they believe, or how much money they have.

This is a book about liberty and justice for women. But everyone's rights are at stake. If the government may interfere in the private lives of some of our citizens, everyone's privacy is threatened. If the government bans abortion and forces women to bear children against their will, or if we fail to support and cherish the choice to have a child, the fabric of our society is at risk. The ramifications of a woman's freedom to choose reach far beyond a single issue.

This is a matter of liberty and justice for *all*.

CHAPTER TWO

FTER MY ABORTION, I BEGAN THE LONG JOURNEY OF GET-
ting my family back onto solid ground. The first order of
business was finances. Even before James left, we were barely making ends meet. Academic life was hardly the most lucrative.

Shortly before we settled in Pennsylvania, our family returned
from a stay in Greece, where James completed research for his
Ph.D. However glamorous that might sound, we, in fact, lived the
entire time on a modest graduate school grant of about $4,000. We
could afford little. A washing machine was an expensive extrava-
gance, which meant scrubbing diapers by hand in the bathtub. Our
budget was so tightly scripted that I knew exactly how much elec-
tricity we could afford. Each morning, I read the meter and made
an exact note of how many kilowatt-hours we could use that day.

The year in Greece was an arduous time, but there was also an
element of adventure to our stay. We lived at the foot of a moun-
tain, below a medieval monastery. Every morning, a local woman
rode down on her donkey to sell goat cheese and yogurt, and the
girls loved running out to meet her. We often took trips in our
Volkswagen bus, exploring ancient ruins, as well as taking weekend excursions to nearby countries.

When we moved to Pennsylvania for James's first teaching job, he was earning a very modest salary, but enough at the time to put a down payment on a small house. We looked forward to settling into a comfortable life in academia with our family.

With James's departure, the fragile state of our finances collapsed. All I had was the very little money remaining in the checking account on the day he left.

It was clear from the start that James would not provide much in the way of financial support. He earned little to begin with, and the child support laws were not very favorable to single mothers. It appeared to me that James was focused solely on his own interests, and chief among them was getting a divorce as quickly as possible. What little we owned was in his name, including the (by then) dilapidated bus, which James took, leaving the girls and me without any means of transportation. For a brief period, he paid the mortgage on the house, but eventually, those payments stopped.

Unable to afford the payments, we sold the house and the girls and I moved into a small, rental town house. It took several court appearances before an unsympathetic judge to obtain an order for minimal child support. James's payments were so irregular that I was often forced back into court to ensure compliance with the order. Eventually, I gave up. It was a losing battle, financially, legally, and emotionally. Fighting for scraps from James was not a viable solution to our financial problems. I had already rejected a doctor's advice that I be hospitalized for treatment of blood clots because I did not have health insurance and could not afford the bill. It was quickly becoming clear to me that I could not survive without help. There was no alternative. I had to apply for welfare.

A county welfare office is not exactly designed to lift one's spirits. Ours was a prototypical government space—drab and utilitarian, packed with cluttered desks and unsmiling people doing what one does in a welfare office: waiting. The place reflected my feelings—sad and dreary. I went to the receptionist and whispered the words I had dreaded: "I need to see someone about going on welfare."

I was motioned to a waiting room, where I reflected on the drastic and sudden turn my life had taken. How did I get here? The breathtaking speed with which I fell from the middle class illustrates the vulnerability of women when they become single mothers. A caseworker handed me the paperwork I was required to fill out in order to prove my need. The review of my application, which resembled an audit, took several weeks. The waiting seemed interminable—waiting to be questioned about my assets, or lack thereof, waiting for approval, waiting for checks.

When the paperwork cleared, I qualified for a small monthly stipend, food stamps, and Medicaid. I quickly learned the absurdity of myths about welfare. The idea that the benefits are lavish is laughable. So is the notion that people on welfare are lazy and do not deserve public support. I remain grateful that our government provides at least a minimal safety net. As difficult as that time was, welfare was a lifesaver for my family, and we grew stronger through it.

Nothing focuses a family on one another like having no money. There are no trips to the movies, shopping expeditions, or vacations. Instead, we had walks in the country, family reading time, and talks over dinner. Trips to the grocery store, as hard as they seemed at the time, were a source of special experiences. Without a car, the four of us walked about a mile to the market, with one of the girls inevitably finding something—a pile of leaves, a bug on the sidewalk, a puddle, a flower—to explore. Our shopping was carefully calibrated. We never bought more at one time than the four of us could carry back home.

We survived, but I lay awake at night worrying that we were a single financial setback away from catastrophe, and there was no one we could count on for help. Once, I went into the local five-and-dime and asked to open a small charge account to buy some school supplies. The cashier asked a handful of cursory questions and told me point-blank that I did not qualify. I took my case to the store manager. My credit was excellent. James and I may not have had much money but we always paid our bills on time. "Please believe me," I insisted. "I'm good for this tiny amount."

His reply was equally insistent: "No." The reason, he admitted, was that I was unmarried. I was incredulous. How could I ever be self-sufficient if I could not even get a charge account at a five-and-dime?

As soon as I was able, I looked for work. A friend told me about a part-time job in the Rare Books Room of the local university library. I applied and was hired. The income didn't quite replace the small stipend I was getting on welfare, and I lost my health coverage, too. As worrisome as that was, I felt more independent and useful.

A few months after I took the position, a young professor of French and French-African Literature named Fred Michelman came in looking for a rare eighteenth-century book. I probably did not give him a second thought. The last thing on my mind was a relationship. I had my hands full with a job and my daughters, and I was not yet prepared to place my trust in anyone again. Emotional vulnerability was too dangerous, and I had decided I would never again become dependent on another person.

Thankfully, though, Fred did give our encounter a second thought—enough of one to inquire about me through a mutual friend. Our relationship began slowly. In addition to my own issues about trust, I had my daughters to think about. Anyone who entered my life had to be carefully screened by how he interacted with them. Fred, a quiet, gentle man, passed the test with flying colors. Almost immediately the girls fell in love with him. So, in time, did I. We were married in 1972.

I believed Fred would be a good husband, but I never imagined how much he could mean to the girls. To begin with, *any* man who could fit in with my bunch had to be someone special. Lisa, our oldest, was introspective, an expressive girl who loved to read and be read to. Tasha was an intensely curious child, full of life, the type to whom everything—from an insect on the sidewalk to a plant on a neighbor's windowsill—was a subject for excitement. Anya was an imaginative and artistic little girl, often teaming up with Tasha to perform plays—rearranging the furniture to make stage scenes, fishing through old clothes for costumes. Every night, we read together, and Fred fit right into the scene. Before long, the girls were squabbling over who got to sit in his lap when we piled onto the couch to read our nightly selections from books like *The Hobbit, A Wrinkle in Time,* or *The Secret Garden.*

The girls and I spent every moment together. Fred had little privacy, which was difficult for him. He was forty years old when we met, ten years older than I, and had no children, so the change in his life was dramatic. Eventually, we refurbished a study for Fred adjacent to the house so he would have a private retreat from the intensity of our family life. The adjustment was a challenge for us all. A new father might have been difficult for the girls to accept. But Fred won them over with such exotic novelties as playing board games, grilling hamburgers outdoors, and posing bedtime riddles. Fred provided dependability, structure, and, most of all, gentle, calm, and unqualified love.

James was still occasionally present in the girls' lives then, and Fred and I were careful not to make them feel as though their biological father was being replaced. At first, they called him "Fred," but gradually, of their own accord, they started calling him "Dad." By the tender power of his example, Fred demonstrated that a father is defined by more than biology. Fathers protect their children, not just physically, but emotionally; cheer for their triumphs; encourage and challenge and love, endlessly, unconditionally, every day. By that measure, Fred was as fine a father any three little girls could ever have.

Later that year, we moved to Gettysburg, where Fred had an assistant professorship in the Department of French at Gettysburg College. We rented a home on the Gettysburg battlefield on a ridge overlooking the town. We were finally settling in as a family.

Back then, Fred and I began a ritual that we've kept up for more than thirty years. Every day, we read the *New York Times* together. Fred would pick up a copy at the college bookstore and bring it home in the afternoon. On January 23, a headline at the top of the front page announced: LYNDON JOHNSON, 36TH PRESIDENT, IS DEAD; WAS ARCHITECT OF "GREAT SOCIETY" PROGRAM. Just under it, albeit in smaller type, another headline caught my eye.

High Court Rules Abortion Legal the First 3 Months

Washington, Jan. 22—The Supreme Court overruled today all state laws that prohibit or restrict a woman's right to obtain an abortion during her first three months of pregnancy. . . .

[T]he plaintiffs had based their protest on an assertion that state laws limiting the availability of abortion had circumscribed rights and freedoms guaranteed them by the Constitution: due process of law, equal protection of the laws, freedom of action and a particular privacy involving a personal and family matter. . . .

I burst into tears. Surprised and concerned, Fred asked what was wrong. For the first time, I told him my story. It may seem shocking today that I had not told him before, but it was simply not something I talked about. Most women who underwent abortions before 1973 would understand why. The law punished us for a choice we deemed right for ourselves and our families. Society judged us harshly.

But Fred did not. He was understanding, loving, and respectful of my decision. Now, in a case involving an anonymous woman known in the courts as Roe and a Texas prosecutor named Wade, Justice Harry Blackmun wrote for a 7–2 majority that the constitutionally protected right of privacy guaranteed women the freedom to make decisions about abortion without the permission or interference of the state.

I had not heard of the case before that day, but I knew immediately what it meant. Women would no longer have to endure the shame and humiliation society heaped on them for exercising personal responsibility. If the Supreme Court said abortion was a private matter and a constitutional right, society's condemnation might well end.

I wrote to Justice Blackmun to express my appreciation and describe what his ruling meant to me. More than twenty years later, I met him after his retirement from the Court. Justice Blackmun was a humble person with extraordinary integrity, enormous character, a fine mind, and an empathetic sensibility. All this was contained in a compact frame that grew frail as he gave up the rest he deserved in his last years to serve on the Court until he could be replaced by a president who shared his values.

I asked whether he remembered my letter in 1973. Justice Blackmun looked up from beneath his trademark bushy brows and broke out in a self-deprecating grin.

"Kate," he said, "I got a lot of letters back then, and not very many of them were nice."

CHAPTER THREE

AFTER WE MOVED TO GETTYSBURG, I BRIEFLY WORKED FOR Lutheran Social Services before being named director of the local Easter Seals Society, which provided support for children and adults with disabilities. In 1975, the local Community Action Agency hired me to run the "Wee Care" Day Care Center and then to coordinate all their early childhood services, including a local Head Start program. My career in early childhood development was under way.

Not long after I started work with the day care program, Fred and I bought our first house, a pre–Civil War era inn a few miles outside Gettysburg. The girls were all in school. Lisa, in seventh grade, was an accomplished flute player whom we often ferried to Baltimore on weekends to study at the Peabody Institute of Music. Tasha, a sixth-grader, had developed a passion for horses. Anya was the soccer and field-hockey star of her fifth-grade class. Our weekends alternated between trips to Baltimore, Tasha's horse competitions, and Anya's games.

I had long been interested in children's development, which was a focus of my undergraduate studies in developmental psychology. I have always had an intense fascination with babies and young children. Perhaps my interest stems from their vulnerability and innocence, coupled with the unfolding of their amazing developmental journey. My study in this area was driven by an intense interest in shaping environmental conditions to foster positive and healthy growth in children. I wanted to understand human development, what factors contributed constructively to that process, and what forces inhibited it.

My experience as a single mother was especially important training for my career. My daughters had suffered from the breakup of our family, and I understood the impact that the stresses I'd faced had on them. I wanted to devote my career to helping both parents and children cope with these kinds of challenges. As director of the day care center, I was responsible for developing curricula, training teachers, and managing the organization. One of my favorite activities was reading to the children. They were delighted when I joined them as they chose a book for story time, which often involved a delicate process of negotiation. Most of them called me Kate. (I know that many people object to a first-name relationship between children and adults, especially in an educational setting. Many prefer a more formal mode of address, but I am not among them. For me, intimacy and openness are essential to authentic contact with people, particularly children. Such was the topic of a friendly family scuffle that took place in the middle of a restaurant in 1991, when my oldest daughter, Lisa, announced she was pregnant for the first time.

"What do you want the baby to call you?" one of my daughters asked.

"Kate," I replied. It was the first thing that occurred to me.

"Mom," Lisa chided, "you just don't want to face the idea of being old enough to be a grandmother."

"No," I insisted, "I just don't relate to 'Grandma.' I'm not 'Grandma.' I'm 'Kate.' "

Five grandchildren later, the compromise we struck—Grandma Kate—still holds.)

Directing the center was a demanding job, but I made time to be personally involved in the program and work with the children whenever I could. I loved reading to them because it is one of the most intimate and important activities in a child's life. I read aloud with my own children nearly every night of their lives from infancy well into adolescence, all of us piled in a heap on the couch or my bed. They got so big that one night the bed collapsed right in the middle of *Watership Down*.

Watching children react to the sound of a voice, the rhythms of a story, the stirring of their imagination, is almost magical. At the day care center, I always made a point of sitting on the floor with them as I read. We made certain the classes were small enough that every child could gather in closely. As I read, I would often stop and elaborate on the story, asking the children what characters they liked best and why. Even the simplest of stories opened a valuable window into their lives. *Goodnight Moon*, a favorite, provided a chance to invite the children to say goodnight to those people and things important to them. Their choices were usually good for a few giggles and, if you listened carefully, you could also glean important insight into their psyches.

Providing a safe, secure, and developmentally appropriate environment for these children was important work, and I loved it. I have always felt strongly that parents should have confidence that their children are in high-quality child care programs with highly qualified personnel. This is one of the most formative periods of a child's life, and that is exactly why society must invest in quality child care. Yet still today, more than three decades after I began working in the field, many parents are still forced to leave their children alone or in substandard programs because they cannot find or afford quality child care.

I often worked with children with developmental disabilities, many of them from socially and economically disadvantaged environments. No matter their situation, they shared a common need—specialized early intervention to address developmental delays or learning disabilities. Generally, the earlier a developmental problem is identified and addressed, the more successful the child's experience will be.

Getting the services each child needed was a challenge, and I grew increasingly frustrated with the fragmented approach to serving these children and their families. Often, a single child with developmental problems would see a speech therapist, a developmental specialist, a physician, a psychologist, a social worker, and countless other service providers. They were usually in different locations and rarely worked together to improve the child's treatment program, much less the child's experience in the one place he or she spent the most time: the home. Each specialist focused on a particular area of development rather than on the whole child. By the time these children reached the first grade, they were often stigmatized and labeled as problem children—and even more tragic, the early childhood years when intervention would have been most effective had been lost.

I decided to design a comprehensive approach that would be both interdisciplinary and multidisciplinary. We would treat the whole child as well as the discrete developmental disabilities, and do so in one location. In 1978, with help from the Pennsylvania Department of Health and Welfare and the Bureau of Education for the Handicapped, Adams County Early Childhood Services—ECS, as it came to be known—was born.

ECS launched in the fall of that year. Over the summer, I spent several days each week in Philadelphia at the Benjamin Franklin Research Institute, whose facilities I used to train our staff. The training required an enormous commitment from Fred, who agreed to spend his summer caring for the girls. Lisa and Tasha had moved on to high school and Anya was in the eighth grade. Looking after the girls was commitment enough, but Fred also had to take charge of their extensive—and, to him, often irksome—menagerie of pets. At various times, we had a horse, ducks, turtles, a goat, dogs, and a bird, who was quickly dispatched by one of our cats. By summer's end, Fred was ready for me to be home, and I was eager to return so I could launch Early Childhood Services.

Every child at ECS had an individualized developmental treatment plan. We worked with the Department of Psychiatry at Hershey Medical School to coordinate care. The program provided most of the services the children and their families needed—psychiatry, educational and speech therapy, psychology, social work, family therapy, and more. We emphasized intensive intervention, so we assigned three therapeutic teachers to every class of ten children. Classrooms were equipped with one-way-vision glass so parents, specialists, and psychiatric interns could observe children interacting with teachers and one another. Our goal was to create an environment that would stimulate development and self-esteem while providing security and confidence.

Each of these children was a part of my life. I came to know every one of them—their strengths, their vulnerabilities, their desires, their struggles—as if they were my own. Many of the children were starved for self-confidence and lacked even a minimal sense of their own value. The cases of abused children were the most heart-wrenching. They had so little self-esteem that they would respond to positive feedback by misbehaving, as if to prove that everything negative they believed about themselves was true. Many of the children suffered classic hyperactivity, an inability to focus and concentrate. Sometimes, their greatest accomplishment was just being able to sit through a book. Most of the children progressed in tiny, delicate steps, but each step was a major accomplishment.

Parents were always closely involved in our programs. We brought them into the classroom and modeled appropriate parent/child interaction. I was struck by how often parents were treated as afterthoughts rather than as integral parts of their children's progress. Children thrive best in dependable family units. That need not mean a "traditional" nuclear family. The key is an environment that is stable, secure, predictable, and reassuring so that children can feel safe and develop the self-confidence to form healthy relationships and take risks. Providing that environment and understanding children's development are enormously complicated and important challenges, yet our society provides less training for this most critical of all jobs—parenting—than for virtually any other undertaking in life.

In many ways, I saw my own struggles in these parents' lives. Like many of them, I knew what it was like to raise children completely alone, with no financial security, while coping with difficult emotional issues myself. I knew they wanted to be good parents, but they faced enormous hurdles. Some were single mothers; most were barely surviving; and many were simply overwhelmed with keeping body and soul together. For any parent, especially one who is single and poor, parenting is an overwhelming responsibility that is only made harder by having a child with emotional or developmental problems. Our program helped parents learn to manage and foster their children's development and understand the conditions that promote emotional health. Most of all, it helped them gain more confidence in their parenting skills.

As I worked with these mothers, I noticed a pattern in their lives. Many lacked even the most basic reproductive health care. They exercised little or no control over the circumstances under which they became pregnant and brought children into the world. Some were in a position to raise more children, but many were not. They were already stretched to the limit personally, socially, and financially.

I was increasingly troubled by how little information many women had, how little control they felt they had over their lives, and how many barriers stood in the way of even the most informed parent. Some had to choose between putting food on the table for their children and obtaining birth control. Many measured their self-worth by how a man felt about or treated them. They were prey to many myths, such as the canard that the Pill caused cancer.

The more I worked with these women, the more profoundly I realized the impact of informed and deliberate reproductive choices on the emotional health of women and children and the stability of families. This growing insight into my own experiences, along with my work with mothers and children, forged a keen understanding of how reproductive choices, or the lack of them, permeate the fabric of a woman's life.

These interests were combining in my consciousness when I saw an ad in the local newspaper: WANTED. EXECUTIVE DIRECTOR. FAMILY PLANNING SERVICES.

Chapter Four

A WAVE OF CELEBRATION SWEPT THE BUILDING. AS THE NEWS spread, everyone leapt to their feet and cheered. The Clarks (not their real names) were expecting. From the exuberance that erupted at Family Planning Services—where I had been named executive director—it was obvious that something wonderful had occurred.

For two years, we had worked with the Clarks, a couple in their midthirties, as they struggled with fertility problems. Like so many couples in similar situations, the Clarks vacillated between disappointment and exhilaration. During my tenure at Family Planning Services, only a few couples were able to conceive. Each cycle of treatment offered promise, only to end in frustration. Then the process would begin again with no guarantee of success. The Clarks were close to abandoning fertility treatment and beginning adoption proceedings when they came in one day for the results of a routine pregnancy test. For nearly two years, those tests had brought disappointment. This time, the result—quite unexpectedly—was positive.

The clinic was in Harrisburg, Pennsylvania, a forty-five-minute drive from Gettysburg. Lisa, who graduated from high school a year early, was attending Gettysburg College, where she lived on campus. Tasha's restless energy and creativity made a conventional educational setting difficult for her, so we enrolled her in a Quaker boarding school near Philadelphia for the last two years of high school. The school was smaller, with more personal attention from teachers, and students were given the freedom to learn in the style that worked best for them. Tasha flourished, writing short stories and poetry and studying languages and Eastern philosophy. She graduated as valedictorian of her class. Only Anya was living with Fred and me at home, so we transferred her to a high school in Harrisburg, where I drove her each morning on my way to work. She was socially outgoing, still a star athlete and a top student as well. Somehow she managed to balance her studies with a busy so-cial schedule as well as field-hockey and softball games.

Among the important decisions I made as executive director of Family Planning Services was to affiliate with Planned Parenthood Federation of America. My goal was to elevate the organization's presence in the community, establish standards of excellence in medical care, and become a forceful advocate of women's rights and health. I approached the job with a simple but powerful guid-ing belief. The right to choose whether, when, and under what cir-cumstances to bear a child was fundamental to women's freedom and equality and the health of families. Abortion was only one of the reproductive choices protected by the Constitution and guar-anteed by *Roe*. I believed *Roe*'s ultimate promise was that women would have both the right to choose and the meaningful ability to act on their choices free of legal, economic, or social barriers. Re-productive choice meant the right not to become pregnant, the right to end a pregnancy, or the right to bear a child, and for that reason, I saw fertility treatment as a core service of Tri-County Planned Parenthood (our new name).

When I first proposed an infertility program to our board of di-rectors, they were reluctant. The organization had previously provided family planning and routine gynecological services as well as treatment for sexually transmitted diseases. Many on the board believed that infertility fell outside our mission.

"We say we offer 'family planning,'" I insisted. "That should mean every family planning option—including the option to have a child."

It required some effort to convince them that our mission must be to offer or facilitate the full range of reproductive choices, from contraception and abortion to fertility treatments and prenatal care. Some board members wondered about the wisdom of this approach. They assumed they were overseeing a fairly low-key organization that provided a relatively simple, mostly noncontroversial range of services, and I was proposing to cover the full range of reproductive health options.

My first day on the job, a staff member took me on a driving tour of our seven clinics, which primarily served low-income women. I was highly impressed by the quality of the medical services and staff but distressed by the environment in which those services were delivered. Many of the clinics were dilapidated. The furniture was decrepit. The medical staff wore T-shirts and jeans. I worried that women coming into these clinics might feel as though they were not deserving of medical settings comparable to those more prosperous women would expect. I made the same point to our board at their next meeting.

"We should not provide medical services in these settings, and the fact that we serve mostly poor women does not justify the conditions of these clinics. It's an insult to poor women to strive for anything less than what other women would expect." I proposed professionalizing the operation by investing in respectable-looking clinics, new furniture, and lab coats for the medical staff. Some of the staff resisted.

"You have to understand the population we serve," one protested. "If we wear lab coats, the patients won't be able to relate to us."

"Why?" I asked. "Because they're poor they don't expect to be treated with the respect other women expect? How we personally interact with these women is what's important—the compassion and support we convey and the quality of care we provide. Many people are opposed to our work, and they try to characterize us as outside the medical mainstream. If our clinics or our staff look less than what any of us would expect to encounter in our family doctor's office, we will play right into those stereotypes."

We began offering a complete women-centered reproductive health care program. We hired a medical director and found new sites and refurbished others, creating a warm but professional medical atmosphere. For many women we were the sole source of medical care. Our routine screenings often discovered serious problems ranging from high blood pressure to diabetes.

Pregnancy testing was one of our most utilized services. While we treated all kinds of women for all kinds of reasons, most women who requested a pregnancy test were concerned about an unplanned pregnancy. For some, pregnancy was a welcome discovery. For others, it was a crisis. No matter what the situation, our goal was to provide information and help guide women through all the options so they could make the best choices for themselves and their circumstances. If a woman was pregnant unexpectedly, we asked her whether she wanted counseling about her options. If she did, we helped her identify the issues she needed to consider when weighing her decision. Was she married or in a stable relationship? What was her financial situation? Did she have medical insurance? Was her life stable and healthy enough to have a child?

If she wanted to continue the pregnancy, we provided or helped her obtain prenatal care. If she was interested in adoption, we referred her to reputable agencies and worked with her through the process. If she decided on abortion, we facilitated that option as well. No matter what her choice, we worked with a network of partners—

public agencies, doctors, social workers, and others—to enable her to act on her choice in the healthiest, safest, and most dignified manner. We never rendered value judgments on what the woman should do. That was her choice. *That* was *Roe's* ultimate promise.

Many of my memories from that period are more troubling. One day, a nurse practitioner named Deb Reed came to my office appearing worried. Deb was an extraordinary medical professional who developed several programs for us, including clinics that provided testing and treatment for sexually transmitted diseases. She knew more about reproductive health than most gynecologists I encountered, and she was also phenomenally warm, compassionate, and energetic. Our patients loved her. She took me to an examining room where an eleven-year-old girl, referred by a school nurse, was sitting. An examination revealed that she was nearly twenty-eight weeks pregnant. The girl was completely unaware of her condition and had assumed she was merely gaining weight.

I vividly remember her complete ignorance about what was happening to her body. We had to explain the birds and the bees in detail so she could comprehend her situation. She did not understand how she got pregnant, much less what it meant to be in her twenty-eighth week without having had so much as one prenatal visit.

I explained that we had to contact her parents. She resisted at first. "Honey," I said as gently but firmly as I could, "we have to."

Later that afternoon we met with her mother. She was totally overwhelmed by the news, which came as a double shock: first, that her eleven-year-old daughter was pregnant, and second, that she was in her twenty-eighth week. When we learned she had a thirteen-year-old daughter as well, we suggested that she come in for a visit. The thirteen-year-old was pregnant as well, although not nearly as far along as her sister. She knew about her pregnancy but had not told her mother.

Still today, with the media more saturated with sexual imagery than ever before, it is tempting to believe that young girls who are old enough to become pregnant understand at least the most basic biological facts. In truth, they often do not. Nor is the problem limited to young girls. Students in the Pennsylvania college towns who used our clinics were also awash in myths. Some believed they could not become pregnant the first time they had sex. Others believed certain sexual positions would protect them from conception.

Now, as then, society has no uniform, integrated program for educating young people about sexuality beyond the most basic information. The anti-choice movement has waged a concerted and often successful effort to derail comprehensive, age-appropriate sex education. In many cases, they have enacted programs that provide either dangerously limited or blatantly inaccurate information. As a result, young people often obtain their sexual "knowledge" from peers, magazines, or television shows.

In addition to providing health screenings, contraceptive services, and fertility treatments, I also suggested providing abortion services in order to facilitate our overall goal of providing a comprehensive reproductive health program. It was particularly critical to ensure access to abortion for low-income and young women, our primary patient population. I believed we should work to make abortion less necessary, but medically safe abortion must always be available.

Women who chose abortion did so for many reasons, often provoked by conditions beyond their control. Some feared losing their jobs because they were pregnant. Some could not afford child care. Some were stuck in the netherworld between not having a job good enough to provide health insurance and not being poor enough to qualify for Medicaid. Their stories are stark evidence that quality child care, affordable health care, and tough laws against discrimination in the workplace are just as important to reproductive freedom as accessible contraception and abortion.

Other women felt their financial situation too precarious to have a child. Some were teenagers who themselves had been born to teenage mothers and did not want to repeat that experience. For some, pregnancy presented serious health risks. And often, women reached a deeply personal conclusion that they were simply not prepared to be mothers. In my experience, teenagers in particular, for all the ignorance they often display about sex, possess an innate wisdom about whether they can handle the enormous responsibilities of motherhood. No matter what the circumstances, abortion is not a choice any woman deliberately sets out to make.

My primary goal at Planned Parenthood was to deliver a full range of reproductive health services. But I was soon drawn into the world of political activism. From very early in my life, social activism seemed a natural extension of who I was. In high school, I organized a campaign to expose the discriminatory treatment of Hispanic students—children of Mexican farm workers—by several teachers in the high school of the town where we lived. As treasurer of my senior high school class, I bypassed the usual fundraisers for social activities and instead organized to raise money for the farmworkers and their families.

Like many other young adults, the moment I saw the gruesome television images of Sheriff Bull Connor's deputies brutalizing marchers on the bridge at Selma, I decided immediately to head south for a second march, which Martin Luther King Jr. was already planning. It was simply impossible not to do something. I was pregnant at the time, and my father—who never fully understood my activism—thought it was dangerous to return to the scene of such violence. I thought it would be morally irresponsible not to go. While in Selma, I stayed with an African-American family headed by a courageous, dedicated woman. After I returned home, I learned she had lost her job as a housecleaner for having

the audacity to harbor supporters of the march. Upset and outraged, I organized a small amount of financial support and sent
periodic packages of clothing and household items.

In 1963, I joined the March on Washington and was later active in the anti-war movement. For me, all these activities were
about far more than single demonstrations. On a personal level,
they provided an opportunity to express and live my values. On a
larger societal level, they raised consciousness and changed the direction of our nation.

At Planned Parenthood, my immediate political concern was
closer to home: our budget. Anti-choice politicians were constantly attacking our state funding, even for services like family
planning that were, or should have been, noncontroversial. Meanwhile, the national anti-choice movement had picked up steam.
The far right gained legitimacy with the election of Ronald Reagan in 1980, for which they claimed credit—a claim buttressed by
the national press. They adopted a strategy to reverse *Roe* through
a state-by-state, year-by-year, legislature-by-legislature approach.
One of their chief tactics was passing state laws restricting abortion. Under *Roe v. Wade*, the laws were bound to be struck down,
but that was no deterrent. Every law that was challenged in court
was another opportunity to weaken *Roe v. Wade* piece by piece,
case by case, until, finally, they could bring it down. At the same
time, they concentrated on building political power at the grass
roots. Pennsylvania was a key battleground. At the state capitol, I
had a front-row seat to deliberate and aggressive attempts by politicians to dismantle a woman's right to choose.

Once, I sat in the gallery of the State House and listened as a
virulently anti-choice representative railed against contraception
and abortion, likening women to "caged animals" who were captive to their hormones. Some legislators actually opposed outlaw-
ing spousal rape; they could not see how anything a man did to his

wife could be considered a crime. I was astounded by the way legis-lators demeaned and publicly disparaged women, and even more outraged that they paid no political price for doing so.

Public advocacy and grassroots organizing became more impor-tant. It seemed everything was at stake. If we failed to organize, elect pro-choice officials, and make our voices and values heard, women would lose their rights. Organizing became a major focus for our affiliate. Soon I was asked to join the board of directors of Pennsylvania NARAL—an affiliate of the National Abortion Rights Action League.

NARAL's national executive director announced her resigna-tion in the spring of 1984. In a fortuitous coincidence, NARAL hired an executive search firm in Philadelphia to conduct a na-tional search for a new executive director. I assume the fact that the firm was located in Pennsylvania accounts for their knowledge of my work and their interest in speaking with me. Initially, I de-clined an interview, unable to conceive of making a professional leap of that magnitude. The position also required moving to Washington, D.C., where NARAL was headquartered. The girls were in college by now. Lisa had started an M.D./Ph.D. program at the University of Virginia Medical School, but, after two years, de-cided medical research was not her calling and became a lab in-structor at Gettysburg College. Tasha was attending Bard College in New York, and Anya was a student at Goucher College in Mary-land. Fred was teaching French and African literature at Gettys-burg College, where he was now chair of the French department. Even though my daughters had begun their adult lives, my family, my home, and my heart remained in Pennsylvania.

That night, I told Fred I had turned the recruiter down.

"Why?" he asked. "You'd be terrific at that job."

That summer, the headhunter called again. "Just come to Phila-delphia and have lunch with me," she insisted. "We'll just talk.

What have you got to lose?" I couldn't argue with that, so I got on a train. Over a long lunch, she persuaded me to consider the job seriously, and my view of the challenges facing the pro-choice movement intrigued her as well.

"We are losing ground on the issue," I said. "We are being increasingly marginalized. Pro-choice values aren't well understood. We are labeled as pro-abortion and our message often sounds strident and harsh. The press paints us as extreme. The paramount challenge for the movement is to position the issue in the mainstream. That's the only way to ensure our support is broad and deep enough to resist attacks. And even more important, that's where the issue belongs. It is about women's bodies, but also so much more. And it certainly is about more than just one medical procedure. Our nation's laws and policies must value women's lives and respect their choices.

"We need to explain that we value childbearing. Women who choose motherhood are being left out of the discussion. I was a struggling young mother, and the woman's movement, as portrayed by the media, did not seem to speak to me or my experiences. We should be talking not only about women's rights, but also about healthy children and families. Until we start communicating in those terms, we cannot build a mainstream movement."

As we talked, my interest in the position intensified. My personal experience with abortion in 1969 had shaped my conviction that the right to choose was fundamental to women's lives and health. Without it, women could not achieve autonomy or equality. And I increasingly believed politics was the key battleground for protecting that freedom.

NARAL seemed to connect the dots. It was a place from which I could affect the lives of women across the country. My reluctance gave way to excitement. By the time the January snows were falling in 1985, I was unpacking at my new desk in Washington.

CHAPTER FIVE

———

THE TRANSITION TO LIVING IN WASHINGTON WAS MORE DIF-
ficult than Fred and I anticipated. Fred remained in Gettysburg to continue teaching, which meant we only saw each other
on weekends. Initially, we alternated weekends traveling between
Gettysburg and Washington, but after long and exhausting weeks,
the commute was draining. And soon, even our weekends together
became rare as I traveled the country giving speeches, meeting
with NARAL's affiliates and activists and introducing myself to financial supporters. As many as three or four weeks could elapse in
which Fred and I would not see one another. Neither of us expected living apart to be easy, but we had hoped that nightly telephone calls would at least engender the closeness and emotional
support on which we both depended. No matter how skilled we
became at long-distance telephone calls, there was no substitute
for coming home to someone who was always there for you.

I also missed being close to my daughters. Lisa still taught at
Gettysburg College, so I saw her only on weekend visits. Tasha was
living in the Hudson Valley of New York, where she worked as a
horse trainer. But not long after I moved to Washington, my youngest daughter, Anya, graduated from college and began working in
the Capitol Hill office of Senator Barbara Mikulski. We saw each

other as much as possible, which helped both of us adjust to living in Washington.

When I assumed leadership of NARAL, the organization was facing serious internal challenges at exactly the time that the religious right was ascending. Ronald Reagan, a staunch opponent of a woman's right to choose, had just been elected to a second term and was at the height of his power and popularity. NARAL needed stronger financial management and sharper organizational focus. The days were long and intense, and I had few personal friends or allies in Washington.

Moreover, leading a national organization was a challenge whose scale vastly exceeded any I had confronted before, a fact of which I was reminded when—during my first month on the job— I was asked to make my first national television appearance: an interview on CNN on the anniversary of *Roe v. Wade.*

I had appeared on local television before, but never before a national audience or in a format of this nature. The segment was an interview alongside Nellie Grey, a zealous anti-choice activist who leads an annual anti-choice march in Washington on *Roe's* anniversary. I was anxious about appearing on national television knowing that most pro-choice activists from around the country would be seeing and hearing me for the first time. As we were questioned by an interviewer in Atlanta, Grey and I were sandwiched so close together in the Washington studio that our bodies were touching. Grey, whom I had never met before, seemed to bristle with hostility. Her answer to every question appeared antagonistic and uncompromising. The interviewer allowed her to interrupt me repeatedly.

I was unsure of how to respond. Public confrontation was antithetical to my personal style and approach. Most important, it was counterproductive to civil discourse. In retrospect it seems naïve, but I had expected to engage in a constructive dialogue in which Grey and I would make our points forcefully but respectfully. As I gained more experience, I learned to ignore such hostility and instead focus on conveying my own message. But at the time, I was unnerved. At one point, I simply placed my hand on Grey's arm and said, "It's okay, you really don't have to be so angry." It was as close as I came to a memorable sound bite for some time.

I devoted most of my first two years at NARAL to the organization's internal needs: strategic and financial planning, board and staff development, and fund-raising. Then, in July 1987, President Reagan's nomination of Robert Bork to the Supreme Court plunged the issue of a woman's right to choose into a major crisis. Reagan was already moving the judiciary rightward. Just a year earlier, he had made William Rehnquist chief justice and put Antonin Scalia on the Supreme Court. But Bork represented a new extreme even by Reagan standards. A foe of many of the Supreme Court's landmark decisions, including *Roe v. Wade*, Bork argued in an extensive body of legal writings that the Constitution did not guarantee Americans a right to privacy. Bork even opposed the Court's ruling in *Griswold v. Connecticut*, which recognized the right of married couples to use birth control. He might as well have argued that the founding document of our nation did not guarantee individual liberty.

Bork embodied what NARAL had long warned was a serious goal of the Reagan Administration: overturning *Roe v. Wade* and ending legal abortion. Justice Department memos later revealed that the administration pursued a deliberate strategy of packing the courts with jurists like Robert Bork in order to enact right-wing social policy and to roll back the progress of the 1960s and 1970s—a strategy now being employed by George W. Bush.

Bork's views may have been far outside the mainstream, but

defeating his nomination looked like a decidedly uphill battle for NARAL and his other opponents. Despite the brewing Iran-Contra scandal, Reagan was highly popular, especially in the South. Southern Democrats had repeatedly voted with the administration on budget, tax, and other issues, and Reagan was counting on them to carry the day on the Bork nomination. All he had to do was hold his Republican base while attracting a handful of the Democratic crossover votes he routinely enjoyed. The South was electing Democrats then more often than it does now, but many were nearly as conservative as Republicans are today.

Opponents of Bork faced the formidable task of holding swing Democrats together *and* persuading moderate Republicans to break ranks with Reagan to defeat the nomination. Moreover, we were up against the Senate's long tradition—which would change during the Clinton years but was then still respected—of giving extreme deference to presidential nominees. But the stakes were too high for defeatism. Bork was not simply another judge who opposed *Roe v. Wade*. He was an activist who would be a force on the Court for overturning the right to privacy altogether. If his vision for America prevailed, women's lives and rights once again would be at the mercy of politics and judges. They would be forced to endure hospital review board interrogations to obtain permission for abortions, as I did, or resort to the back alley, as so many women of my generation were forced to do. Bork's constitutional philosophy was a serious threat to women's progress in a variety of areas—including the right to contraception and abortion, both of which he believed the states should be allowed to ban.

NARAL was determined from the very beginning to take our case directly to the American people. In the summer of 1987, shortly after the nomination, Ralph Neas, director of the Leadership Conference on Civil Rights, called a meeting of advocacy organizations that opposed Bork, including NARAL. We began as a working group, and Ralph steadily organized us into a powerful political coalition, skillfully managing a diverse array of organizations that encompassed a wide range of interests and issues. The coalition included labor, women's, civil rights and civil liberties, and environmental groups. The Leadership Conference—a coalition of civil rights groups, including the U.S. Conference of Catholic Bishops—did not take a stand on a woman's right to choose. Because I had not been on the national scene long and was therefore relatively unknown, some coalition members were uncertain about what to expect from my presence. They were also initially uncomfortable with NARAL and other pro-choice groups taking a prominent public role in the fight because of the controversial and divisive nature of the abortion issue. They did not want opposition to Bork to be defined by abortion rights alone.

I was somewhat surprised by the coalition's discomfort. This was nearly fifteen years after *Roe v. Wade*, a decision that had recognized a woman's right to choose as a constitutional liberty, yet some of my colleagues were reluctant to address the issue directly. I understood the need for a message that appealed broadly to mainstream America, but choice was both a mainstream value and a fundamental right. I believed it should not be relegated to lesser status among the constitutional rights that were threatened by the Bork nomination.

The reluctance of some in the advocacy community to embrace the issue fully was emblematic of the impact of the anti-choice movement's strategy to demonize and sensationalize abortion. Even people who called themselves pro-choice were reluctant to publicly identify with the issue. It was imperative that the pro-choice movement define and communicate the values that underlie pro-choice policies more effectively. As president of NARAL, I wanted to demonstrate to the coalition that we could talk about the right to choose *and* Bork's record in a way that would mobilize Americans. I also argued that, given Bork's extreme views, it was impossible to avoid the issue.

During the nomination battle, I hired a pollster for the first time to help us understand what would motivate Americans to take action against Bork. Harrison Hickman, whom I knew about from his work on a pro-choice campaign in Arkansas, conducted focus groups and listened to everyday Americans discuss the Supreme Court, *Roe v. Wade*, and Bork's views. The participants were decidedly upset about Bork's belief that the Constitution did not protect a right to privacy, the fundamental underpinning of a woman's right to contraception and abortion. Harrison briefed the coalition leaders, who agreed that privacy should be a central theme of our opposition to Bork.

When Bork's hearings before the Senate Judiciary Committee got under way, the leaders of the coalition huddled in late-night strategy sessions across the street from the Capitol. One night that fall, after Bork had testified for several days, the issue of the coalition groups' testimony before the Judiciary Committee arose for discussion. My approach was, to say the least, unconventional. During one of the most visible and heavily covered political controversies in years, I was trying to convince my colleagues to do something unusual in Washington: remain quiet.

Earlier that afternoon, I had met with Senator Joe Biden of Delaware, the chairman of the Judiciary Committee and a firm Bork opponent, to discuss strategy. A passionate leader known for his thundering orations on the Senate floor, Biden felt Bork was far out of the judicial mainstream, and he recognized the nomination as part of a larger strategy to shift the federal courts to the right. Biden always speaks his mind frankly, and he did so immediately.

"Kate, I am very worried about all the coalition groups testifying before the committee. At the same time, I respect the hard work everyone has done. The fact is that Bork is his own worst enemy. Every time he says there's no constitutional right to privacy, he convinces the public that he's out of the mainstream. But if all of the groups testify, you'll become the issue. We're going to be distracted by a debate about your agendas instead of Bork's views. This is a real danger. I need you to raise this with the coalition."

Biden and I grew close during the hearings. He trusted my judgment and viewed NARAL as reasonable and politically skilled. I agreed that our best strategy was to keep the focus on Bork. He was undermining himself with every word he spoke. He had already condemned *Griswold v. Connecticut* and *Roe v. Wade*. Bork was frightening people with his own words, and additional testimony by the coalition would only be a distraction. I promised Biden I would make the case to the coalition.

It wasn't an easy sell. Leaders such as Molly Yard of the National Organization for Women and Faye Wattleton of Planned Parenthood were eager to testify, and they would have been compelling witnesses. Other coalition groups, like labor unions, represented causes that they thought were not fully aired during the hearings, and many felt a responsibility to speak for their issues.

"I understand all the arguments in favor of testifying," I said. "I'd like nothing more than to testify myself. I'd like NARAL to be front and center in this debate; our donors and members expect it. But it isn't worth losing the momentum we now have. We need to stay clearly focused on defeating Robert Bork. And right now that means keeping a low profile. If we testify it could hurt our chances for success."

The meeting lasted several hours. Groups like the National Women's Law Center and the National Women's Legal Defense

Fund that worked actively on Capitol Hill most readily saw the wisdom in refraining from testifying. Gradually, most of the coalition acknowledged that silence was our best course. There were only a few holdouts who were adamant about testifying, including Ralph Nader. Nader argued that it was important for him to testify because the issues he advocated would not receive a hearing otherwise. A career of activism on behalf of consumer causes had justifiably made Nader a legend, and I respected him for that. But something about his attitude in that debate disturbed me. He was too eager, insistent and impervious to other arguments. I felt he was putting his and his organization's interests above the greater good.

After a lengthy and sometimes heated discussion, coalition leaders finally agreed that testifying was not in our best interests. Bork kept talking—and with every word, he reinforced our message that he was radically out of step with the mainstream of American constitutional values.

But that alone wasn't enough to defeat Bork. We needed a majority of votes in the Senate, and the battle would begin in the Senate Judiciary Committee. If we could defeat Bork in committee, the nomination might be withdrawn. To prevail, we would need Republican votes. Additionally, if pro-choice Republicans opposed a Republican president's nominee, that in and of itself would illustrate the extremism of Bork's views. While there is no disputing the reality that more Democratic public officials than Republicans are pro-choice, I have always believed that we need as broad a base of support as possible in order to protect and defend a woman's right to choose. Polarizing is a tactic the anti-choice movement has employed for years, but it does an enormous disservice to the American people, dividing them along ideological lines instead of uniting them around shared values.

Arlen Specter, a pro-choice Republican from Pennsylvania who served on the Judiciary Committee, looked like our best hope on the GOP side. I knew him to be smart and independent-minded. I met with him several times in the summer of 1987 as the nomination battle took shape, emphasizing that Bork's judicial philosophy posed an imminent threat to freedoms about which Specter cared deeply, especially the right to privacy and the right to choose. Specter was understandably torn between his belief that judges should be thoughtful moderates rather than activist ideologues and the call of loyalty to a president of his own party. He always listened courteously to me, but did not commit himself.

Meanwhile, the coalition worked to persuade other swing votes on the Judiciary Committee, like Democrat Howell Heflin of Alabama. As a Southerner with a large African-American constituency, we believed that Heflin could more easily be persuaded by concerns about Bork's civil rights record, so the NAACP took the lead on lobbying him. The outcome was uncertain until the Judiciary Committee voted on October 6, giving opponents of Bork a resounding victory—nine to five against confirmation, with both Specter and Heflin voting to oppose the nomination.

In most cases, that would have been the end of the battle. Without the committee's endorsement, Bork had little chance of approval by the full Senate, but it was clear he would not give up. Bork insisted on taking the fight to a Senate vote.

A vote in the full chamber made it all the more important that we attract moderate Republicans to our side. Combative tactics would hardly be persuasive with Republican senators, who already faced a difficult political situation. Combat was never my personal style, and I had had extensive experience working with moderate Republicans, who were Planned Parenthood's strongest pro-choice allies in Pennsylvania.

One unseasonably warm October afternoon, I met with Senator Robert Stafford, a moderate pro-choice Republican from Vermont. Gracious but with a New Englander's sense of reserve, Senator

Stafford had a well-earned reputation as both an advocate of women's rights and a courageous leader willing to defy his party when his principles were at stake. Another women's-rights organization visited the senator just before me. I learned later that they had been heavy-handed and confrontational, threatening to publicly chastise Stafford if he supported Bork. Their strong-arm tactics were disrespectful of Stafford's unblemished pro-choice record and, more important, they were unpersuasive. I took a different approach.

"I believe voting against Judge Bork would be consistent with your long history of support for women's rights and the right to choose. Bork's views are antithetical to everything you have stood for," I told Stafford. "But I do know how difficult this vote is for you. I'm asking you to oppose a president of your party. If you decide you must support the president—and I certainly hope you won't—it will not mean everything you have done to protect women and their rights has been meaningless. NARAL will not attack you. But, Senator, the women of America need you and are counting on you."

I handed Senator Stafford NARAL's report on Bork's beliefs and record, knowing he would read it. A few days later, he phoned.

"I'm about to announce my opposition to Bork, and I wanted you to know personally before the news comes out," he said. "Your visit with me was very helpful—not just the information you provided, but the respectful tenor of our discussion as well."

"Senator, this is tremendous news!" I replied. "I understand how difficult it is to vote against a president of your party. This is a very principled stand and I appreciate your courage."

Other moderate Republicans such as Lowell Weicker of Connecticut and Bob Packwood of Oregon came out against Bork as well.

One-on-one lobbying was only one element of our strategy. Politically, Bork was a formidable nominee. President Reagan's popularity, especially in the South, could go a long way toward peeling
off Democratic votes. The coalition felt it was important for senators to hear directly from the people whose interests they were
elected to represent. Unless we had the support of the voting public, our chances of success were limited. It was no small task to
convince the American people that a Supreme Court nomination
would have a daily impact on their lives—an impact so serious and
grave that they should actively oppose it. I knew it was time to
bring NARAL's traditional emphasis on grassroots organizing into
sharp relief.

This would be NARAL's largest-ever national grassroots campaign, and the media spotlight on the Bork nomination intensified
its importance. Along with Althea Simmons, Washington director
of the NAACP, and the AFL-CIO, I cochaired the coalition's
grassroots task force aimed at mobilizing everyday Americans to
contact their senators and urge them to oppose Bork. Althea was
larger than life, literally and figuratively. She had an imposing physical presence and a long-standing status as the premiere civil rights
activist in Washington, D.C. The NAACP had no official position
on the right to choose, and Althea was initially wary of both the
issue and me. But as the grassroots campaign geared up over the summer and continued into the fall, Althea and I grew closer. When
the battle was over, we were celebrating at lunch in the Senate
cafeteria. She reached across the table in a warm and affectionate
gesture.

"Kate," Althea said, "you're all right." It was one of the highest
compliments I ever received—and one of the most important al-
liances NARAL ever formed.

The NAACP, AFL-CIO, and NARAL devised a strategy that

harnessed each of the organization's strengths. Our national office disseminated our Bork report, talking points, and other materials. NARAL organized our national membership as well as our state-level affiliates, who in turn contacted their members and activists.

By reaching pro-choice Americans one at a time, the coalition unleashed a torrent of phone calls and letters on the Senate. In the end, the Senate defeated Bork 58–42. Ever since, the right wing has claimed that Bork was a victim of character assassination by the coalition that opposed him. Not true: This was a battle about Bork's judicial philosophy and views of the Constitution. NARAL never questioned his professional qualifications or his integrity. The Bork nomination provoked a national discussion on the constitutional guarantee of individual liberties and the right to privacy. Its ramifications would be felt for years. The far right would harbor lasting and deep resentment over Bork's defeat, anger that prompted a permanent strategy—one that endures to this day—of using judicial appointments and the courts as weapons against social and political progress.

Ultimately, Bork was replaced by Justice Anthony Kennedy. Today, Kennedy's record on a woman's right to choose is mixed. He is certainly no Harry Blackmun, but neither is he Robert Bork. And subsequent years would prove just how much of a difference defeating Bork would make.

CHAPTER SIX

A MPLIFIED BY BULLHORNS, CRIES OF "DON'T KILL YOUR BABY!" filled the air. Protestors, waving gruesome pictures, rushed cars. A swarm of cameramen and reporters shouted questions to no one in particular and anyone who would respond.

It was the summer of 1988, and I was in Atlanta, site of the Democratic National Convention and scene of a massive anti-choice protest at a local women's health clinic. Operation Rescue, the radical anti-choice group run by a firebrand named Randall Terry, a former used-car salesman from upstate New York, was in charge. The protestors' tactics—publicly harassing and humiliating women and blockading clinics—were detestable but increasingly common. As patients of all ages and backgrounds attempted to exit their cars and walk inside, the crowd formed what can only be described as a gauntlet of terror. Among the patients were middle-aged married women, single and young women, students, as well as women of all faiths and economic backgrounds.

The protestors, most often led by men, rushed in, many carrying pictures of bloody fetuses. "Don't let the murderers make you do this!" they shouted. Many of the women had not even told their families they intended to have abortions, but whatever hopes they had for privacy were shattered when protestors surrounded the clinic and blocked the entrance, subjecting them to public harassment and humiliation. Some protestors tried to rush the women and beg them to reconsider. Others held up pictures of mutilated fetuses and shouted, "This is what you're about to do to your baby! You'll regret this for the rest of your life! This may be your only chance to have a baby!"

The circumstances that brought each woman to the clinic that day were of absolutely no interest to the protestors. Had she been raped? Had she, like me, been abandoned with other children to care for? Was she a woman desperate to have a child who had just discovered her fetus had a terrible defect and no hope of survival? Was she a young woman responsibly using contraception that had failed, who knew she was not yet prepared to be a mother? The protestors simply did not care. To them, these women were faceless caricatures, not people with individual stories who deserved compassion.

While I was there to attend the Democratic convention, I decided to join a pro-choice counter-demonstration. Initially I was hesitant. I worried that the hostile rhetoric of the protestors was already inflaming the public debate, and I did not want to contribute to an increase in tensions. In the end, I knew it would be wrong to remain silent in the face of such a virulent attack on women and their right to choose, particularly with the convention going on. But I also wanted to do more than speak at a rally. Since the mid-1980s, thousands of courageous and dedicated volunteers across the nation have eased women's walks along the "gauntlet of terror" by escorting them into clinics. Joining them was the least I could do.

As I waited my turn to escort, my heart ached for the women who had been brave enough to subject themselves to harassment and intimidation. Many women canceled their appointments or turned back when they saw the mob scene at the clinic. I wondered if they would find the courage to come back or, if not, what would become of them. I could not alleviate the personal burden on these women, but in this environment that denied their humanity, I could offer a strong arm and a human connection.

As the woman I was to escort arrived, I reached out with that single-minded goal. "Hi," I said. "I'm Kate." As I placed my arm around her shoulder, I could feel her trembling and the tension in her body. "These people are going to say things that may upset you," I whispered. "Don't react to them. And please try not to worry. We're going to get you into the clinic quickly."

We walked together, eyes looking straight ahead. Protestors tried desperately to reach this woman, some pledging support and pleading softly for her not to "kill your baby." Others were outright abusive. "Don't let these people murder your baby!" they yelled. The fact that the demonstrators invoked Martin Luther King Jr.'s legacy of civil disobedience made their actions all the more offensive. When I marched with Reverend King, it was to win long-denied rights, not to take them away; to lift the yoke of discrimination and restore human dignity. These women and medical professionals were being deprived of their dignity in an attempt to prevent them from exercising their lawful rights.

That fall, Operation Rescue descended on cities across the nation for protests that shut down clinics in several cities and harassed women mercilessly in others. The radical fringe of the anti-choice movement was taking center stage. Among its most extreme elements, lawlessness seemed to abound. A single word from two leaders the protestors venerated—Ronald Reagan, the incumbent president, or George H. W. Bush, then on his way to victory in his own presidential campaign—might have restored a semblance of sanity. But Reagan and Bush opted for silence, refusing even to advise their own partisans to behave decently and obey the law.

In August 1991, with Bush in the White House, Operation

Rescue came to Wichita, Kansas. Dr. George Tiller, one of the few physicians in the country who would still perform late second-trimester abortions, was the target of a massive demonstration that gripped the entire city. Pro-choice leaders flew in from around the country to speak on behalf of pro-choice Americans. I wanted to be a voice for those women who were being harassed and denigrated. I was also determined that Randall Terry's public display of hostility and hatred not go unanswered. The tension had escalated. The screams seemed louder, the harassment more dangerous, Terry's rants more rabid. The protests made it nearly impossible for Wichita's only two abortion clinics to operate, so a federal judge found it necessary to issue an injunction against the protestors. I felt they had gone far beyond their constitutional right to protest, a right I fully respect. Instead, I believed they were waging a full-scale campaign of intimidation, invasion of privacy, and aggressive interference with private clinics' ability to provide lawful health care.

The U.S. attorney general, Richard Thornburgh—a former governor of Pennsylvania whose anti-choice record I knew from prior experience—took the extraordinary step of filing a court brief urging that the judge's ruling be overturned. This aggressive action by the Bush administration was a jarring illustration of how far it would go to support the goals of the anti-choice movement. By that time, I had given up any realistic hope of the administration exercising moral leadership to discourage anti-choice extremists. But Thornburgh's action was extraordinary. A sitting attorney general, the nation's highest law enforcement officer, actually went to court to thwart the rule of law.*

*He insisted that he was intervening only on a legal technicality, not to defend the protestors' tactics. But his obvious, if unstated, motive was political, and there was at least some solace in knowing that it backfired: The public disapproval of his actions in the face of the Wichita protests contributed to his stunning defeat when he ran for the U.S. Senate in Pennsylvania.

Anti-choice harassment was not a new phenomenon. As far back as my tenure with Planned Parenthood in Pennsylvania in the early 1980s, extremists glued the locks of our clinics, broke windows, and even, on one occasion, slipped a gaseous green substance into our ventilation system that fogged several rooms and filled them with a noxious odor. No one was hurt, but we were forced to close the clinic for a day. As my public profile rose at NARAL, so did the number of personal threats against me. Letters and phone calls threatened to "punish" me for my work. On rare occasions, they contained outright death threats. I rarely worried about them, but there were times when anti-choice violence was especially intense that it was difficult to banish the threat entirely from my mind.

An especially ominous sense of foreboding hung over me in the fall of 1988. I had seen the protestors up close, felt their rage, watched them dominate the television airwaves with their presence. An atmosphere that combustible could not be maintained forever. I could not shake the unsettling feeling that it was only a matter of time before something more horrendous—and tragic— happened.

As anti-choice demonstrations neared the boiling point, the Supreme Court heard arguments in what was widely expected to be one of the most important reproductive rights cases since *Roe*. *Webster v. Reproductive Health Services* involved a Missouri law that prohibited the use of public funds or facilities for performing abortions or even counseling women about the option. Missouri's law was a perfect example of what has proven to be a highly effective strategy to weaken the foundation of *Roe v. Wade*: State legislatures enact restrictions that on the surface appear reasonable but in reality severely undermine the right to choose and have access to abortion. The Missouri law under review would effectively deny poor women who depended on Medicaid—as well as women who live in areas served only by public hospitals—the ability to exercise reproductive choice.

Webster presented an increasingly conservative Court, which included several Reagan appointees, with its first opportunity to eliminate the protections guaranteed by *Roe*. The first Bush administration argued in a brief supporting the Missouri law that the Court should overrule *Roe* outright, an argument the Reagan administration had also made.* There might actually now be enough votes on the Court to reverse sixteen years of reproductive freedom for American women. The climate had changed, and not just in the Supreme Court. The anti-choice movement, fragmented and disparate after *Roe v. Wade*, had spent nearly two decades consolidating and building a formidable political base. With the assent of the press, they claimed credit for Ronald Reagan's election in 1980, providing them political legitimacy and a stable home in the Republican party. Their grossly misleading ultrasound film, *The Silent Scream*, aired in 1984 and was the centerpiece of a multiyear effort to portray the fetus as a living person in the public's mind—a necessary precondition for legally declaring abortion to be murder. Yet as the anti-choice movement attempted to establish the fetus as a full-fledged person, it also ignored the very existence of women, dehumanizing them in the process.

Dawn Johnsen, NARAL's legal director, suggested that we submit a brief to the Supreme Court that told the stories of real women whose lives would be affected if *Roe* was overruled. "It's never been done before," Dawn said, "so it could really help the

---

*In the 1985 case of *Thornburgh v. American College of Obstetricians and Gynecologists*, Reagan Justice Department official Carolyn Kuhl coauthored a harshly worded brief urging the Supreme Court to reverse *Roe v. Wade*. President George W. Bush later nominated Kuhl to a lifetime appointment as a federal appeals judge.

justices understand the personal, human impact of losing the right to choose."

Dawn and I presented the idea to the staff.

"We have perhaps the greatest challenge the pro-choice movement has ever faced," I said. "Legal arguments simply aren't enough. The Court needs to hear women's voices, and we need a national campaign to alert the American people to the threat we face. The public doesn't realize how close we are to losing the right to choose. People need to know and speak out. While the Court doesn't directly respond to political pressures, they don't make decisions in a vacuum either. The American people need to make it clear where they stand on this issue."

NARAL put out a nationwide call for women to share their personal stories. We sent thousands of letters to NARAL affiliates, clinics, women's groups, and other organizations around the country. We were asking women to publicly reveal a profoundly personal, intimate decision, often made under painful and difficult circumstances. Shortly after our letters went out, responses began to pour in. Women told us how important it was that people understand what they endured. They told their stories in intense, revealing detail. A nurse wrote:

> In 1965, I had to care for a nineteen-year-old girl as she lay dying of infection following an illegal abortion. The fact that she denied having an abortion up to the time of her death and the tearful disclosure by her mother after her death underscored the fear these two people were experiencing.

Another woman remembered undergoing an abortion on a bed with her legs resting on two chairs. "I experienced an extreme amount of pain and was told that if I didn't shut up, [the doctor] would leave and not complete the operation." While recovering at home, the woman passed out on a hot-water pipe in her bathroom, causing second-degree burns. The abortion was botched so badly that she spent sixteen days in the hospital, undergoing major surgery to save her life.

One of the most moving stories came from a woman who was the first person in a family of thirteen to graduate from high school. She became pregnant when she was twenty.

> I was told that I shouldn't be afraid. "Don't worry. There is a guy in . . . Ohio who is safe. All the mob guys take their girlfriends there . . ."
>
> We arrived at dusk and pulled into an alley behind a very old house . . . I waited, afraid of what was going to happen, and then the pain began. Hour after hour of the most intense pain I have ever experienced. Then the bleeding began, a hemorrhage so bad the memory of it still frightens me. The hours in the bedroom of my apartment, my roommate begging me to call a doctor, go to the hospital, call my mother, do something, are still with me. But . . . I was afraid to do anything, because I was convinced that . . . I would go to jail.

Another woman spoke for many pro-choice activists frustrated that the battle we had won less than twenty years earlier had to be fought anew: "It was over! I want to shout. My closest childhood and young-adult friend, [who had an] abortion on her dining room table . . . with no sterilization and the crudest of instruments . . . is already dead. Why do I have to fight for her life again?"

We fashioned these stories and more—2,887 in all—into what must be one of the most unconventional yet powerful briefs the justices of the Supreme Court have ever read. The press covered the stories extensively. But it wasn't enough. In June, the Court handed down its opinion in the *Webster* case upholding the Missouri law.

That in itself was disturbing. But a close reading of the opinions revealed that four justices also voted to overturn *Roe v. Wade* outright. All it would take to cast *Roe* aside was one more anti-choice justice. Justice Blackmun, author of *Roe*, captured the danger in his dissent: "I fear for the future," he wrote. "I fear for the liberty and equality of the millions of women who have lived and come of age in the sixteen years since *Roe* was decided. . . . [T]he signs are evident and very ominous, and a chill wind blows."

It was 1989, only sixteen years after *Roe*, yet we could see its legal underpinnings beginning to fracture. It was increasingly clear that—in order to protect a woman's right to choose—we would have to appeal to the American people directly and build an active movement in support of choice. The afternoon of the *Webster* decision, I rushed to an editing studio to put the finishing touches on a TV spot that NARAL had already produced for just this eventuality. It was to be the pro-choice movement's first national ad campaign in years. The right to choose was gravely threatened and the nation needed to know that a fundamental American value was at stake.

CHAPTER SEVEN

I N THE AFTERMATH OF *WEBSTER*, ANTI-CHOICE POLITICIANS COR-
rectly perceived that the protections of *Roe v. Wade* were highly
vulnerable. Emboldened, they moved aggressively—sometimes
shockingly—to seize an opening to further their goal of ending the
right to choose. Utah rushed through a statute banning abortion
and classifying it as a capital offense. Through what its supporters
later characterized as an inadvertent loophole, the law could have
allowed zealous prosecutors to seek the death penalty for women
who chose abortions. In special session, the legislature closed the
loophole and clarified that abortion was not capital murder, but it
left the underlying abortion ban intact. Louisiana passed a sweeping law that criminalized abortion as well as commonly used forms
of birth control like the IUD. Doctors who violated the law were
threatened with up to ten years of hard labor. Sponsors of the
Louisiana statute described it as a deliberate attempt to test how
much the courts would permit the state to restrict reproductive
rights. Far-reaching abortion bans like Louisiana's and Utah's were
overturned by the courts, but each court case presented a clear
threat to *Roe* and, ultimately, women's health and lives. Within a
year, politicians had introduced hundreds of restrictions on abortion in more than forty states.

Webster made the threat to a woman's right to choose a stark and imminent reality, shaking many pro-choice Americans from their complacency. It even motivated some previously anti-choice lawmakers to reconsider their views. Congressman Frank Pallone, a Democrat from New Jersey who had voted consistently anti-choice, delivered a speech in the House of Representatives that fall explaining why he could no longer vote to deny women the right to choose.

"I have thought about it a lot," he said, "and the bottom line is that I do not feel that I have been elected to come down here and make those individual decisions for women."

When I called Pallone to say how moved I was by his remarks, he explained that *Webster* had inspired him to reconsider his anti-choice stance.

"I have always felt that with *Roe* in place, I could vote on the basis of my personal opposition to abortion," Pallone said. "Now it's clear that *Roe* may not always be there. And I just don't think it's my role as a congressman to make decisions for women."

In Florida, the state legislature—with the support of Bob Martinez, the far-right Republican governor—moved to pass an abortion ban as Utah and Louisiana had. Led by several courageous pro-choice members of the state legislature, pro-choice Floridians mobilized and spoke out. NARAL organized a campaign against the abortion ban, holding demonstrations and encouraging pro-choice voters to contact their representatives. The ban was defeated—and, when he ran for reelection the next year, so was Martinez.

In order to protect women's rights, we needed a nationwide mobilization such as the one we had organized in Florida. To broaden our movement, we also had to broaden our message. I have been committed throughout my career to changing the tone of the national discussion on reproductive rights and inspiring people to take action to protect the right to choose. The religious right had been working to convince the public that women chose abortion casually and frivolously. The national debate was narrowly focused on the act of abortion rather than women's lives and needs and the conditions surrounding their choices. And at this point in time—in 1989, after enduring eight years of Ronald Reagan in the White House and facing another four with George H. W. Bush—our movement needed to reach mainstream Americans with a message they could hear.

The "it's our bodies" language, which emanated from the women's movement of the 1970s, motivated grassroots feminists. But in focus groups, we often heard that many ordinary women did not identify with that message. To them it sounded strident and polarizing, defiant rather than positive. Americans needed a broader context to better understand the value and importance of women being able to decide whether, when, and under what circumstances to bear children. Harrison Hickman, our pollster, described the public's perception of the debate as two extremes yelling at each other across a chasm while the vast majority in the middle were left out, unable to relate to the rhetoric of either side.

Webster necessitated a national effort to inspire Americans to resist attempts to take away the right to choose. Without a vital, passionate, and strong movement of Americans defending women's rights, politicians and the courts would accede to the demands of the far right, jeopardizing women's rights and health.

Achieving such a strong national movement would take far more than a press release, speech, or even an advertisement. A full-fledged national campaign was necessary to mobilize pro-choice Americans and inspire them to take action in support of the right to choose. They needed to understand that women's health was threatened and that Americans were in serious danger of losing a fundamental right. We opened dialogues with pro-choice voters to hear their concerns. During a focus group in Tampa, Florida, pro-choice people—mostly women—sat around a table discussing the issue as I watched from behind a two-way mirror. After several minutes of discussion, one woman—quiet until then—spoke up.

"What it comes down to," she said, "is who makes the decision."

She had captured the very essence of the issue. I turned to a NARAL colleague who was observing the session with me. "That's it!" I said. "She's got it!" The woman had identified the central question in the abortion debate. "Who Decides?" The issue was not whether abortion was morally right or wrong; that was a matter of individual conscience. The question was who had the right to decide—women or the government? Our "Who Decides?" mobilization was born.

"Who Decides?" was a multifaceted campaign with a clear goal: to motivate pro-choice Americans to act on their values by contacting their elected officials, calling radio shows, writing letters to the editor, and other efforts. Our affiliates organized house parties across their states where people discussed their pro-choice beliefs. Frank Greer, NARAL's media consultant and one of the sharpest political minds in Washington, produced a compelling advertising campaign built around the "Who Decides?" theme. We held rallies, aired ads in states where polling showed we could make an impact, and used the "Who Decides?" message each time we communicated.

If pro-choice Americans considered the question in those terms, we were confident they would be inspired to oppose government restrictions on a woman's right to choose. The message proved compelling, and it was persuasive to both women and men. Women instinctively understood the intimacy of pregnancy and childbearing, but men in our focus groups also responded strongly to the essence of "Who Decides?": that government should not interfere with private decisions.

The "Who Decides?" campaign required increasing our membership and raising significantly more money than we had in the past. Advertising, lobbying, electing pro-choice candidates, and grassroots organizing on a national level were expensive. Having worked for nonprofits my entire career, I had raised large sums of money, but this was fund-raising on a new scale: an annual budget that would soon exceed $10 million. It was the equivalent of raising enough money to run a statewide political campaign every year. Few people enjoy asking strangers for money, but fund-raising is an opportunity to educate, to build and deepen support, and, ultimately, to inspire activism on behalf of the cause. It is also an opportunity to meet unique—and uniquely dedicated—people.

A wealthy donor once called from her home in Idaho to say that her mother—a voracious art collector and an ardent supporter of women's rights—had just passed away. The family was donating most of her collection to the Hirshhorn Gallery in Washington, D.C., but they were reserving a small number of pieces for women's-rights groups, including NARAL. The donor informed me that we would receive a portrait by the early twentieth-century Italian painter and sculptor Amedeo Modigliani. The painting—a woman's head with Modigliani's signature elongated neck—was exquisite. We were reluctant to part with it, but the point of the gift, after all, was to support NARAL's work to protect the right to choose. I traveled to New York to meet the family at Christie's, where the painting was to be auctioned. When it was unveiled by the auctioneer, an audible gasp filled the room. We were anxious as the bidding began slowly. But just as the auctioneer was about to close the sale, bids erupted from all around the room as well as over the phone from collectors across the world. The painting fetched $1.5 million.

Another donor, an owner of racehorses in the Midwest who

was passionately pro-choice, adopted NARAL as his favorite cause shortly after "Who Decides?" debuted. He began naming horses after us—one was called "Kate's Choice," another "Who Decides?"—and he donated their purses to NARAL when they won.

Some of the most famous stars of movies and television were also among our leading contributors. The actors Amy Madigan and Ed Harris—two of the most passionate individuals I know—became close friends and longtime supporters of NARAL. Amy later joined our board of directors. Stars like Robin Williams, Susan Sarandon, Glenn Close, Ashley Judd, and others have supported us financially, opened their homes for receptions, and, most important, lent the power of their voices to our cause. Brad Whitford of NBC's drama *The West Wing* has brought his dry wit to many of our events ("Here we stand, one broken hip away," he once noted of the fragile state of the Supreme Court), and has been a prominent activist on behalf of our cause. The late Ossie Davis, a personal hero for his leadership in the civil rights movement, once spoke eloquently at a NARAL dinner of a woman's right to choose as a natural extension of his lifelong devotion to equality.

Other donors have become close friends too. Dagmar Dolby—whose husband, Ray, founded Dolby Sound Systems—was a Republican whom I met through a mutual friend. Dagmar was pro-choice, but she was known in her community of San Francisco mostly as a patron of the arts. When we met, she was both alarmed and inspired to learn of the extent to which a woman's right to choose was being threatened. The meeting, Dagmar told me later, changed her life. She became a devoted pro-choice activist, personally building a broad base of NARAL supporters in San Francisco. The more she saw the stranglehold the far right held over her political party, the more difficult it became for her to remain a Republican. In the late 1990s, she gave up her Republican registration because of the party's opposition to a woman's right to choose.

Relationships forged over such an intensely personal issue become exactly that: intensely personal. One donor who supported NARAL generously over the years called one afternoon and spoke in a calm and measured tone that moves me still.

"Kate," she said, "I am calling all the people who are special to me in my life. I want you to know how important it was for me to have worked with you and NARAL in the struggle for a woman's right to choose. It has meant a great deal to me. You must know I am dying and this is probably the last time we will talk." She died several days later.

Webster dramatically changed the political landscape surrounding a woman's right to choose. The nation's conversation was no longer an academic discourse conducted with *Roe v. Wade* as a safety net. The Court had made it clear that *Roe* could be overturned with one more vote. I made it a priority for NARAL to engage Americans in the conversation, mobilize our base, and make a meaningful impact in the political arena to save the right to choose.

As the 1990 election cycle approached, I named a skilled political operative, James Wagoner, a longtime Capitol Hill veteran, as political director at NARAL. At the time, James's hiring raised some eyebrows within the movement. It seemed to suggest that I was, in the parlance of old-school feminism, "male-identified," the derogatory label for someone who believed that the women's movement should involve men who shared our passion for equality and had skills to contribute to our cause.

NARAL's roots were in the feminist movement of the 1960s and 1970s. I wanted to harness the passion of that time while focusing the organization on mainstream politics, but the old and new still clashed occasionally. James got a taste of that conflict early in his tenure, when he joined me for his first meeting of the Core Group, a coalition of the heads of major women's organizations. I opened the meeting by suggesting we discuss the congressional seats that would be competitive in the 1990 elections.

"In the post-*Webster* era," I said, "it is more important than ever that we place a high priority on electing pro-choice candidates, and to do that we need to identify and reach pro-choice Americans."

One participant responded that it was elitist to talk only about "Americans," since many women in the country were illegal immigrants.

James surged forward in his seat. *"What?"* he whispered to me, just barely under his breath. "If we're going to talk about voters we *have* to talk about Americans."

"Remain calm," I whispered back. This woman was raising an issue important to many in the women's movement. But the interchange illustrated the difference in approach that sometimes arose between movement politics, which tends to be concerned with raising consciousness and maintaining ideological purity, and governing politics, which is about getting votes and achieving concrete political results. Both are valid approaches, but they do sometimes conflict.

The success of "Who Decides?" convinced me that we could make a woman's right to choose a winning political issue. That notion was first put to the test in 1989 in off-year elections in which New Jersey and Virginia held gubernatorial races. Congressman Jim Florio was running in New Jersey; Lieutenant Governor Doug Wilder was on the ballot in Virginia; and both were pro-choice moderates. We endorsed Florio in his primary against an anti-choice Democrat. He won the nomination and soon pulled comfortably ahead in the general election, which he went on to win.

But Wilder, an African-American running in the capital of the Confederacy, faced a more difficult campaign. Wilder was controversial within the pro-choice community because he had said he was willing to consider a parental notification law. Moreover, Virginia was trending Republican and the campaign would be highly expensive. Some members of our staff were reluctant to get involved both because of Wilder's comments on parental consent and because of the long odds and enormous expense. Others disagreed. They felt the race could be won and that NARAL should be involved in what could turn out to be a historic campaign. I agreed and made the case for Wilder to our team.

"Doug Wilder may become the first African-American governor of Virginia. This is a critically important and historic campaign, and it would be wrong to sit this one out. Once he's elected governor we can work with him on parental notification. The Supreme Court is now beginning to allow state restrictions on abortion, so it's more important than ever that we elect pro-choice officials at the state level, not just in Washington. And if that doesn't convince you, look at his opponent." The Republican nominee, Marshall Coleman, was strongly anti-choice.

Still, the Wilder campaign was a gamble. It would be the first major electoral test of the "Who Decides?" message, and if we failed, it would be a serious setback for NARAL and the pro-choice movement. But there was far too much at stake not to engage in the campaign. Pro-choice Americans had been silent for too long, and it was time their voices were heard and their votes counted.

NARAL hit the airwaves with ads highlighting Coleman's anti-choice positions. We hired a firm to identify pro-choice voters and initiated a mail and phone program to educate them. This was old-fashioned grassroots politics: defining a message voters would respond to, reaching them however we could—on the phone, in the mail, door-to-door, on the public square, and over the airwaves. The effect was immediate: Not only did Coleman begin slipping in the polls, but he was also forced to respond to NARAL's campaign, which meant he had to talk about an issue he would rather have avoided. Wilder himself aired a spot highlighting his pro-choice position, something that was quite rare in 1989. Our theory was proving itself right: Anti-choice views could be a distinct disadvantage for a politician; being pro-choice could be a real asset. Going into election night, polling showed Wilder in the lead.

But almost as soon as the votes started coming in, his lead shrank until the race was suddenly neck and neck—then Coleman pulled ahead. I was mystified. How could the polls have been so wrong?

"It's simple, Kate," Harrison, himself a Southerner, explained. "We've come a long way on race, but this is still the Deep South. If someone's not going to vote for Wilder because he's African-American, they don't advertise that to a pollster. They just don't tell the truth, then they go into the voting booth and pull the lever for the other guy."

By late evening, it was too close to call. I was devastated by the possibility of losing a historic opportunity to elect a pro-choice African-American governor in Virginia, especially with race apparently playing a role in his loss. And NARAL had a great deal at stake as well. I had made this election a priority. We had been highly visible, and if we lost, the press would say the choice issue hurt rather than helped Wilder. A woman's right to choose as a positive political message might well die in Virginia.

In the morning when the final ballots were counted, Wilder won by only a few thousand votes. We were relieved and elated.

Political experts said an important factor in his victory was our "Who Decides?" campaign, which pulled pro-choice Republicans across party lines to support Wilder. And the next year, when Virginia's assembly sent Wilder a parental consent bill, he was convinced by the merits of our arguments and vetoed it.

The following year brought another string of electoral successes, this time at the federal level. In Iowa, where Senator Tom Harkin was in a tough race for reelection, we ran a series of "Who Decides?" ads spotlighting his opponent's anti-choice record. We learned through the rumor mill that Harkin was initially concerned the ads would inflame an already controversial issue. When they actually ran, however, he was delighted with the message.

"The ads were exactly the right tone," Harkin told me after the campaign. "They were thoughtful, they weren't strident. It's just how this issue should be discussed."

In Montana, we taped an ad of a rancher speaking directly to the camera about the government staying out of private decisions. Pro-choice representative Pat Williams went on to win a close campaign. But one loss that year was particularly painful. Senator Jesse Helms, perhaps the Senate's leading—or certainly loudest—anti-choice member, was widely seen as vulnerable to a challenge from Charlotte's African-American mayor, Harvey Gantt. We began airing an ad on Helms's radical anti-choice record, and within days, North Carolina Republicans tried to pressure television stations not to air it. It was plain, old-fashioned intimidation.

Gantt was closely competitive in the race—many pundits, in fact, were predicting victory—when the Helms camp pulled one of the most notorious and despicable stunts in modern politics: an ad in which a pair of white hands crumpled a job application while the announcer said it was given to a minority because of affirmative action. It was blatant race-baiting, and what was worse, it worked. Gantt began to slip almost immediately in the polls and never recovered. His loss was especially heartbreaking both because Helms represented the extreme fringe of the anti-choice movement and because his tactics against Gantt represented the very worst in politics. North Carolina Republicans went to the Federal Election Commission to complain about our ads, claiming that we illegally coordinated our efforts with the Gantt campaign. We had kept extensive records and were careful to follow the law to the letter. We were vindicated, but not before we spent a considerable amount of money on legal fees.

Still, there was good news: The fact that Helms tried to muscle TV stations in North Carolina and filed an FEC complaint was proof that the "Who Decides?" message was working. In a string of political victories at both the state and national levels, we now had proof that choice could be a winning political issue. Just as important, after years of defeats in the Reagan/Bush era, we now had the victories to demonstrate that activism could make a difference. Our success had advanced a goal I had been pursuing since I took the helm at NARAL: positioning a woman's right to choose where it belonged—in the political mainstream.

CHAPTER EIGHT

NARAL MAY HAVE BEEN REACHING MORE AMERICANS WITH our message, but two of the most important people in my world were still absent from the discussion: my parents. Nearly thirty years after one of the defining experiences of my life, I still had not told them about my abortion. I had long since overcome the humiliation I suffered when I had my abortion, but my parents were devout Catholics. I was hesitant to reveal that I had done something they might regard as a grave sin, in part because I was reluctant to risk incurring their disapproval. They had followed my career closely and proudly. I had never shied away from expressing my views about reproductive rights, and they had always been respectful of my beliefs and supportive of my work. The fact that they did not know about one of the most formative experiences of my life created a barrier for me in what was an otherwise intimate and open relationship. And even if they disagreed with my position on abortion, it was very important to me that their understanding of the issue not be informed exclusively by the rhetoric of the anti-choice movement.

I had often thought about telling them. At the time I had the abortion, I contemplated confiding in my mother. She was one of

the most accepting and loving people I knew, and her support during that difficult period would have been a comfort. But my parents were already very upset over the breakup of my marriage. I did
not want to inflict more pain by telling them about the abortion.
Several times over the years, I planned to talk with them, but always found a reason to draw back. I worried about their reaction. I
worried they would be hurt that I had not told them earlier.

The truth is, I had simply not been ready to tell them. Yet in my
own way, I had been setting the stage for many years. As my career
progressed, we had talked about reproductive freedom many times—
why I believed it was central to women's equality, the many ways
in which it touched women lives, and how it shaped their ability
to be successful mothers. Perhaps, subconsciously, I was establishing a basis for them to understand my own choice more fully.

In 1990, I was invited to speak at an event for Texas gubernatorial candidate Ann Richards in Tyler, an East Texas city about
an hour's drive from where my parents had recently moved. This
seemed the perfect opportunity, but I still feared they were so
rooted in their Catholicism that they would be unable to accept
the reality of my experience. My desire to be honest overcame my
fear of their reaction; continuing to keep this defining experience
from them was harder than sharing it. It was time. I picked up the
phone and called them—still nervous, but certain it was the right
thing to do.

"Mom and Dad," I said, "I would like you to come to a speech
I'm giving."

They were excited about hearing me speak in public for the
first time.

"But first, I need you to know something," I continued, somewhat anxiously. "I am going to talk about a personal experience
that I have never discussed with you."

I didn't go into more detail. I never doubted my parents' love and support. My mother was always reassuring, accepting, and encouraging. But my father was harder to please. His standards were as rigid as they were high, and no matter how old I was, I was always seeking his approval. There was a real possibility that we might clash strongly over one of the most profoundly personal experiences of my life. At a deeper level, I was worried that he would believe I had done something wrong. No matter how clear I was about my choice, the prospect of a harsh judgment by my father—something he was quite capable of—was still devastating to me.

"I really want you to be there," I said. They assured me that they would.

As I drove from the airport in Dallas on my way to the speech, I thought about my parents, my early years, my life growing up, and how the seeds of my own activism were planted early in my life.

Both of my parents were children of poor Catholic immigrants. My father's parents emigrated to the United States from northern Italy in 1913. Orphaned and destitute at the age of four, he was placed in a Catholic boys' home where he often had only one meal a day, which was frequently infested with maggots. One among four hundred boys, he was lonely and desperate for love. The orphanage only kept children until they were sixteen, so when my father reached that age, he was forced to leave to make his way in the world.

I am convinced this experience was responsible for two of his most enduring character traits: No obstacle ever daunted him, and he was imbued at a deep and personal, almost genetic, level with an ethic of helping others. When I was young, we lived in a working-class neighborhood outside Camden, New Jersey. Good friends of our family owned a struggling grocery store with a butcher shop. My father was always there, helping out, making repairs, even though he was struggling himself to make ends meet. When he rose through the ranks to become a plant supervisor for the Campbell Soup Company, he walked the floor of his plant every day to greet each of his employees personally. Well into his seventies, he was climbing onto his neighbor's roof to help with repairs.

In many ways, my father devoted his life to helping others—not through any earth-shaking achievement, but through small actions. He started his career as a tool and die maker, and perhaps it was that skill—taking things apart and putting them back together—that gave him both his problem-solving skills and his appreciation for the small things in life. One of his personal trademarks was carrying a pouch of butterscotch candies, which he gave as a treat to checkers at supermarkets, tellers in banks, and other people he encountered, along with a word of praise and thanks for whatever they had done to help him. When he pulled up to a gas station, he hopped out of the car, and in the time it took to fill the tank he learned the attendant's name, where he was from, what was important to him and the challenges he faced in life. He gave advice, encouragement, and inspiration. My father viewed it as his personal mission to make a difference in the life of every person he met.

But it seemed, at times, as if he was more generous with other people's lives than he was with ours. My father was a stern man, occasionally temperamental, and a perfectionist to the bone. He taught us responsibility from an early age—not just about chores, although we had plenty of those, but moral responsibility as well. His own childhood was consigned to a private and painful place in his memory that was off-limits for discussion or probing, but hints of it erupted any time he heard us complain, especially about food. *"You have no idea what it's like to be hungry!"* he would say.

In my father's eyes, it was wrong to find fault with something without trying to fix it. That, I think, inspired the roots of my own activism, an ethic that emerged at an instinctive level at an early age. As a Catholic teenager, I noticed that the migrant worker families in our community always sat in the back of the church, isolated and apart, as if they believed that was where they belonged. I went to our parish priest and told him he should do something about the situation because they should not feel less than equal to the rest of us. He thought I was a little crazy, I imagine, but he did stand in the pulpit and invite the migrant families to join the rest of the congregation at the front of the church. At first, they were reluctant to move from their customary pews. But over the course of the next few weeks, a handful of families moved forward each Sunday. In time, they became more comfortable, seeing themselves as a part of our community.

In high school, I witnessed the discriminatory treatment of Hispanic teens. They were often targeted for disciplinary problems that were not of their making, and they were always punished harshly. It was clear to me that some of the teachers were biased against these students. I organized a petition drive to demand more equal treatment and was suspended from school for three days.

For the most part, my father supported my activism. When I organized a town drive to collect and distribute toys to poor children in our community, he drove me around to deliver them. When I chaired a senior high school Christmas tree sale to raise money for migrant worker families, he was there with me in the cold, selling trees every day. I know my parents were not sure how they ended up with a daughter who had such strong views. Little did they realize it all started at home.

My mother was the perfect complement to a sometimes overbearing father: quiet, steady, stable. She was our emotional rock, the shoulder we could cry on. Without us saying a word, she knew when her children were hurting. A traditional woman, she would never criticize my father in front of us, but she could tell when his disapproval wounded us. In these situations, my mother's way of communicating her displeasure to my father was the silent treatment. It rarely modified his behavior, but it was still comforting to know she understood and cared about how we felt. Both of my parents were great influences in my life, each in different ways.

All those memories were vivid as I arrived to give my speech to the Ann Richards supporters in Texas. I was there to inspire activism on behalf of reproductive rights and Richards's quest for the governorship of Texas. My personal story was a cautionary tale of a world without *Roe* and an illustration of the need to elect pro-choice candidates. My parents and I were seated in the back of a restaurant, and as I heard the emcee introduce me, I rose, put one hand on each of my parents' shoulders, squeezed gently, and made my way to the front of the room. I was nervous about their reaction but also relieved that I was ending the secrecy and inviting them into this important aspect of my life. When I arrived at the podium, I thanked the emcee, greeted the audience, and turned to my parents.

"My parents are here today," I said, "and they have never heard the story I am about to tell you. I invited them because I want them to know this part of my life."

I began to tell my story. It was a speech to a hundred or so of Ann Richards's supporters, but in my mind, they were simply spectators to an intimate conversation between my parents and me. I spoke directly to my parents most of the time, searching for a sense of their reaction. I talked about how James abandoned us. That part of the story, they knew. But when I explained the pregnancy, the abortion, the indignity of the review board, and the humiliation of having to obtain James's permission, we were on uncharted waters.

My mother was in tears. She was an understated woman, hard to read sometimes, but I knew she was moved. When I looked over at my father, he looked serious but I could tell he was touched. When our eyes met, he smiled, and that one glance said it all: "It's all right."

I finished my speech, walked off the riser, went straight to our table, and embraced them both.

"We had no idea," my mother whispered. She told me she felt badly they were not there for me during that difficult time.

"I am furious about how they treated you," my father added.

And from both of them, the words that were most important: "We're proud of you."

Chapter Nine

I T HAD ALL THE HALLMARKS OF A PRE–*ROE V. WADE* TRAGEDY: a desperate young woman, an illegal abortion, a promising life truncated by a shortsighted law that assumed politicians, rather than women, knew best. But when Becky Bell, a high school junior, died of an illegal abortion, the year was neither 1958 nor 1968. It was 1988, fifteen years after *Roe* declared that the constitutional right to privacy guaranteed a woman's right to choose abortion safely and legally.

Becky lived in Indiana, where state law required that young women seeking abortions obtain permission from either their parents or a judge. The family was close, but—like many teenagers—Becky was afraid of disappointing them by revealing the pregnancy. The idea of appearing before a judge, discussing this intimate situation with a complete stranger who was in a position of authority, must have been terrifying as well. Rather than go to court, Becky had an illegal abortion. A few days later, she complained of feeling sick. At first, her parents thought she had pneumonia or the flu. Her fever spiked to 104. By the time her parents got her to the emergency room, Becky was so weak they had to carry her inside.

Her mother later recounted what happened when they arrived: "I heard the nurses say her veins had collapsed. They put oxygen on her, but Becky pulled the mask off. I leaned down and said, 'Honey, tell Mom, tell me, honey.' She said, 'Mom, Dad, I love you, forgive me.' And that was it. Her heart stopped."

I met Becky's parents, Bill and Karen Bell, in late 1989. We were each testifying before a committee of the Michigan House of Representatives that was considering a parental consent law. Michigan's governor at the time, Jim Blanchard, was strongly pro-choice, but Michigan's anti-choice movement was one of the most aggressive and well organized in the country. The anti-choice movement was pressuring the legislature to pass a measure they believed would seem reasonable. Who, after all, does not agree that parents should be involved in their daughters' decisions? But the Bells knew the issue was more complicated. They had agreed to travel throughout the country to tell their story so legislators and others would understand the real dangers of state-mandated parental consent and notification laws. Their willingness to speak out is one of the most personally courageous, selfless acts I have ever seen.

I already knew the Bells' story, but I was nonetheless heart-broken meeting them for the first time. As a mother, I could only imagine the pain they must have endured. Before the Michigan hearing began, I saw Bill and Karen across the room. Bill is a big, blond, garrulous man, the kind whose warmth envelopes you. Karen is more reserved than Bill, but every bit as engaging and caring. Bill was interested in politics, but neither of them was politically active before Becky's death, and certainly not on this issue. They were friendly, middle class, and hardworking. If a tragedy like Becky's death could happen to them, it could happen to anyone. I walked up, introduced myself, and embraced them both.

"I'm just devastated for you," I said. "As a mother, I don't know how you bear the pain. It must be very hard to tell Becky's story, but I want you to know how grateful we are that you're willing to talk about your experience so that it doesn't happen again to another family. I don't know how to thank you for what you're doing."

Bill was in tears as he evoked painful memories. "At first, we were not sure about telling our story. But we needed to give some meaning to this tragedy. Nothing can make up for this loss, but we have to try to salvage some good from it by making sure society learns from Becky's death."

State-mandated parental involvement laws like the one Michigan was considering are emblematic of a tactic the anti-choice movement has employed since Roe v. Wade was decided. Rather than trying to ban abortion outright, which most politicians acknowledge the American public does not support, they instead chip away at the right to choose, one restriction at a time. In the case of parental involvement laws, anti-choice legislators—for all their claims about promoting family values—are not social workers or family therapists. They are politicians intent on bending the law to their own purposes and denying women the right to choose regardless of the consequences. They take complicated issues and reduce them to emotional, highly charged rhetoric and simplistic solutions that often sound perfectly reasonable on the surface.

Parental involvement laws would certainly sound reasonable to me, as a mother, if I did not know the harm such requirements can cause. Having raised three daughters, I also know how challenging parenting teens can be, especially when it involves issues of their emerging sexuality. Anti-choice politicians believe government can and should force families to communicate regardless of the fact that family communication is sometimes nonexistent or dysfunctional. Even in families where communication is healthy, teenagers become more private at exactly the same time they become aware of their sexual feelings.

My daughters certainly did. I thought we had as close and open a relationship as parents and children can have, but throughout adolescence our communications were often strained. It worried me, as it does many parents. I worked hard to keep the lines of communication open. I talked frankly with them about responsible sexual behavior and especially their right to say no to sex.

But I was the one doing the talking, not the girls, and that's the key. The simple fact is that a high percentage of teens say they are sexually active, and not all of them talk to their parents. All parents assume their own daughter would tell them about a pregnancy, and the reality is that a majority voluntarily do so. The younger the teen, the likelier she is to involve her parents in a decision about pregnancy. Many young women who do not involve a parent have good reasons, including the fear of abuse or being kicked out of their homes. Pregnancies that are the result of rape or incest add an especially tragic dimension to the problem.

The idea that young women who are unable to talk with their parents should be forced to appear like criminals before a judge is absurd. Many adolescent women are confronted with abusive judges. A Louisiana judge asked one such young woman what she would say to her fetus if she had the abortion. Another judge in Ohio refused to grant permission for an abortion to a seventeen-year-old college-bound student because she "had not had enough hard knocks in her life." Their condescension is outdone only by the irony: Girls willing to endure judicial hearings to obtain an abortion because they believe they are not ready for motherhood are actually engaging in one of the most mature and thoughtful acts of their lives.

Ideally, of course, teenagers *will* talk with their parents about being pregnant. But government cannot mandate healthy family communication, and politicians should not risk the health and lives of teens by interfering in private family matters. The real question is what society can do to educate young people about sexuality, and thereby reduce the number of adolescent pregnancies and the need for abortion. And in cases where young women do not talk to their parents and are unwilling to see a judge, should we risk their lives by denying medically safe abortions? These are complex issues that do not have easy solutions.

I understand the swirl of emotions parents feel, and I respect the fact that there are divergent views on this question. Many people have counseled me to drop the issue. It's futile, they insist, and it makes the pro-choice movement look extreme. After all, who could possibly be against a law mandating that parents be involved in something as serious as choosing an abortion? My answer is: anyone who knows Bill and Karen Bell.

CHAPTER TEN

I N OCTOBER 1990, OUR OLDEST DAUGHTER, LISA, BROKE THE news to Fred and me that she was pregnant and that our first grandchild was due the following July. I was thrilled and excited about sharing the experience of pregnancy, birth, and motherhood with Lisa. Early in her pregnancy, I was traveling several days a week campaigning for pro-choice congressional candidates. The House and Senate elections that fall were the first campaigns for federal candidates in which we used our "Who Decides?" message.

Lisa, who still lived and taught in Gettysburg, remained vigorous and healthy throughout her pregnancy, even jogging daily. And in February 1991, our family increased once more when our youngest daughter, Anya, was married.

By late June, as Lisa's pregnancy was nearing its end, the "chill wind" of which Justice Blackmun had warned in the *Webster* case grew stronger when Justice Thurgood Marshall announced his retirement from the Supreme Court. NARAL knew from the narrow decision in *Webster* that *Roe* might not survive the departure of a justice who supported the constitutional right to privacy and choice. And as a lifelong civil rights activist, I was especially saddened to see such an icon of the civil rights movement leave public life.

NARAL was also wary about whom President Bush, an avowed opponent of a woman's right to choose, would nominate to replace the legendary Marshall. On July 1, the president announced federal judge Clarence Thomas, a relatively unknown conservative, as his choice. Thomas's written record was not nearly as extensive as Robert Bork's, nor was his judicial philosophy as well known. We needed to understand Thomas's views fully before charging into the public debate. Under the direction of Dawn Johnsen, NARAL's legal director, our legal team began an urgent review of Thomas's record and writings.

"We have to learn whatever we can before the White House spin on Thomas takes over," I told Dawn. "Go all night if you have to."

In the predawn hours the next morning, July 2, I was awakened by a call from Dawn.

"We've found something important," she said. In a June 1987 speech to the Heritage Foundation, Thomas had praised an article in which conservative scholar Lewis Lehrman condemned abortion and argued that a fetus had a right to life under natural law. That view was completely incompatible with *Roe*. As an official in the Reagan administration, Thomas had also been a part of a group that produced a report criticizing the Supreme Court's expansion of the right to privacy as "fatally flawed."

I was deeply concerned, if not surprised, by the extremism of Thomas's views, which left no doubt that he would cast the decisive fifth vote to overturn *Roe v. Wade*. It was critical that we inform the public without delay about what we had learned.

"Dawn," I said, "we need to prepare immediately to release this information."

Later that day, NARAL held a press conference to announce our findings and call on the Senate Judiciary Committee to conduct a thorough review of Thomas's record and judicial philosophy.

We were the first major organization to oppose Thomas's nomination publicly. Other groups within the anti-Bork coalition were proceeding with caution. Many of them were reluctant to speak out, in part because Thomas's record was unknown. It also seemed undeniable that Thomas's race played a role in their reticence. Indeed, the nomination was a cynical ploy by President Bush: He assumed that some groups in the Bork coalition would be unwilling to oppose an African-American candidate for the high court even though Thomas's views were fundamentally opposed to those of Thurgood Marshall. But it would have been the antithesis of Marshall's legacy to treat Thomas differently from any other nominee simply because he was African-American. In the end, most of the coalition unified in opposition to Thomas because of his extreme views. In so doing, they made clear that judicial philosophy was what mattered, not a nominee's race, gender, creed, or color.

Our press conference was the first evidence that the Thomas nomination would face serious opposition. But as this important battle was taking shape, I also had other priorities to balance. The day after the press conference, I returned to Gettysburg for the Fourth of July weekend to be with Lisa when the baby was born. In the middle of the night of July 5, Lisa called to tell us that she was in labor and on her way to the hospital. After a long and difficult labor, lasting nearly 24 hours, Matthew, our first grandson, was born. From the hospital hallway, Fred and I heard the baby's first cry.

The moment I heard it, I knew immediately there was a problem. Something about the sound of his cry—something almost imperceptible—instinctively told me he was struggling to breathe. I began pacing the halls. Fred was mystified.

"What's wrong?" he asked.

"Something's wrong with Matthew," I said. "I can tell."

A few moments later, the pediatrician at the hospital who gave

Matthew his preliminary examination emerged from the room, appearing calm and businesslike.

"Is everything all right?" I asked.

"Oh, yes. He's just fine."

"His cry sounded strange. It sounded like he was struggling to breathe."

"No, no," the doctor replied in a tone at once reassuring and dismissive.

"There's just mucous in his lungs. All new babies have it."

I could not specify precisely what disturbed me, but I was not satisfied with the doctor's reassurance.

"Something's definitely wrong," I insisted to Fred. I went into the delivery room, hugged Lisa, and gathered Matthew in my arms. He looked beautiful, but his cry still sounded abnormal. He continued struggling for breath, even gasping audibly. I was growing increasingly concerned, but did not want to alarm Lisa.

"You might want to have the pediatrician check his lungs again," I said before I left the hospital later that night. The next day, when Lisa and Matthew arrived home, Matthew's breathing was still labored. He seemed to struggle for air, and at one point actually started to turn blue. Within hours he was back in the hospital and in intensive care.

It was heartbreaking for me to see Matthew so sick and fragile and to watch Lisa—who was recovering from the difficult delivery—consumed with fear and worry. Eventually, Matthew's pediatrician—a different doctor from the one he saw at the hospital—concluded that he had contracted a lung infection while trapped in the birth canal.

After a week in the hospital, this pediatrician decided that Matthew was out of immediate danger and that, while his breathing and heart would still have to be monitored closely, he was well enough to return home.

With Matthew stabilized, I returned to Washington to prepare for the Thomas nomination battle, but traveled back to Gettysburg every weekend to spend time with the baby. Matthew grew stronger as the weeks progressed, but Lisa developed flu-like symptoms and a high fever. She knew something was amiss, yet her ob-gyn repeatedly assured her that nothing was wrong.

Over the next two to three months, Lisa's health deteriorated badly. I finally insisted she come to Washington, where I would find her a specialist.

Within minutes of examining her, the ob-gyn that I had arranged for her to see determined that Lisa had a raging and life-threatening infection. She immediately admitted Lisa to the hospital. A battery of tests revealed that the entire placenta had not been delivered after Matthew was born. In addition to her grave illness, the infection had badly scarred her uterus. The doctors were bluntly pessimistic about whether she would be able to have more children. (Lisa proved them wrong. She has since given birth to two more beautiful children.) It was, needless to say, a frightening start to this new chapter in our family's life.

Lisa's and Matthew's ordeals were stark examples of how profound an impact reproductive choices have on a woman and her family. They underscored dramatically the fact that pregnancy and childbearing are intense and intimate experiences that can only be undertaken by choice, not by the compulsion of the state.

As we were coping with this crisis in our family, NARAL was also dealing with the crisis of the Thomas nomination and the threat it posed to a woman's right to choose. *Roe v. Wade* and, with it, the lives and health of millions of women were at stake. Because of the nomination's pivotal importance, NARAL had requested to testify before the Senate Judiciary Committee at Thomas's confirmation hearings. By the time I was scheduled to appear that September, many witnesses, including legal scholars, had already made the important constitutional arguments that Thomas opposed privacy rights, that a woman's right to choose was endangered after a decade of Reagan/Bush rule, and that Thomas would vote to reverse precedent and overrule *Roe v. Wade*. I called my team together to discuss whether it still made sense for me to appear before the committee.

"I don't want to testify just for the sake of testifying. If I have nothing to add of significance, I don't think it's necessary." The team urged me to appear before the committee, arguing that the threat Thomas posed to *Roe v. Wade* was critically important and that the message was worth repeating even if other witnesses had already made similar arguments. I remained unsure whether I had anything to add that would enhance the committee's understanding of what was at stake.

As is so often the case, the answer to that question came to me in the middle of the night.

Legal arguments were necessary and important, but they were also often abstract. Senators—as well as the public—had already heard about precedents, penumbras of legal rights, and arguments between explicit and implicit liberties. But there was little discussion of how Thomas's judicial philosophy would affect real women's lives. I was one of untold thousands of women who understood—silently but no less powerfully—the serious, life-altering repercussions of being denied the right to choose. I had told my story in a smaller gathering, like the speech my parents attended in Texas, but I had never spoken out so personally on a national scale.

It was time for me to do so.

Sharing such an intimate story before the Senate Judiciary Committee—and millions of viewers on live television—was a daunting prospect. But I knew it was important for me to give voice to the millions of women whose experiences and views were not being heard. I gave careful thought to the tone and content of my testimony. It was important I convey the impact of my personal experience without allowing emotion to overwhelm the intellectual core of my argument.

Washington's muggy, hot summer persisted on the Thursday morning I was scheduled to testify late that September. With crowds pressing into the Senate Judiciary Committee's hearing room and television lights glaring from every angle, the chamber felt nearly as hot as the ninety-five-degree temperature outside. I knew a great deal was at stake in this hearing, for me personally and for American women. Testifying before a congressional committee is an inherently intimidating experience; revealing intimate details of my personal life to a panel of U.S. senators as well as a national television audience was especially so.

When my panel was called, I took my seat at the witness table beside Faye Wattleton of Planned Parenthood, former governor Madeline Kunin of Vermont, and Sarah Weddington, the Texas attorney who argued *Roe v. Wade* before the Supreme Court in 1973. When it came time for me to speak I was anxious that my message be one of hope for women everywhere. Slowly but with growing steadiness, I began:

> I thought very long and hard about the focus of my testimony today. During this process, I think we must remember a very simple truth. What is decided here will profoundly affect the lives of millions of Americans outside this hearing room. . . . Millions of Americans know firsthand that when we get past constitutional theory, legal precedent, and court rulings, this confirmation process will determine whether millions of women will be forced, terrified and alone, to face one of the most difficult crises of their lives. Mr. Chairman, today I must tell you that I was one of those women.

In detail, I shared my experience—James leaving us, going on welfare, discovering I was pregnant, facing the review board, being told I needed my husband's permission to undergo an abortion.

> Perhaps now you can begin to understand the pain and anger I feel when I hear the right to choose dismissed as a mere single issue. This right is absolutely fundamental; fundamental to our dignity, to our power to shape our own lives, to our ability to act in the best interests of our families. No issue, none—*none*—has a greater impact on the lives and futures of American women and their families.

When I returned to the office, the phones were ringing incessantly. Senator Paul Simon, a friend and member of the Judiciary Committee, called to say he was devastated by my story. A reporter who heard my testimony on his car radio said he was so moved he had to pull over to the side of the road. By far, though, the most gratifying calls and letters came from the ordinary women for whom I wanted to speak. Many wrote of having similar experiences. One eerily echoed my own story: "So I could get permission for an abortion, a group of psychiatrists had to say I was crazy," she wrote. "That's on my record now." Another woman once told me she, too, had to be declared legally insane to obtain permission for an abortion, and—in a tragedy many women faced—her ex-husband used that fact against her to try to take away her children.

A year later, in August 1992, Congressman Robert Dornan, a rabid anti-choice extremist from California who has since been defeated for reelection, said on the floor of the House of Representatives that "Kate Michelman . . . aborted her fourth child to get even with her husband. . . ." The statement was insulting, of course, but those familiar with Dornan's bombastic style would expect little more from him. By and large, our anti-choice opponents were silent after my testimony. Confronted with the reality of a personal story of this nature, I believe they simply did not know *how* to respond.

I felt we had made substantial progress in convincing the senators of the threat Thomas's nomination posed to women. But in early October, less than two weeks after I testified, Anita Hill's allegations of sexual harassment dramatically altered the debate, drowning out most of the discussion that had come before. In the end, Thomas was narrowly confirmed. The fifth anti-choice justice of whom Justice Blackmun warned had arrived.

Chapter Eleven

IN JANUARY 1992, IN ONE OF ITS FIRST MAJOR DECISIONS since Thomas's confirmation, the Supreme Court announced it would hear arguments in a case called *Planned Parenthood v. Casey*, which challenged the constitutionality of a Pennsylvania law restricting access to abortion. With Thomas now on the bench, speculation was rampant that the Court would use the case as an opportunity to overrule *Roe v. Wade* outright. This would end nearly two decades of legal protection for the right to choose and subject women to a nationwide patchwork of abortion laws whereby a fundamental right in one state was a felony in the state next door. Many states were virtually certain to enact total bans on abortion if the Court allowed them to do so.

While we began immediately to prepare our legal strategy in response to the case, we also knew our longer-term challenge was political. It was now critically important that we elect a pro-choice president. The right to choose was already on the brink of extinction; another Supreme Court nomination in a second Bush term would almost certainly mean *Roe*'s demise. And if the Court did use *Planned Parenthood v. Casey* to overrule *Roe*, any hope women might have for federal protection would depend on a pro-choice president.

The choice seemed stark: Elect a pro-choice president or return to the days of back-alley abortion.

About the time the Court decided to hear *Casey* and just before the first presidential primaries, we invited the ten Democratic pro-choice candidates to speak at NARAL's annual *Roe v. Wade* anniversary gala. NARAL was widely regarded as a primary political force in the pro-choice movement. Our "Who Decides?" campaign had transformed politicians' approach to the issue by empowering them with a positive message that defined the right to choose in terms of privacy and individual choice rather than whether abortion was morally right or wrong. The conventional wisdom had been to avoid talking about the right to choose, but the Florio and Wilder campaigns, as well as the congressional elections in 1990, proved that embracing the issue and talking forcefully about keeping government out of private decisions was a winning political strategy. Now it was time to take that strategy to the national stage.

Arkansas governor Bill Clinton's candidacy was already attracting growing attention that January, but few knew precisely where he stood on a woman's right to choose. Clinton was known to be moderately pro-choice, but his beliefs on specific policies were less clear—and on a woman's right to choose, the details are critical. For example, a policymaker who believes a woman should have a legal right to choose but refuses to support Medicaid funding essentially renders the right meaningless for poor women.

As he so often does, Clinton captivated the crowd that night, infusing a woman's right to choose with a sense of moral purpose. He masterfully cast the issue as one of privacy, personal and religious liberties, and freedom and equality for women. With that speech, Clinton spoke of his commitment to pro-choice values and signaled his intent to embrace the right to choose as an impor-

tant issue in his campaign. That evening, a close working relationship with the man who was to be the forty-second president of the
United States began.

As the presidential election loomed on the horizon, the National Organization for Women announced a march on Washington for April of 1992 to demonstrate broad-based support for a
woman's right to choose. It would require the dedicated involvement of many organizations—including NARAL—for the march
to succeed. NOW's plan for a large-scale mobilization was a perfectly good idea, but a march of this scale costs millions of dollars
and involves countless hours of hard work. Still, I agreed immediately that NARAL should cosponsor the event. I believed that organizing a demonstration of strong and visible support for choice
was exactly what was needed to awaken the public's consciousness
to the danger of losing their right to choose.

But the importance of the march's success could not be under-
estimated. The press, the public, and those in political office in
Washington and throughout the nation would judge the power
and relevance of the entire women's movement by the size and
scope of this march. In 1986, the March for Women's Lives attracted 250,000 people; in 1989, half a million supporters marched
and gathered on the lawn of the U.S. Capitol. It was imperative
that the 1992 march exceed that turnout in order to deflect media
stories alleging that the strength of the pro-choice movement was
in decline at exactly the moment we faced our greatest challenge in
years. Surpassing five hundred thousand would be an exceedingly
difficult task. Persuading people to vote a certain way, write their
senator, or sign a petition is challenging. Convincing them to forgo
a weekend, spend money and time, and climb aboard a bus to Washington for a march is even more so.

Our message needed to convey the gravity of the threat and the

urgency for action. Pro-choice Americans had to be inspired to believe they must participate in the march. When attempting to
persuade people to take extraordinary action, the medium one
chooses is just as important as the message. A radio advertisement
might influence people's votes, but it is not enough to motivate
them to travel halfway across the country. That would take persua-
sion of a personal nature—familiar faces using the most powerful
political tools that exist, person-by-person organizing. Mobilizing
more than half a million pro-choice Americans to travel to Washington would require a massive grassroots campaign. We knew the
risk and embraced it.

Grassroots organizing is equal parts obsessive detail and controlled chaos, and so I tapped the skill and drive of a political operative seasoned in both: Bob Bosch. Bob was a veteran of several
progressive causes, including the environment and women's rights.
He was especially passionate about both a woman's right to choose
and the importance of grassroots organizing itself. Bob was a rail-
thin, chain-smoking, hyperactive, brilliant organizer who never
seemed to sleep and who lived, as far as I could tell, on cigarettes,
coffee, and Coca-Cola. Bob took charge of the operational details. He began by targeting the key states—Massachusetts, New
York, Pennsylvania, Illinois, Virginia, Maryland, and Delaware,
among others. Experience had taught us that their close proximity
to Washington, D.C., could produce large numbers of activists. He
mobilized an army of volunteers who went door to door, setting up
tables in malls and outside grocery stores, organizing on college
campuses, holding house parties, running phone banks, and spread-
ing the message one person at a time in any way they could.

Managing an operation as diffuse as this presented its own challenges. Our thousands of NARAL volunteers had to be trained
and on-message. Moreover, chaos has its limits. Without careful

organizing, for example, competing sets of volunteers might canvass the same neighborhoods. Bob worked with NARAL affiliates to conduct trainings around the country where volunteers learned how to communicate our message; how to organize a neighborhood canvass; what kind of information to compile; and how to target those who were most likely to march.

Armed with maps and clipboards, these volunteers fanned out across the country and literally started knocking on doors. The life of the organizer is not glamorous. It consists of long days, cold pizza, repeated rejections, and few material rewards. After an initial round of organizing—in which, among other things, the canvassers compiled lists of phone numbers, addresses, and names of people who pledged to attend—volunteers began contacting these targets. In any grassroots campaign, whether the purpose is getting out the vote or organizing a march, follow-up is crucial. For every person who indicated interest, we checked back repeatedly to see whether she or he had bought a bus ticket, found lodging, and made other necessary arrangements.

Bob focused my time on providing the motivation the march needed to succeed. In press conferences, interviews, speeches, and other venues around the country, I urged pro-choice Americans not to take a woman's right to choose for granted. Bob kept tabs on the details with a level of sophistication and energy that would have made the wealthiest and farthest-flung global conglomerate envious. Every morning, he held a conference call during which key organizers in target states reported on activities. Time zone was irrelevant. Bob convened the call at precisely nine a.m. eastern time, and people in California were required to be up with a cup of coffee in one hand and progress reports in the other. He spent his day allocating resources and solving problems based on what he had learned on the call. Detailed crowd estimates percolated up from around the country, first from precinct captains, then to regional organizers, then state affiliates, who finally conveyed them to Bob.

Other logistical hurdles loomed. We wanted our "Who Decides?" message to be visible at every level of the march. If we expected more than a half million marchers, that meant we needed at least a quarter million "Who Decides?" signs. But where, exactly, does one assemble and store 250,000 signs? NARAL rented a storefront office in downtown Washington where we hammered and stapled around the clock. In the hectic weeks leading up to the march, Clinton, by then the leading Democratic candidate, visited the storefront—an encouraging sign that he had embraced a woman's right to choose as a positive, proactive, and central issue in his campaign.

By April 5, the day of the march, signs were stored in rented semitrailer trucks parked at strategic locations near metro stops, all around the metropolitan Washington area. Indications pointed to a strong turnout, but until marchers actually took their first step, nothing was certain. By four a.m., Bob was scurrying around the distribution points for signs, prowling the march route, calling every organizer we had on the ground and peppering them with questions. I checked in with Bob by phone around five a.m. I had fixated on the sign distribution as the one detail on which I would vent my nervous energy. After all, the only dilemma more difficult than how to store 250,000 signs before the march was how to get them into the hands of marchers. Bob, who was the only person in the operation more intense than I and doubtless in no mood to deal with my anxieties, assured me that everything was proceeding according to plan.

Everything that could be done was done, so I put on my sweat suit and headed out of my Capitol Hill apartment for a six a.m.

sunrise run to the Washington Monument. The day was crisp and brilliant, the sky porcelain-blue. Marchers were not scheduled to begin assembling for another four hours, but signs of life were already evident on the national mall: hundreds of buses rolling in, marchers with handmade signs beginning to appear, a handful of groups scattered from the Capitol to the Washington Monument. As I rounded the monument and headed back east toward home, even more marchers—several hundred by then—were gathering along the mall.

This was going to be an incredible day, I thought.

By the time the march set off down Pennsylvania Avenue toward the Capitol, I knew we had made history. We needed to exceed five hundred thousand, and estimates were already suggesting the crowd was at least seven hundred thousand strong. It was the largest demonstration ever held in the nation's capital. The marchers represented Americans of every conceivable background—young and old as well as all religions and ethnicities, and generations of families. Delegations from as far away as Europe and Latin America attended as well. The extraordinary sight of so many women and men who came so far to make a personal stand for the right to choose was inspiring. It was also bold confirmation that Americans did not want government to dictate their personal decisions. In addition, every marcher who attended represented many more pro-choice people back home who were unable to make the trip.

The march had accomplished its purpose. The six months of organizing and recruitment had made history. It was an enormous achievement for all the women's-rights groups involved. NOW did a superb job leading the effort. NARAL was one of many groups, including Planned Parenthood, that helped to drive turnout. We banded together to prove how serious and relevant a woman's right to choose was to the American people. We knew the political impact of the march would be tremendous. The more than seven hundred thousand people mobilized by the march represented the potential margin of victory in the presidential election. The marchers would return to their respective communities more motivated to get involved in political campaigns.

And perhaps, we hoped, the nine Americans whom we desperately needed to reach, the justices of the Supreme Court—whose chambers were located behind the Capitol—were listening.

CHAPTER TWELVE

LATER IN APRIL, THE SUPREME COURT HEARD ARGUMENTS IN *Planned Parenthood v. Casey*. From the moment the arguments concluded, an anxious waiting game ensued. Based on prior decisions, we expected at least four justices would vote to overrule *Roe v. Wade*. Potentially, millions of women were at risk of severely restrictive state abortion laws. All that was needed was a fifth vote, and there was every reason to believe that Thomas, the Court's newest addition, would provide it. On June 29—toward the end of the Court's term and nearly a year to the day since Thomas's nomination—the decision was imminent. NARAL largely existed in a collective state of anxiety as we contemplated the very real prospect that the right to choose could be lost less than twenty years after it was recognized.

We also knew a different outcome was possible. In prior legal opinions, Justice Sandra Day O'Connor suggested she might argue to leave *Roe* outwardly intact but seriously diminish its protections. In *Webster*, O'Connor had said that states could not ban abortion outright, but could restrict the circumstances under which women could choose it far more than *Roe* allowed. We spent months educating reporters about the danger such a weakened and unclear standard of protection would pose for women.

It was unusual for me to attend Supreme Court sessions, but when the decision in *Planned Parenthood v. Casey* was announced, I wanted to be there. *Roe* was hanging in the balance, and women's lives, rights, and health were at stake. The fact that the underlying case dealt with a Pennsylvania law requiring a woman to notify her husband before obtaining an abortion—a law similar to the obstacle I faced as a young woman seeking an abortion in Pennsylvania—made the case all the more personal to me.

"I feel as if my life is coming full circle," I whispered to Dawn Johnsen, NARAL's legal director, before the Court came into session. We were sitting together in the middle of the courtroom, a few rows back from the dais where the justices would soon appear. An anti-choice demonstrator who often followed me at public appearances had managed to find a seat immediately behind us. He menacingly whispered that he was certain the end of *Roe* was at hand. Dawn was extremely nervous, both about the outcome of the case and what she knew would be the intricate and difficult task of explaining to the media the impact of the Court's decision.

"I'm very worried about what we're facing," was all she said.

The tension in the chamber was palpable as the session began, and the Court's strictly enforced standards of decorum, which forbid noise of any sort, produced an eerie quiet. As I entered the chamber, the marshals ordered me to put away the notes I was holding. Even the rustling of paper might be a distraction.

As the justices entered the courtroom, I was chilled at the thought of witnessing the final moments of *Roe v. Wade*. I flashed back to my own experience and feared the Court was about to condemn untold thousands of women—and future generations—to repeat it. Then, to my surprise and relief, O'Connor began reading an opinion that not only upheld *Roe*, but also reaffirmed a woman's right to choose in some of the strongest and most eloquent language the Court had ever pronounced:

[Matters of childbearing], involving the most intimate and personal choices a person may make in a lifetime, choices central to personal dignity and autonomy, are central to the liberty protected by the Fourteenth Amendment. At the heart of liberty is the right to define one's own concept of existence, of meaning, of the universe, and of the mystery of human life. Beliefs about these matters could not define the attributes of personhood were they formed under compulsion of the State. . . . The destiny of the woman must be shaped to a large extent on her own conception of her spiritual imperatives and her place in society.

As O'Connor spoke, I was both incredulous and ecstatic that the Court would continue to protect women's fundamental right to privacy. Just moments before, we were nearly certain that the right to choose—a liberty on which women's lives depended—would be lost. When we realized that the Court upheld *Roe*, Dawn and I looked at each other in amazement and delight.

But as O'Connor continued, it became clear that a compromise that left the shell of *Roe* intact but hollowed out many of its protections was taking shape. Under *Roe*, states could not interfere in a woman's private choice unless they demonstrated a "compelling state interest" for doing so. O'Connor introduced an entirely new and murky standard. While states could not ban abortion outright, they could impose restrictions as long as they did not place an "undue burden" on women. States no longer had to demonstrate a compelling reason for restricting the right to choose. Under O'Connor's new standard, almost all of Pennsylvania's restrictions were upheld, including many the Court had previously ruled unconstitutional.

The essential problem was, and remains today, that no one knew exactly what "undue burden" meant. It was a new concept in jurisprudence that relegated a woman's right to choose to second-class status among constitutional liberties. It was still a right, but a lesser one; it was still central, but would receive less protection than other fundamental liberties. Federal judges, many of whom were opposed to *Roe*, would have wide discretion in interpreting the standard and imposing their views on women. The Court had, in essence, preserved a woman's legal right to reproductive choice but made it harder to exercise.

After O'Connor spoke, Justice Antonin Scalia announced a dissent on behalf of the remaining four justices—including Thomas. His opinion was a scathing critique of *Roe* and an ominous reminder of how many justices were eager to overrule the right to choose entirely. Years later, after Justice Harry Blackmun died and his private papers were made public, we learned how perilously close the decision had been. According to Blackmun's notes, as reported by Linda Greenhouse in the *New York Times*, the Court had actually decided to overrule *Roe* in the *Casey* decision. Chief Justice Rehnquist was in the process of writing the majority opinion when, at the last moment, Justice Anthony Kennedy—who joined the Court after Bork's defeat—changed his vote and sided with O'Connor's opinion.

When the session ended, everyone filed out of the courtroom. Only Dawn and I remained, sitting in stunned silence at the complexity of the ruling. Our exhilaration had given way to trepidation over how to communicate what had just happened. Dawn rushed up to the clerk to obtain a written copy of the opinions and began reading through them to gain a more detailed understanding of the Court's momentous decision. With reporters waiting on the steps of the court, I faced a difficult challenge: how to convey the impact of the decision to the press and the public.

The media widely expected the Court to overturn *Roe*. The fact that *Roe* had survived would dominate the headlines while the legal technicalities of the "undue burden" standard—which had

now opened the floodgates to state restrictions on abortion—
would be lost. With states now free to legislate against reproductive freedom and choice, the vigilance of pro-choice Americans
was more urgently needed. If all they heard was that *Roe* had survived, they might fall into complacency.

"Dawn," I said quietly, "this could be the beginning of the end."

States were free to impose a wide range of restrictions on the
right to choose, restrictions that would fulfill a long-standing goal
of the anti-choice movement. Each measure could provide a vehicle for court challenges that could steadily weaken *Roe* until it was
overturned. The states could also be used as laboratories to test the
viability of restrictions that the anti-choice movement could then
introduce at the federal level.

When I commented on the potential impact of the *Casey* ruling to the press, I sounded that warning. I was accused of over-
reacting. But in the years since, our warning has been vindicated.
Since 1995, states have enacted more than four hundred restrictions on reproductive rights, from arbitrary waiting periods for
women seeking abortions, to parental consent laws that endanger
young women's lives, to onerous regulations designed to harass
providers of reproductive health services. Access to abortion is
now restricted in a majority of states. The impact of these laws on
women's lives has been coercive and financially and emotionally
devastating. Indeed, women today have fewer rights than their
mothers did in 1973, when *Roe* was first decided.

Preserving *Roe* was, of course, an important legal victory, but a
frighteningly narrow one. The close margin on the Court underscored the importance of electing a pro-choice president. By the
time *Casey* was decided, Clinton had secured the Democratic
nomination. We knew he would be asked to comment on the ruling, so Clinton's staff arranged in advance for me to call him when

the decision was announced. On my way out of the court, I dialed his number.

"Governor, the decision contains good news and bad news," I said. "The Court upheld *Roe*, but also weakened its protections. If you go into the legal details, your message may be lost. My advice is that you emphasize that four justices wanted to overturn *Roe*, and that if President Bush is re-elected, they'll get the fifth. If you're elected, we hope you will appoint justices who will uphold fundamental constitutional rights."

"It's awfully good news that *Roe* was upheld," he replied. "But I understand the danger of this new standard. I want you to know that you can count on me to continue to stand up for a woman's right to choose."

Throughout the presidential campaign, NARAL's strategy was to position the right to choose—especially the future of the Supreme Court—in the forefront of the national political debate. We were also determined not to treat a woman's right to choose as a partisan issue. I believed it was important to work across party lines, so I flew to Houston for the 1992 Republican National Convention. A number of courageous pro-choice Republicans were attempting to repeal the official party platform's opposition to *Roe v. Wade*. The moment I stepped off the plane at the Houston airport, I saw a throng of anti-choice demonstrators. Operation Rescue had learned the details of my arrival—a disconcerting invasion of privacy that remains a mystery to this day. They carried pictures of mutilated fetuses and called out chants such as "Baby killer!" and "You're on a losing mission!"

The latter turned out to be true. All efforts to make inroads at the platform committee failed. The convention was steeped in so much hostile rhetoric that at times I found it hard to believe I was in America. Pat Buchanan's mean-spirited speech to the delegates in Houston probably won more votes for Clinton than all the words spoken at the Democratic convention combined. Finally, I gave up and decided to return home. Hotel arrangements at political conventions have to be made through the sponsoring party, so it was no surprise that I was booked at a rundown motel miles from the convention site. When I packed to check out, I found roaches in my suitcase.

While our political and field operations were intensifying around the presidential and congressional races, NARAL was also organizing support for the Freedom of Choice Act, or FOCA, a bill to codify the protections of *Roe v. Wade* into federal law. With federal statutory protection, women would no longer have to depend solely on the Supreme Court to safeguard the right to choose. FOCA emerged as a strategy in the aftermath of the 1989 *Webster* decision and gained momentum as *Casey* approached and we faced the real possibility of *Roe* being overturned. Senator Alan Cranston of California led the effort in the Senate, while Representatives Don Edwards and Barbara Boxer of California introduced the bill in the House. The Freedom of Choice Act arose out of legal necessity, but it also presented a political opportunity. If FOCA passed the Democratic Congress, President George H. W. Bush would be forced to veto the bill to appease his far-right base on the eve of the presidential election. With irrefutable evidence, he would demonstrate to mainstream Americans his fundamental opposition to a woman's right to privacy and choice.

Late that summer, while on a family vacation in New Hampshire with Fred and the girls, I received a call from Senate Majority Leader George Mitchell. The FOCA strategy hinged on his leadership and support, and some on our staff were concerned about whether or not we would have them. Earlier, on a related choice issue, Senator Mitchell had made a speech criticizing pro-choice groups for putting too much pressure on the Senate. James Wagoner, NARAL's political director, had expressed his frustration.

"Senator Mitchell's a good man," I replied. "He's pro-choice, and he cares about women's rights. Let me talk with him."

I had spoken with Mitchell several times, making both the cases that a woman's right to choose needed federal statutory protection and that FOCA could be politically advantageous. When he reached me in New Hampshire, Mitchell had encouraging news: He supported the FOCA strategy, both legally and politically.

"I'm on board," he said. "I'm ready to make this happen."

Our first major challenge was addressing the scope of the bill. Ideally, FOCA would both embody the legal protections of *Roe v. Wade* and ensure its full promise. The law would guarantee that abortion was both legal *and* accessible. At the same time, we had to be realistic about what a single bill could accomplish.

Mitchell, a careful and cautious realist, was direct: "Parental consent and Medicaid funding are nonstarters." If FOCA either preempted state parental consent laws or provided Medicaid funding for abortion, senators with ambivalent views and mixed voting records on the issue would oppose the bill. Such an outcome would play directly into anti-choice hands. Rather than forcing a presidential veto, we would hand our opponents a victory. They would claim we were incapable of mustering the support to pass a bill. And the entire debate would focus on two of the most difficult and controversial issues rather than on a woman's right to privacy and choice. The challenge was how to protect both poor and young women's rights while achieving federal protection.

In the first draft of the bill, parental consent and Medicaid funding were left deliberately vague. Senator Mitchell now felt their exclusion had to be explicit.

"We will be forced to confront the issues eventually," he said. "It's better to address them at the outset."

Mitchell introduced a substitute bill making it clear that FOCA did not compel Medicaid funding for abortion or forbid states from imposing parental notification requirements.

Leaders of the pro-choice coalition met in Senator Alan Cranston's office to discuss whether to support Mitchell's substitute. Many of Congress' foremost pro-choice leaders were there: Cranston, Barbara Boxer, Don Edwards, and Senators Bob Packwood and Howard Metzenbaum among them.

"I understand that Mitchell's bill is not exactly what we would each prefer," Boxer said. "But it's the only bill with a realistic chance of success."

I agreed. "It's difficult," I said. "Medicaid funding and parental notification are very important, so we must address them in a parallel but separate strategy. But our immediate imperative is passing the best possible bill."

After a lively discussion, most of the group endorsed Mitchell's approach.

In the late fall, during a strategy meeting in Mitchell's office, one of the senator's aides informed him that George Stephanopoulos—one of Clinton's top aides—was on the phone.

"They're concerned about moving the bill during the campaign," Mitchell said. "I've already heard them out and have told them I'm moving forward. Kate, this is a decision for you and the coalition to make. You must decide whether we proceed or not."

James Wagoner left the room to take the call on my behalf. If Clinton won the presidency, Stephanopoulos assured, the White House would support the Freedom of Choice Act. But at the time, they were concerned that FOCA would distract from the campaign's economic message. I was skeptical of their reasoning. NARAL's experience clearly demonstrated that a woman's right to choose was a winning message. In the end, we decided to err on the side of caution and agreed to delay moving the bill. NARAL had made electing a pro-choice president a top priority, and I did not want to do anything that might interfere with that goal.

Throughout the fall, NARAL conducted an independent expenditure campaign to elect Bill Clinton. In the field, we established a broad-based and highly professional operation aimed at undecided and swing voters. A key objective was to persuade pro-choice independents and Republicans, particularly women, that the threat to women's rights and lives was real and important enough to warrant crossing party lines. We concentrated our efforts in the swing states, including Florida, Minnesota, Ohio, Oregon, Pennsylvania, Washington, and Wisconsin. In each state, we conducted polling, aired advertising, and undertook get-out-the-vote activities with the single-minded purpose of educating, persuading, and mobilizing the pro-choice vote. Typically, a national advocacy group like NARAL would have engaged in the election from a distance through advertising or financial contributions. Instead, we treated the issue of a woman's right to choose, itself, as though it were a candidate on the ballot in each state.

The 1992 campaign marked NARAL's first use of the "Who Decides?" strategy in a presidential race. Research showed that women were likelier to vote on the basis of the right to choose once they understood the threat. We employed a political consulting firm to identify pro-choice women in our targeted states, then initiated a voter contact program to educate, persuade, and mobilize them. We believed our strategic focus on women, emphasizing a message about the threat to their right to choose, would fuel a gender gap necessary to Clinton's victory.

While the presidential campaign was our most important priority, we also focused on electing congressional candidates who would fight for a woman's right to choose on Capitol Hill. In the aftermath of *Webster* and *Casey*, with state legislators wielding increasing power to restrict reproductive rights, it was especially important to build relationships in Congress. The emergence of several talented women candidates for the Senate—Barbara Boxer and Dianne Feinstein in California, Patty Murray in Washington State, Carol Moseley-Braun in Illinois, and others—provided the opportunity we needed. In 1992, politics was still a mostly male bastion. Many skeptics were reluctant to believe that so many women could rise to positions of prominence in a single election year. But as I traveled the country campaigning for these women, I could sense momentum building.

For me personally, the campaign was simultaneously exhausting and exhilarating. I was on the road for weeks on end, visiting every swing state, briefing the media, and speaking at rallies. There were long periods of time when I was rarely in the office. Early one morning, I awoke in a hotel room with literally no idea where I was or even what day it was. I had to think about what I had done the day before in order to locate myself in time and space. (I finally realized I was in San Antonio, Texas.)

Fred was still teaching full time at Gettysburg College, which meant we only saw each other intermittently on weekends. Even those sparse visits evaporated as I spent more and more time traveling in the fall. The separation placed tremendous strain on us both. We had to work especially hard to maintain our emotional intimacy and support one another using the telephone as our main point of contact. Lisa was disappointed that I could not spend more time being a grandmother to Matthew, and I was equally sad that I was missing many special moments in his young life. But my entire family was unfailingly supportive. They understood the extraordinary stakes of this election and the strong responsibility I felt to the women whose lives would be at risk without a pro-choice president.

Excitement mounted as Election Day approached. The threat to a woman's right to choose, combined with a backlash against the shameful treatment of Anita Hill, generated what went down in history as the "Year of the Woman." Boxer, Feinstein, Murray, and Moseley-Braun all prevailed in their senate races. Clinton won the presidency by a comfortable margin.

Most political pundits credited the economy as the major force behind Clinton's victory. But deeper analysis showed that a woman's right to choose was a driving, even decisive, issue. After the election, Alan Abramowitz, a political scientist at Emory University, scrutinized election returns and found that fully 17 percent of Republican voters defected to either Clinton or Ross Perot over the right to choose alone. He summarized his findings in an article whose title put a new twist on the widely publicized motto of the Clinton campaign: "It's abortion, stupid."

American women had traveled an extraordinary distance from June, when the end of *Roe v. Wade* seemed all but a forgone conclusion, to November, when the first fully pro-choice president in history was elected. In just that brief period, women emerged from peril to great possibility and hope. Not only could we defend against attacks on a woman's right to choose, a forward-looking, progressive, pro-choice policy—investing in women's and children's health, expanding women's options, and making abortion less necessary—seemed to be within our grasp.

CHAPTER THIRTEEN

T HE ELECTION OF PRESIDENT WILLIAM JEFFERSON CLINTON
marked a monumental turning point in the struggle for a
woman's right to choose. For the previous twelve years, two suc-
cessive presidents had used all the power at their disposal to deny
women their right to choose and to make access to the reproductive health services they needed more difficult. The *Webster* and
Casey decisions had positioned *Roe v. Wade* a single vote away
from being overturned. Clinton's election as the nation's first fully
pro-choice president halted the anti-choice movement's inexorable
march toward a Supreme Court with enough votes to destroy *Roe*.

Since assuming leadership of NARAL, we had been on the defensive against attacks on reproductive rights. Political activism
usually meant battling a threat from the White House, Congress,
or legislators at the state level. With Clinton preparing to take the
oath of office, we had a meaningful opportunity to move beyond
the endless attacks on legal abortion and toward a positive, comprehensive vision for a pro-choice society. I made the case in an
op-ed in the *Chicago Tribune*:

> The immediate challenge to this new administration is to
> pull together the pieces of a comprehensive reproductive health

policy—a policy that goes well beyond abortion to contraception, education and nurturing. A policy that makes clear to women and men the options and the consequences of having children—free from dogma and ideology. Not just the joys—but the responsibilities. Not just the gifts—but the costs.

With both Congress and the White House in pro-choice hands, this was the moment to invest in pregnancy prevention, family planning, comprehensive sex education, prenatal care, child care, and other social supports necessary to strengthen women and families. Rather than judging and controlling the decisions women made, the nation could focus on improving the conditions that shaped their lives and choices.

The Clinton era began on a propitious note for the pro-choice movement. In the days leading up to his inauguration, NARAL approached the Clinton transition team with a proposal to mark *Roe v. Wade*'s twentieth anniversary with a series of executive orders repealing a number of the Reagan and Bush administration's most egregious anti-choice policies. Reagan and Bush had imposed a gag rule prohibiting doctors in federally funded family planning programs from giving women complete and accurate information about their reproductive options. They had banned FDA testing of the new drug called RU-486, a promising early medical alternative to surgical abortion. In a devastating rule known as the "Mexico City policy," they had stripped foreign family-planning organizations serving the world's neediest women of U.S. funding if they used their own money to perform or even discuss abortion.

The Clinton team accepted our suggestion of using the *Roe* anniversary to overturn the Reagan/Bush policies. They appointed Walter Dellinger, a highly respected constitutional scholar—and later the solicitor general of the United States—to work with

NARAL to formulate the measures. Dellinger and Dawn Johnsen closeted themselves away for days, drafting President Clinton's first presidential executive orders. On Clinton's second day in office, I was thrilled to be in the White House with other leaders of the women's movement to witness the president's first official act on behalf of women's rights.

This milestone was both awe-inspiring and a powerful reminder of the importance of elections. For the preceding twelve years, the White House would never even have returned our telephone calls, much less agreed to a policy suggestion and invited NARAL to see it implemented. Now, with the stroke of a pen, Clinton single-handedly transformed millions of women's lives. A pro-choice president made all the difference.

But the elation of those early days of the Clinton administration was short-lived. Convinced the election of a pro-choice president had put an end to threats to reproductive rights, many pro-choice Americans relaxed their guard and retreated into apathy. The impact was dramatic. Our fund-raising and membership support, which had shattered records throughout 1992, precipitously declined.

This dramatic downturn in revenues was an example of a problem the pro-choice movement has faced repeatedly over the years: Victory often weakens our resolve. Many of our supporters are lulled into indifference by the fallacy that a single achievement can change our world permanently. The reality is far different. Opponents of women's rights and freedoms are tenacious and determined, even in the face of defeat, to deny women the right to choose. Organizations like NARAL will always be necessary to protect and defend freedom of choice and will always require the financial resources to remain effective. A businessperson might assess NARAL's groundbreaking successes in 1992 as worthy of additional investment. In social movements, success often produces the opposite result: Effectiveness means people believe it is safe to give less. (The environmental movement faced the same challenge.)

After twelve years outside the corridors of power, fending off one attack after another, we struggled with one of the most vexing dilemmas in political activism: how to make the transition from opposing to governing. When the Freedom of Choice Act began moving through the Senate that spring, that dilemma fractured our movement.

Clinton's ascendance to the White House fundamentally transformed the environment in which FOCA was originally conceived. We now had a serious opportunity to enact a federal law that would resolve the uncertainty women faced in the aftermath of *Webster* and *Casey*, both of which gave the states broad leeway to restrict the right to choose. In ever-increasing numbers, state legislatures were seizing the opportunity to intrude into reproductive privacy. Women faced growing barriers to the medical care they needed. And their lives and health were threatened as a result. We needed to act quickly.

Some in the pro-choice coalition, such as the National Organization for Women and the American Civil Liberties Union, remained concerned that the bill did not address issues like Medicaid funding and parental notification. Both issues were critically important, but NARAL and others in the coalition believed we would more likely succeed if we addressed them in parallel but separate strategies. Our difference of opinion was purely tactical rather than substantive in nature. While we worked with our allies to promote a companion bill ensuring access to reproductive health services for low-income women, I urged the coalition groups to support moving on FOCA immediately, while the political environment was favorable.

Prior to the election, we had embarked on an aggressive strategy of recruiting cosponsors for the bill. The goal was to achieve early and strong support from our allies in Congress to build momentum and lend FOCA a sense of inevitability. Senator Carol Moseley-Braun, who had just been elected from Illinois, was one of our earliest supporters, but the National Organization for Women, opposed to FOCA because of the Medicaid and parental consent issues, quietly convinced her to withdraw her support. The moment she removed her name as a cosponsor, the strategy began to unravel. I knew it was the beginning of the end. The controversy would make it difficult for other senators to continue supporting the bill without appearing to be less committed to the needs of minors or poor women. One by one, senators began withdrawing their support. I took to the op-ed page of the *Washington Post* to make the case for the bill:

> The challenge for pro-choice America is to show that we do care, that we are too smart and too determined to be polarized. If we sacrifice the Freedom of Choice Act because it does not in itself embody the entire pro-choice vision, we miss a rare opportunity to make progress. If, ultimately, we accept nothing because we cannot get everything, we hand opponents of choice a victory they did not win. The election victories still offer real hope for significant, lasting progress. But for the Democratic leaders who promised the American people they would support a woman's freedom to choose, and for a pro-choice movement in transition, this is a moment of truth.
>
> Today's fight over the Freedom of Choice Act isn't about rich and poor, black and white, urban and rural, or young and old. It is about standing together and facing down the religious right, about refusing to squander last year's election gains and about making a real commitment to the long-term battle for the multifaceted legislative program that will secure true reproductive choice for American women.

But that view was not shared by the entire coalition. Even if it meant defeat, some of the groups believed it was more important to insist that this single bill achieve everything we ultimately aspired to rather than accept an imperfect but still substantial step forward. In my view, this was movement politics at its least effective. I urged the other groups to hold together, but to no avail. Senators were calling saying they had no desire to take sides in what appeared to be a public squabble among women's-rights groups. Once the cascade began, it could not be stopped.

I called Senator Mitchell, who was, as always, direct: "It's hard to see how we move forward."

"I know. I'm sorry. I'm very grateful for your support, and I can't tell you how disappointed I am."

Personally, I was frustrated with the coalition's actions and with my failure to foresee the problem and to resolve the differences before the bill moved forward. To this day, it stands out as one of the greatest disappointments of our movement. The White House and leadership of Congress were pro-choice, polling found public support for FOCA to be strong, and we had a real opportunity to guarantee women, no matter where they lived, the right to make reproductive choices free from government intrusion. The law could have protected women from the humiliation and burden of many of the more than four hundred state restrictions that have since interfered with their choices. It may be years before we wield that much political power again. A time would come when we would have readily accepted a fraction of FOCA's protections. But the moment was lost. Within a year, it was too late.

CHAPTER FOURTEEN

I T WAS NO LESS STUNNING FOR HAVING BEEN, IN RETROSPECT, so inevitable. On March 10, 1993, one of my staff rushed into my office, obviously distraught.

"A doctor's been shot!"

That morning, Dr. David Gunn, an ob-gyn, stepped out of his car and headed for the back entrance of a Pensacola, Florida, clinic that had been besieged by protestors. The graphic signs and provocative chants—"David Gunn kills babies!"—were familiar, but what happened next was tragic. A man chased Dr. Gunn down, pulled out a snub-nosed .38 caliber revolver, shouted "Don't kill any more babies!" and shot him three times in the back at point-blank range. Dr. Gunn died within hours.

Several anti-choice groups condemned the murder, but there was no escaping the movement's responsibility for contributing to a menacing climate in which violence was acceptable. Some even called the killing justifiable homicide. The leader of one extremist group, Rescue America, set up a fund for the murderer's family, explaining, according to the *Chicago Sun-Times*, "We know that the abortionist is well taken care of. But there is a financial strain for the assailant." It was chilling to hear murder condoned so openly.

The public was now witness to the deadly tactics of the more extreme elements of the anti-choice movement.

That day I joined Gloria Feldt of Planned Parenthood, Patricia Ireland of NOW, Ellie Smeal of the Feminist Majority Foundation, and other pro-choice leaders in calling for federal legislation to protect clinics against invasive, threatening protests that crossed the line from free speech to hostile aggression, violation of privacy, and blocking both clinic operations and patients' access to care. Such a law, the Freedom of Access to Clinic Entrances Act, or "FACE," was already pending before Congress. FACE was carefully drafted to balance the rights of demonstrators to freedom of speech with women's rights to obtain the health care they needed. We had been advocating for the law since the Atlanta and Wichita protests, but it had been met with resistance from labor unions. They, along with the ACLU, were concerned about its effect on lawful picketing and the rights of assembly and free expression. In the face of Dr. Gunn's murder, we urged Congress to take up the legislation without delay.

Leaders of pro-choice and women's-rights groups met with Attorney General Janet Reno to seek her endorsement of FACE as well as an immediate infusion of federal funds for clinic security. Merely the fact that the Justice Department was willing to meet face to face with us was another sign of the significant impact of the presidential election. For twelve years, the Justice Department was off limits to pro-choice advocates. It was also the place from which Reagan and Bush initiated many of the most serious attacks on *Roe v. Wade* in the form of legal briefs to the Supreme Court arguing that *Roe* should be overturned.

Reno was known to be pro-choice, but she also had a reputation as a highly independent person who did not respond well to pressure. And whatever her views about a woman's constitutional right to choose, she was responsible for safeguarding all liberties, including those of anti-choice protestors. Our task was to present the facts regarding the climate of violence that had taken hold at clinics and the compelling need for increased federal law enforcement to protect them.

Reno is not an outwardly emotive person, but she listened intently as Ellie Smeal and Gloria Feldt reported their findings. Each of their groups had conducted an extensive analysis of clinic violence, providing empirical evidence that protestors were creating serious barriers for women seeking to exercise their constitutional right to choose.

"I share your concern about the growing wave of violence," Reno said. "We need to balance the rights of protestors with the rights of women seeking health care."

"We are confident the FACE law achieves a fair balance," I responded, emphasizing the fact that pro-choice and women's groups were just as concerned about preserving our right to demonstrate as anyone. "There is a difference between peaceful protest and protest that infringes on other people's rights," I said. "The clinics have become battlegrounds of violence and fear."

As the meeting concluded, Reno thanked us for the information and pledged that she would take any constitutionally permissible steps to protect access to the clinics. When Congress held hearings on FACE, the attorney general testified in favor of the law.

Shocked by Dr. Gunn's murder, clinics dramatically increased their security. Physicians began taking extra precautions. Dr. George Tiller, a friend and courageous ob-gyn who was determined to provide services when few others would, told me with grim humor, "Every time I turn that ignition key I expect to find myself blown to smithereens." His clinic had been blockaded during anti-choice protests. Dr. Tiller was cautious (he wore a bulletproof vest) but always compassionate. Earlier that year, he had lowered his fees so his services would be more affordable, provoking intense outrage and aggression from protestors.

In the aftermath of Dr. Gunn's murder, we were especially concerned about copycat shootings, a worry that became all too real one evening that August when someone told me a woman in Wichita had shot a doctor outside a clinic.

"Oh, my God!" I cried. "Who was it?"

"George Tiller."

When I reached Dr. Tiller by phone in his hospital room, he assured me his injuries were not life-threatening. He had been shot in both arms, however, and had narrowly escaped losing all function. Had the injury been worse, it might have ended his medical career.

"I'm okay, Kate, but it was a shock. I thought it was the end of my days," he said, before adding a statement especially befitting a physician of his character. "I'll tell you this: If they think they're going to stop me from providing women abortions, they've got another thing coming."

As they had been after Dr. Gunn's murder, anti-choice extremists were blunt in commenting on the shooting of Dr. Tiller. "The chickens have come home to roost in Tiller's house," one said. The continuing wave of anti-choice violence finally sparked congressional action. In 1994, under the leadership of then representative Charles Schumer, Congress passed FACE and President Clinton signed it into law. By the following year, even as sensible an idea as protecting health clinics against violence stood no chance on Capitol Hill.

As the 1994 midterm elections for Congress approached, we faced a difficult political landscape. Pundits expected the elections to be a referendum on President Clinton's early record and policies, and his popularity was unsteady at best. Clinton's health care reform plan had antagonized the right wing and was headed for failure. The president's party almost always loses seats in midterm elections, but few predicted what was coming.

The right to choose was not a major issue in the 1994 elections. Many pro-choice Americans believed reproductive freedom to be safe under a pro-choice president, so they did not focus on the threat posed by Congress or state legislatures. Two of our staunchest pro-choice allies—Senators Ted Kennedy of Massachusetts and Chuck Robb of Virginia—were facing difficult campaigns. Kennedy, one of the Senate's champions of women's rights, was challenged by Mitt Romney, a millionaire businessman. Romney declared himself to be pro-choice, but while he had no record on the issue because he had never held elective office, there were reasons to doubt Romney's claim. NARAL's research revealed that he been endorsed by a far-right anti-choice group in Massachusetts and that he favored restricting a woman's right to choose.

A number of candidates across the country adopted a misleading strategy of claiming they were pro-choice, even though they supported serious restrictions on reproductive rights. Politicians increasingly recognized the political danger of openly declaring their anti-choice views. NARAL responded with our "Great Pretenders" campaign, in which we targeted certain of these candidates, including Romney, Texas senator Kay Bailey Hutchison, Georgia senator Paul Coverdell, New York gubernatorial candidate George Pataki, and California senatorial candidate Michael Huffington. The fact that our "Great Pretenders" campaign was necessary was in and of itself encouraging. Candidates pretending to be pro-choice were powerful evidence of what our polling routinely indicated—that most Americans believe that women, not politicians, should decide.

In Virginia, Marshall Coleman—who had called for a ban on abortion as a candidate for governor in 1989—ran as an independent. Robb's most serious opponent, however, was Republican Oliver North, who was making his debut as a political figure after his key role in the Iran-Contra scandal. Unlike some other Republicans, North was absolutely forthright in his position on abortion: He wanted to make it a crime, even in cases of rape and incest, and he did not hesitate to declare his intentions openly. North's prominence would make this campaign a national bellwether. That—combined with Robb's strong and uncompromising pro-choice stand—made it especially important that Robb prevail. I was disappointed, if not surprised, when some women's groups refused to support Robb because of an allegation that he had had an extramarital affair. One even endorsed a Democratic primary challenger whose only real effect in the race was to weaken Robb against North. Robb was not being accused of either a pattern of harassment or abuse of his public office. The allegations dealt with a personal indiscretion that was a matter for Robb and his wife to resolve. For the women's movement, and the voters, the more important question was whether Senator Robb or Oliver North— whether a strong pro-choice advocate or a radical opponent of *Roe v. Wade*—would serve in the United States Senate.

NARAL endorsed Robb early and campaigned aggressively for him. Robb made his pro-choice views a prominent issue in his campaign. Meanwhile, the North candidacy caught fire quickly. Right-wing money poured in from across the nation. The Republican National Committee made North's campaign a national priority. Polls showed him leading or at least neck and neck heading into the final days. It was a perilous sign for a pro-choice incumbent like Robb.

I spent most of election night at Robb's headquarters in the Virginia suburbs of Washington. When he was declared the winner by a narrow margin, I was both relieved and overjoyed. This was a victory achieved against difficult odds for a courageous pro-choice leader, and reports of Kennedy's solid win in Massachusetts made it even sweeter. But as news from races across the country came in, a complete political catastrophe began to take shape. Democratic members of the House were defeated in large numbers, including some of our closest allies. House Speaker Tom Foley, whose support had been critical during the battle over the Freedom of Choice Act, was defeated by a political novice. Jim Sasser—a pro-choice Democrat from Tennessee and a possible senate majority leader—lost his seat to anti-choice Republican Bill Frist.

By the end of the night, thirty-four House members and two senators had lost their seats, and anti-choice Republicans had solid control of both bodies for the first time in decades.

One night not long after the election, I was in my kitchen when the phone rang. A journalist was on the other end of the line.

"I need to ask you some questions about Senator Packwood," she said.

Senator Bob Packwood of Oregon was one of NARAL's closest allies on Capitol Hill. He was among the last of a vanishing breed of moderate, pro-choice Republicans. But Packwood was more than a reliable pro-choice vote. He was an outspoken leader on women's rights. Even before *Roe v. Wade*, he had offered a bill to legalize abortion. He and another pro-choice Republican, Senator Lowell Weicker of Connecticut, often led filibusters against anti-choice legislation, sleeping on cots in their offices while taking turns speaking around the clock.

During the 1980s, as the religious right began to overtake the Republican establishment, pro-choice moderates like Packwood felt increasingly isolated. "Kate," Packwood once told me, "I don't even feel welcome at the Republican convention anymore." Senator John Chafee, a pro-choice Republican from Rhode Island, told me years later that one of the reasons he had decided to retire from the Senate was that he no longer recognized his party and detested the mean-spiritedness that took hold on Capitol Hill after the 1994 elections.

"Our party is in the grip of a right-wing minority," he said. "It's getting worse, and I just don't want to be a part of it."

In addition to being a courageous pro-choice leader, Packwood was also a personal friend. When I assumed NARAL's leadership, he held a reception in the Capitol to welcome me, and the senator and my husband shared a love of jazz. But from what the reporter described on the telephone that night, there was a great deal about Packwood that I did not know. She revealed several allegations of sexual misconduct, including inappropriate behavior with members of his staff. What, she wanted to know, was my reaction as a women's-rights leader?

I was dumbstruck. The behavior she was describing was unconscionable, and coming on the heels of the Clarence Thomas nomination, public consciousness about, and media interest in, sexual harassment was intense. From the beginning, I knew Packwood faced a political catastrophe. I felt torn between my admiration for Packwood's lifetime of advocacy for women's rights and my abhorrence of the behavior of which he was accused. Regardless, I had no firsthand knowledge of the allegations, and I had no desire to participate in what amounted to a public hanging. I told the reporter that, if the allegations were true, Packwood must be held accountable, but I declined to comment further. I simply did not know enough, I explained.

The reporter was incredulous. After the Packwood story broke, many people suddenly claimed to have known about the allegations for years. But the truth is that they were not common knowledge either at NARAL or in the circles in which I traveled. Many of our critics, especially anti-choice leaders, took advantage of the situation to accuse women's-rights groups of hypocrisy. They said we refused to condemn Packwood because he was a leader on women's rights. Once the truth about Packwood's conduct was established, I forcefully condemned the behavior, but felt no need to heap gratuitous scorn on someone whose career was already being destroyed. Soon enough, the inevitable occurred: Packwood resigned. It was at once gratifying to see the country take the allegations so seriously and terribly painful to watch a friend being publicly humiliated.

As the Packwood scandal wore on, the newly Republican Congress, led by Newt Gingrich, overreached on one issue after another. They attacked long-standing and broadly supported institutions from public television to the Department of Education as they implemented the "Contract with America." Their mistake was a classic example of political hubris. They falsely interpreted the election of 1994 as a sweeping public mandate for a far–right-wing agenda. There was no question that the election resulted in a profound reordering of the political landscape. But the most important reason for the Republicans' success was turnout, not ideology: The religious right flocked to the polls, and moderate voters stayed home.

The anti-choice Republican majority began proposing restrictions on reproductive rights almost immediately. Legal abortion was only the beginning. In July 1995, House Appropriations chairman Robert Livingston tried to undermine the federal family planning program for poor women by permitting states to decide whether or not to offer these services. When he introduced the measure, he did not mince words. "Today," he said, "is payback time."

President Clinton often was forced to veto bills to prevent anti-choice measures from becoming law. But some prevailed, such as a ban on servicewomen or military dependents using their own money to obtain abortions at overseas military hospitals. They have all but faded from public consciousness, but their personal impact remains real.

Army general Claudia Kennedy once publicly testified about the experience of a pregnant American soldier in Germany who needed to have an abortion. Even if she paid for it with her own money, the soldier could not have the procedure at a U.S. military hospital. Flying home to a private hospital in the United States might have been an option, but she could not afford the trip and did not want to divulge her pregnancy to her superiors in order to obtain leave. Her only option was to leave the base for an abortion in Germany. As Kennedy told the story:

> [T]he experience [was] both mortifying and painful. . . . no pain killer of any sort was administered for the procedure; the modesty of this soldier and the other women at the clinic had been violated (due to different cultural expectations about nudity); and neither she nor the soldier understood German, and the instructions were given in almost unintelligible English. I believe that they were able to get some follow-up care for the soldier at the U.S. Army medical facility. But it was a searing experience for all of us—that in a very vulnerable time, this American who was serving her country overseas could not count on the Army to give her the care she needed.

Congress also renewed the Hyde Amendment, which prohibited the use of federal funds to perform abortions except in cases of rape and incest or to save the life of the woman. The law often triggers an inhumane calculus, a fact I learned late one night when my phone rang while at NARAL. The voice on the other end of the line was distressed.

"I'm desperate to get help for my niece," the woman said through tears. The caller's niece, who was married to an enlisted man in the navy, was diagnosed with a malignant brain tumor while she was pregnant. Doctors advised her to begin radiation and chemotherapy but, because the treatments could harm the fetus, they recommended that she have an abortion. Under the Hyde Amendment, though, the abortion could only be covered by her military health insurance or performed in a military hospital if the pregnancy threatened her life. In this case, it was the brain tumor, not the pregnancy itself, that posed the threat.

"My niece already has one child," the elderly aunt pleaded. "I don't want that child to be an orphan. What can I do?"

Under federal law, there was little she could do but plead for private help. NARAL arranged for her to have an abortion at a Washington-area hospital. It was a travesty that a woman whose husband was serving our country had to beg and plead for help to save her own life.

The Hyde Amendment's impact on poor women who depended on Medicaid was equally devastating. A case from Louisiana illustrated the implications of the policy in compelling terms. Michelle Lee, a twenty-seven-year-old mother near Shreveport who was awaiting a heart transplant, became pregnant when her contraception failed. She was single and poor, two qualities on which many politicians do not look favorably. Michelle's cardiologist advised an abortion, warning that her fragile heart might not be able to bear the strain of a pregnancy. Pregnancy would also make her ineligible for a heart transplant.

Under the Hyde Amendment, Medicaid could only pay for Michelle's abortion if it was necessary to save her life. Michelle's situation should have been an obvious case, but Louisiana, an extremely anti-choice state, imposed a stricter standard. In order for

Medicaid to cover the abortion, a panel of doctors had to decide that Michelle would *probably* die without it. The doctors' conclusion was chilling: She only had a 50 percent chance of surviving the pregnancy. Michelle *might* die, but they could not say definitively that she was *likely* to. Her request for Medicaid coverage was denied. With no money of her own, she was out of options, with her life literally on the line.

The news of Michelle's story was shocking but also typical of the attitude many anti-choice politicians display toward women, especially poor women. The simple fact is that Michelle's life counted less to them. She was a single mother, sick, poor, and vulnerable, and because she depended on the government for health care, they believed they had the right to impose their political and religious views on her. Michelle's needs had no place in the discussion, nor did her two living children, who might be orphaned by the policy.

When NARAL learned of Michelle's plight, we helped raise the thousands of dollars it took to transport her by ambulance to Texas, where she was able to obtain an abortion. But there was no way to know how many other women were left without hope because their stories were never heard.

The Republican majority's barrage of assaults on a woman's right to choose and other mainstream values had an ironic result that actually helped their cause. They overreached so many times on so many issues that before long, the media, and therefore the public, were no longer paying much attention. To grab the spotlight, they needed to shock the public sensibility.

"The Partial-Birth Abortion Ban Act of 1995" provided just such a shock.

CHAPTER FIFTEEN

C OREEN COSTELLO, A CALIFORNIA WOMAN IN HER THIRTIES, was a devoted mother, devout Catholic, and conservative voter. She once attended an anti-choice demonstration and recalled being moved to tears when she heard an anti-choice congressional leader deliver a speech on C-SPAN. The anti-choice movement might have held her up as an exemplar of their values. Instead, they condemned her.

That is because, after these earlier experiences, Coreen underwent a procedure that anti-choice politicians call "partial-birth abortion." In the summer of 1995, congressional opponents of abortion began appearing on the floor of the House and Senate with baby dolls and scissors, describing in sensational terms a procedure they called gruesome, wantonly cruel, and never necessary. They spoke of fully delivered, perfectly formed babies being stabbed in the head with scissors and their brains suctioned out. They peddled one distortion after another. But before long, the distortions took hold in the public consciousness as though they were established fact.

The name itself is misleading. "Partial-birth abortion" is a political rather than a medical term. It appears on page after page of the *Congressional Record* but not in medical textbooks. It cannot be meaningfully banned because doctors do not know what it means. In fact, anti-choice politicians drafted bans in terms so vague and broad that they could be interpreted as prohibiting a variety of safe abortion procedures used throughout pregnancy. For this reason, I will not use the term again in this book. Instead, I will describe the "partial-birth abortion ban" in more accurate language: as a "ban on abortion."

Coreen Costello knew better than anyone how distorted and inflamed the debate on the issue had become. She was seven months pregnant and looking forward to the birth of her third child when she learned her fetus had a lethal neurological defect. Because the fetus had become rigid in an awkward position, Coreen's doctors warned that delivering it intact through the birth canal could seriously endanger her health and her reproductive organs. She might never be able to have another child. They recommended that she undergo an abortion procedure known as "intact D&E"—one of many procedures covered by the ban Congress was considering.

I was later present as Coreen told her story to the Senate Judiciary Committee, which was considering the ban. The room was completely quiet as she added a human dimension to what had been an impersonal, sensationalized debate:

> A perinatologist recommended terminating the pregnancy. For my husband and me, this was not an option. I chose to go into labor naturally. I wanted her to come on God's time—I didn't want to interfere. It was so difficult to go home and be pregnant and go on with this life, knowing my baby was dying. I wanted to stay in bed. My husband looked at me and said, "Coreen, this baby is still with us. Let's be proud of her. Let's make these last days of her life as special as possible." I felt her life inside of me, and somehow I still glowed. At this time we chose her name—

Katherine Grace. "Katherine" means pure, and "Grace" represents God's mercy.

Over the next two weeks, Coreen related, she learned that natural birth and induced labor were impossible because of the fetus's rigid position. She described the agonizing choice she faced:

> We considered a caesarean section, but experts at Cedars-Sinai Hospital were adamant that the risks to my health and possibly my life were too great. There was no reason to risk leaving my children motherless if there was no hope of saving Katherine. The doctors all agreed that our only option was the intact D&E procedure.
>
> When I was put under the anesthesia, Katherine's heart stopped. She was able to pass away peacefully in the womb, which was the most comfortable place for her to be. Even if regular birth or a caesarean had been medically possible, my daughter would have died an agonizing death.
>
> When I awoke a few hours later, she was brought in to us. She was beautiful. She was not missing part of her brain. She had not been stabbed in the head with scissors. She looked peaceful. . . .
>
> Because of the safety of this procedure, I am now pregnant again. . . . Fortunately, most of you will never have to walk the valley we have walked. It deeply saddens me that you are making a decision having never walked in our shoes. . . .
>
> We are the families that ache to hold our babies, to raise them, to love and nurture them. We are the families who will forever have a hole in our hearts. We are the families that had to choose how our babies would die.

Coreen's story was the human face of the issue, the living embodiment of the difficult choices women and their families must confront. But it was not a face anti-choice politicians in Congress chose to acknowledge. Under a bill they introduced in

Congress, doctors could be imprisoned for performing procedures like Coreen's, even if they were necessary to protect the woman's health.

These activists understood what the pro-choice movement had, in the case of the Freedom of Choice Act in 1993, failed to recognize. Unable to enact their entire agenda—banning all abortions under all circumstances—they settled for what was politically possible, moving one step at a time, until, eventually, their vision could be achieved. The "Who Decides?" campaign had repositioned a woman's right to choose as a mainstream value, so the anti-choice movement's strategy was to find a way to inflame the issue and demonize abortion. The ban on procedures provided the perfect vehicle. Completely ignoring the stories of women like Coreen, they described the procedures as barbaric and needless.

Anti-choice politicians stooped to distorted theatrics, implying that the procedure was commonly performed on healthy, full-term fetuses. In reality, nearly 90 percent of women who choose to terminate unintended pregnancies do so in the first trimester. Women who have post-viability abortions do so because wanted pregnancies have gone tragically awry.

But the distortions succeeded. The media, especially television networks, presented the anti-choice showmanship without asking critical questions. Because journalists had generally ignored prior assaults on reproductive freedom and choice, these shocking images were many Americans' first introduction to the issue. The pro-choice movement was immediately on the defensive.

The ban appeared headed for certain passage, and NARAL faced a dilemma. Should we fight the battle? Should we engage in a protracted legislative debate that we seemed destined to lose and that might imperil our work to position the right to choose in the mainstream? And were we prepared to ask our allies in Congress to cast such a controversial vote if we were unlikely to prevail? I convened NARAL's senior leadership team for a strategy discussion and told them, as I always did, that I wanted a full debate in which everyone freely expressed their views.

Our legal team was adamant that we should oppose the bill.

"This bill is written so broadly that it could be interpreted as a ban on many commonly performed procedures," they explained. "An overzealous anti-choice prosecutor could use this law to prosecute any doctor for doing any abortion. For a doctor facing imprisonment under a vague criminal statute, the safest alternative is not to provide abortions at all."

"I agree," I replied. "The bill is aimed directly at the heart of *Roe v. Wade*. It is part of a long-term public relations strategy to demonize all abortions. And the assumptions beneath the law are degrading and insulting. They imply that women and doctors choose what is being called a barbaric procedure for no reason."

The bill contained no exception to protect the health of the woman. Her needs were completely absent from the debate. I thought of the women who faced these difficult circumstances. The senators parading baby dolls on Capitol Hill were judging these women the same way the hospital review board once judged me.

I understand the strong reactions many Americans had to the graphic depictions of the procedure. If all I knew about the issue was what I read in the newspaper or heard on television, I would be upset as well. But sometimes the choices women have to make about pregnancy are terribly difficult. It may be easy to sit in judgment from afar, but only the woman fully understands her needs. Coreen Costello's story illustrates the impossibility of writing a blanket law that addresses every woman's highly individualized medical circumstances. Congress is not the place to write medical protocols. I knew the issue presented a difficult public relations challenge, but I decided we had to fight this bill.

James Wagoner warned me of the dangers.

"Kate, you have spent years trying to move this issue into the mainstream," he said. "I don't like this bill any more than anybody else, but the fact is that it's likely to pass, and when it's over, we're going to be left looking like we were defending an extreme, horrific procedure. It's tailor-made for sound bites: 'Look at NARAL. They won't even budge on a procedure this terrible.' We have to pick our fights. We should consider passing on this as a legislative fight and instead challenge it later in the courts."

James saw all that was to come, and his forecast was prophetic: "This," he said, "has all the makings of a disaster."

Almost immediately, James's prediction was vindicated. We made several mistakes, beginning with the most common error in politics: being enticed to debate on an opponent's ground. Supporters of the ban said the procedure was used commonly, so we focused our early message on explaining that post-viability abortions were rare. Soon enough, the public debate shifted from our most persuasive message—who should decide whether women can have abortions—to a medically technical discussion of the procedure. The vagueness of the terminology complicated matters further. When reporters asked how often the procedures in question were performed, I confined my response to abortions performed after fetal viability, when they were rare and almost always medically necessary. But when reporters called clinics and asked the same question, they answered based on the broad wording of the bill, including previability abortions. Consequently, their numbers were far larger. NARAL and others appeared to be deliberately underestimating the frequency with which the procedures were used.

Then, in the process of responding to the claim that the fetus experiences pain during the procedure, we sank into another factual morass. During a press conference, I explained what I understood to be the medical facts and what others, including a doctor, had also said—that the anesthesia administered to the woman contributed to the demise of the fetus before the procedure itself was performed. The head of the American Society of Anesthesiologists refuted my statement emphatically. It was an honest mistake on my part, but our credibility was again in question.

When faced with an issue as divisive as this, the earliest moments of a debate often determine its outcome, and our beginning was problematic. Polling showed that even pro-choice voters believed the opponents' rhetoric. Once our factual statements were questioned, it was difficult to overcome the doubts that resulted. We strayed from our message and into areas of medical detail that were neither our expertise nor especially relevant to our cause. The central issue should have been whether politicians or women and doctors knew best what procedure was the most appropriate and safest in each complicated and individual case. We reacted too quickly. Nothing we could have done would have changed the outcome, but our credibility was in doubt. Our management of the issue reads like a case study in how to mishandle a controversy.

Meanwhile, the anti-choice movement stooped to new lows of deception. An alternative bill was introduced that would have allowed the procedure if a physician determined it was necessary to protect the woman's health. In response, the U.S. Conference of Catholic Bishops published a newspaper advertisement listing reasons a woman might choose abortion that would, in its view, be protected under the health exception. Among them were: "Won't Fit Into a Prom Dress: Hates Being Fat: Had an Unhappy Childhood."

I was infuriated. The advertisement reflected a fundamental and demeaning belief that women were immoral, and the fact that it was published by religious leaders made it all the more egregious. Their insulting and condescending rhetoric suggested that women could not be trusted to make our own decisions because we were frivolous, callous, and self-indulgent. The bishops said nothing about women like Coreen Costello, who chose this procedure out of tragic necessity. To them, every woman cared more about her appearance than anything else. I asked our staff to send the ad to every pro-choice legislator on Capitol Hill. I wanted them to know exactly how insulting and demeaning the proponents of this ban were.

As the vote on the bill approached, we surveyed the landscape. I asked our lobbyists what they were hearing from Capitol Hill.

"The House is hopeless," came the reply. "And it doesn't look good in the Senate either. The Republicans are probably going to hold most of their votes and pull enough Democrats to pass. This is going to the president. He's our last chance."

We were lobbying furiously, but we had to face reality. If we were going to stop the bill, there was only one place to turn. I placed a call to the president.

"Mr. President," I said, "I need to talk with you about this horrendous legislation, the 'partial-birth abortion' ban. I hate to even use the term; it's so misleading. I understand how terribly difficult this debate has been. Politically, anti-choice forces have created a tough situation. I'm sure the bill is going to pass. The impact will be serious, especially for women's health and for *Roe*. I know it's politically difficult. But you are the arbiter now. You are the only thing standing between women and a ban on abortion. If you allow this bill to become law, it's a major step toward the demise of *Roe v. Wade*."

Clinton listened intently as I described the threat to women's health if the ban became law. Then he turned to the practical issues at hand.

"How badly will we lose in the Senate?" he asked. I gave him that day's vote count—the bill would probably get between fifty and sixty votes.

"If I veto this bill, we have to sustain it," Clinton replied. Sustaining a veto would require thirty-four votes in the Senate. "I've got to know we have enough votes." He was right. If Congress overrode his veto, we would have more than a terrible law on the books. We would also severely weaken his ability to veto other legislative assaults on reproductive rights in the future. And pro-choice members of Congress would have voted for a highly controversial bill just as they faced reelection in 1996.

"We can sustain a veto, Mr. President," I said. "The House will vote to override, but I believe we can hold the Senate."

"The thing that really troubles me about the bill is the lack of a health exception," Clinton explained. "I'm not going to commit either way today, but you know my position, Kate. Abortion should be safe, legal, and rare."

The White House was clearly worried about the political implications of the bill, but to their credit, they declined to become entangled in the controversy, waiting until more information could come out and cooler heads could prevail. Despite our early missteps, we knew that we must persuade the President of the danger of a bill that would threaten women's health. Women's stories were the most compelling vehicle for presenting the issue to Clinton. We worked with other groups, like the National Abortion Federation, to identify women who underwent abortion procedures outlawed by the ban and were willing to allow their own veils of privacy to be pierced. Coreen Costello was one of them. NARAL helped to arrange for a number of these women to meet privately with the president. Their stories were extraordinary, and Clinton was deeply moved. After the meeting, he held a press conference at which several of the women courageously spoke.

One of them, Mary Dorothy Line, was a registered Republican and practicing Catholic from Los Angeles. She and her husband, Bill, were eagerly awaiting the birth of their first child when they learned the fetus was suffering from a terrible birth defect called hydrocephalus in which the head contains excess fluid that prevents the brain from developing. Mary Dorothy and Bill begged doctors to save the pregnancy, but they were told there was nothing that could be done. As she explained at the press conference:

> This was not our choice, for not only was our son going to die, but the complications of the pregnancy put my health in danger, as well. If I carried to term, he might die in utero, and the resulting toxins could cause a hemorrhage and possibly a hysterectomy. The hydrocephaly also meant that a natural labor risked rupturing my cervix and my uterus.
>
> Several specialists recommended that we terminate the pregnancy. I thank God every day that I had this safe medical option available to me, especially now that I am pregnant again and expecting a baby in September.

Another of the women, Vikki Stella, brought her three-month-old baby boy to the meeting with Clinton—a baby she was able to have because a safe abortion procedure was available to her when a previous pregnancy went terribly wrong. Vikki, who lived in Chicago, discovered in the thirty-second week of her pregnancy that her fetus did not have a brain.

"But the one part I want to stress," she said at the press conference, "is I needed this [procedure] for health reasons. I'm a diabetic. Other procedures would not have been what I needed. I don't heal as well as other people, so other procedures just were not the answer."

Claudia Ades, who lived in Santa Monica, California, explained that her fetus was diagnosed with a lethal chromosomal abnormality called Trisomy 13 and had no hope of survival.

"I say this for the people that say that we don't care and for the people who say we don't want our children, and for the people that say we have no spirit or no soul or no religion," Claudia said. "My husband and I are Jewish and we got the news on Rosh Hashanah. And when we finally had the procedure, the third day of this grueling procedure, it was Yom Kippur, the holiest day of the Jewish year. And Yom Kippur is the day that you mourn those that have passed, and it's the day that you pray that God will inscribe them in the Book of Life."

On November 1, the House passed the ban with no exception to protect the health of the woman, and Clinton announced he would veto it. The Senate added a narrow life exception, but rejected a proposal by senators Barbara Boxer and Dianne Feinstein to allow the procedure in the case of "serious adverse health consequences." The final bill garnered fifty-four votes in the Senate— enough to send it to Clinton's desk but not enough to override his veto. Gingrich and Trent Lott, the new senate majority leader, postponed the override vote for months so it would coincide with a Washington convention of the Christian Coalition—and have the maximum impact on the elections. But we sustained the veto.

We had dodged a bullet. But we did not know that one of our own allies had planted a land mine.

CHAPTER SIXTEEN

"WELL," A SENATOR REMARKED, "*THIS* IS UNUSUAL."

I was appearing before the Senate Finance Committee, and beside me sat a Catholic nun. It was certainly an unusual pairing, but the issue before the committee—welfare reform—was morally compelling enough to bring us to the same witness table though we differed sharply on the legality of abortion.

Both President Clinton and the Republican leadership of Congress had pledged to reform the welfare system. But unlike President Clinton, whose call to "end welfare as we know it" included investments in helping people in poverty regain their independence, many Republican plans seemed punitive. Every day's headlines proclaimed a new welfare proposal as Republicans appeared to be attempting to outdo one another in making poverty a punishable offense. Their proposals suggested a cold, condescending view of welfare recipients, and having been one many years before, I recognized both the devastating impact of the most severe of their plans as well as the myths about poor people on which they were based.

The House Republican bill proposed a family cap—a limit on the number of children for whom a family could receive welfare benefits. The proposal, in fact, revealed the complete hypocrisy of the anti-choice leadership on Capitol Hill. On the one hand, they were intent on denying women the right to choose an abortion, but on the other, were eliminating the support poor women might require if they have children. When facing an unintended pregnancy, many of these women might feel as though abortion was their only option. Moreover, if women decided to continue their pregnancies despite the cap on benefits, the children would ultimately bear the brunt of these punishing policies.

It was my view that NARAL should speak out against the policy, but some on our team were concerned that opposing a welfare reform proposal would alienate the moderate Republicans on whom we depended in close votes.

"We should preserve our political capital for matters that more directly affect a woman's right to choose," they said. Their concern was valid, but I believed this issue lay at the heart of reproductive choice.

"Being 'pro-choice' means more than defending the right to have an abortion," I said. "We must support a woman no matter what choice she makes—whether it is to use contraception, have an abortion, or bear a child. This policy punishes women for making the choice to have a child. It is the very definition of 'anti-choice.'"

A few weeks later, I testified before the Senate Finance Committee with Sister Mary Rose McGeady, president of Covenant House, a New York City–based agency that serves homeless youth. I strongly disagree with the Church on a woman's right to choose, but the Church has had a long and consistent tradition of support for society's least fortunate, a tradition I deeply respect. McGeady had devoted her life to serving the poor, and her testimony was compassionate and compelling. "The national debate on welfare reform is extremely troublesome because the tone of our debate seems so punitive," she said. "Troublesome because I sense the growing feelings of frustration in our country, which result in a negative attitude about helping the poor. Poor people are not evil, they are just poor."

As for my testimony, the fact of my appearance before the committee was probably as important as what I said. Proponents of the welfare reform proposal bombarded members of Congress with stereotypes of welfare recipients manipulating the system for personal advantage. I aspired to counter that stereotype by giving witness as an independent and productive member of society who had also been a welfare recipient. I hoped they would see me as a model of many welfare recipients—people who face a sudden crisis, often through no fault of their own, and who need temporary help. I also wanted to impress upon lawmakers that effective welfare reform must empower women to make responsible decisions, a point I emphasized in my testimony:

> NARAL recognizes the compelling need for comprehensive welfare reform. But true reform lies not in callous policies that punish women for the choices they make, but in helping women make responsible, deliberate decisions about childbearing by providing access to necessary information and health services, rewarding and encouraging economic self-sufficiency, and helping reduce teenage pregnancy.

Later in 1995, I had a unique opportunity on an international scale to advance the same principle—that women and families prospered when women had more control over their own lives. In September, I traveled to Beijing to attend the United Nations World Conference on Women, where women's-rights activists from every continent gathered. Marcy Wilder, NARAL's new legal director, coordinated our strategy to ensure that the U.N. conference's ten-year plan of action for women reflected the centrality of reproductive rights and health to women's well-being.

Simply making that argument proved to be a serious challenge. The highly repressive Chinese regime moved an array of groups that opposed its policy of forced abortion—including NARAL, Planned Parenthood, the Catholic Church, and several human-rights organizations—to a hotel miles from the conference site in an attempt to limit our ability to lobby the delegates. Our every move was closely monitored. The government assigned extra surveillance to the hotel and cautioned us that Chinese law forbade any meeting of more than three people in a single room. Late each night, a man wearing a business suit stopped by my hotel room, as well as Marcy's and those of other attendees.

"Laundry, please," he would say, but his business suit was a poor disguise. The real purpose of his nightly visits was to monitor our compliance with the ban on meetings. Every day, we returned to our hotel rooms to discover obvious evidence—open suitcases and scattered papers—that they had been searched. Our movements were also restricted. To obtain a taxi, we were required to report our precise destination to the authorities, and even then, we were routinely stopped at checkpoints throughout the city for further questioning about our activities. It was terribly unsettling to live, if only briefly, in a society where the deprivation of freedom was so absolute. The entire experience deepened my appreciation for the values of individual liberty and privacy from government, and reinforced my commitment to defend those values when I returned home.

The opportunity to meet and work with women's-rights advocates from diverse world cultures and countries was singularly inspiring. Despite the Chinese government's intrusive monitoring and the Catholic Church's fierce opposition, pro-choice activists secured a statement from the conference endorsing women's right to reproductive health care. It also called on countries to halt the imprisonment of women who chose abortion. They were important achievements for which the international women's-rights community worked hard.

In the United States, other important victories were on the horizon. The Senate ultimately defeated family caps, and in 1996, President Clinton signed a welfare bill without them. In July, the Food and Drug Administration convened a long-awaited hearing to consider approval of the drug RU-486, or mifepristone, an early medical alternative to surgical abortion.

Mifepristone was a highly promising option that could make earlier pregnancy terminations possible. It also offered women more privacy than having a surgical abortion. For many, this was an especially important advantage at a time when visiting an abortion clinic often meant facing a gauntlet of protestors. Research also showed that mifepristone had potential for treating diseases such as breast cancer and other conditions. It was, as Marcy Wilder characterized the drug, one of the most important innovations in reproductive health since the advent of the birth control pill.

While it had been used safely and effectively by European women for several years, mifepristone had been repeatedly blocked in the United States for political rather than medical reasons. The first President Bush banned its importation as a concession to his anti-choice base, a policy President Clinton reversed with one of the executive orders he signed shortly after his inauguration. However, the French company that manufactured the drug announced it would not distribute mifepristone in the United States because of political concerns. Eventually, the U.S. rights to the drug were donated to a nonprofit group, the Population Council, which conducted clinical trials in 1994 and 1995.

FDA commissioner David Kessler was determined to resist

political intrusion into the drug-approval process. A skilled physician and a public servant of profound courage, Kessler was a Republican who was originally appointed by the first President Bush. He was completely impervious to political pressure, insisting that science, not politics, guide his decisions in all medical matters. Kessler decided that mifepristone would receive a scientific hearing no different from any other drug. Because of security concerns arising from the continuing wave of hostile anti-choice protests at clinics, the hearings were held in a windowless, warehouse-like building outside Washington. Marcy testified, traveling to the hearing site with the other witnesses in a specially arranged bus with blacked-out windows.

To Kessler's immense credit, the review panel conducted a rigorous examination of the drug at the hearing, allowing both proponents and opponents of mifepristone to speak freely. In Marcy's presentation, she argued that science alone should guide the FDA's decision, and the medical evidence indicated overwhelmingly that mifepristone was safe and effective. After the hearing, the panel agreed. It took another four years before the FDA issued final approval for mifepristone. In the interim, anti-choice members of Congress attempted unprecedented maneuvers to prevent the FDA from proceeding with the approval process—maneuvers that continue to this day—but the drug is available to women nonetheless. The hearing in July 1996 was an important milestone along the way.

Another pro-choice milestone was reached in November 1996 when President Clinton won reelection. NARAL emerged from the 1996 electoral campaigns wary of the continuing threats we faced from Capitol Hill, but confident in our ability to defeat them. The House and Senate were still under anti-choice control, but President Clinton was in a strong position. And the Republicans' deliberate timing of the veto override of the abortion ban had not harmed him politically. More attacks were inevitable, but at least we knew a pro-choice president would be in office for another four years to neutralize them.

Then the land mine exploded.

In February 1997, the *New York Times* carried a front-page story in which Ron Fitzsimmons, the executive director of the National Coalition of Abortion Providers, revealed that, during the earlier debate on the abortion ban, he had deliberately lied about the number of intact D&Es that were performed. Fitzsimmons now said that the actual number of intact D&Es was higher than he had previously claimed. He also said they were performed earlier in pregnancy and on more healthy women and fetuses than Americans had been led to believe.

The uproar was instantaneous. The *Washington Post* published a lengthy article quoting clinic workers who verified that the procedure was more commonly used. Richard Cohen, a firmly pro-choice essayist for the *Post*, wrote a column retracting his earlier opposition to the ban and implying that "the usual pro-choice groups" had deceived him. He did not accuse NARAL by name, but the inference was clear. Cohen and I had talked many times, and while he always knew I was expressing my opinion, he also trusted that the facts on which I based it were true. My policy with him, as with every journalist, was absolute honesty. I phoned Cohen as soon as I read the column.

"Richard, I thought you at least would have given me a chance to respond to your concerns before going to print," I said. I explained that the numbers were being confused by differing definitions. The numbers I had presented Cohen were those of post-viability abortions; the information he now had included abortions performed in the second trimester as well.

"We are talking about two distinct sets of numbers," I said.

He listened coolly, but it was clear he still felt misled.

The repercussions on Capitol Hill were even more dramatic. Anti-choice legislators immediately reintroduced the abortion ban in both the House and Senate, and congressional committees convened hearings into Fitzsimmons's statements under the banner of "Partial-Birth Abortion: The Truth." I testified, framing the fundamental issues that had, by now, been all but forgotten:

> As you struggle with your vote on this legislation, there are two crucial questions I urge you to consider: First, are you ready, as a member of Congress, to dictate medical decisions surrounding this constitutionally protected choice, even when a doctor considers this procedure the safest and most medically appropriate? And second, does this legislation protect the lives and health of those women whose wanted pregnancies have become medical nightmares?

The pro-choice movement's attempts to clarify the misunderstandings were barely heard amid the controversy. Fitzsimmons had lied, indefensibly and unnecessarily, and the credibility of every pro-choice advocate was now under suspicion. A decade of hard work to move the pro-choice movement into the mainstream of American politics was at risk.

Before long, even some of our allies began to abandon our cause. Senator Arlen Specter, a moderate Republican from Pennsylvania and a usually reliable pro-choice vote, likened intact D&E to "infanticide." On a visit to newly elected senator Susan Collins of Maine, another pro-choice Republican, I was greeted with an ice-cold glare in the lobby of her office. "You've lied to us," she said. "We're in a horrible position." I had not lied to anyone—Fitzsimmons had—but this was no time to exacerbate the tensions. I resisted the temptation to respond and instead presented my arguments as calmly and clearly as I could. Collins eventually voted against the ban.

The most painful defections were those of two of NARAL's closest allies: Tom Daschle, the Senate Democratic leader, and Pat Leahy, the ranking Democrat on the Judiciary Committee. Both had opposed the earlier ban and were now reconsidering. They were very upset over this latest controversy. Daschle was entering a reelection campaign in his predominantly Republican home state of South Dakota. The earlier vote had been difficult for him to explain to his conservative constituents. He might not be able to do so again in a climate in which the pro-choice movement was assumed, however unfairly, to have lied. Daschle was also concerned about the political impact of the controversy on other Democratic senators. My staff and I met with Daschle and his team often, hoping to persuade him to stand firm in his opposition to the ban. Daschle was always open-minded and accessible, but he was also personally disturbed by Fitzsimmons's deception and concerned about its political consequences for Democrats.

"Senator," I told him, "our anti-choice opponents have dramatically sensationalized this issue. The critical point is simple: It is not the role of Congress to dictate to women and doctors what medical procedures they can or should choose."

It was difficult enough to counter the medical myths about intact D&E, but by now, a new misperception was taking hold—the belief that opposing the abortion ban would be politically disastrous. Pro-choice Senator Tom Harkin of Iowa had won reelection handily in 1996 despite a last-minute barrage of ads attacking his opposition to the abortion ban. Yet when he returned to Washington, he began sounding warnings about the political controversy the issue could cause. I went to see him.

"This isn't helpful, Senator," I said delicately but firmly. Not a

single member of Congress who was attacked for opposing the ban
lost because of it, including Harkin. When candidates addressed
the issue forthrightly—defining it as a question of who should make
medical decisions and describing the ban as a threat to women's
health—the attacks could be neutralized. In 1990, NARAL had
generated considerable support for Harkin with our "Who Decides?"
message, but when he ran for reelection in 1996, Harkin avoided
discussing his pro-choice views entirely until he was attacked late
in the campaign. To the extent the ban on abortion was politically
damaging, which was questionable, I believed it was because Harkin
failed to define his pro-choice views and values clearly from the
outset of his campaign. It would have been more effective to high-
light his commitment to protecting women's lives, rights, and privacy. But by the time he addressed the issue, he was forced to respond
to anti-choice accusations rather than discuss it on his own terms.

Daschle later offered the Senate an alternative—a ban on all
post-viability abortions of any type unless the woman's life was endangered or, in extremely limited situations, to protect her health.
NARAL decided not to oppose the proposal. We knew it had no
chance of passing. And Daschle's bill would also serve to expose
the hypocrisy of anti-choice politicians. It offered senators a choice
between enacting an abortion ban by a wide margin or pursuing a
bill whose primary purpose was to inflame and polarize public opinion and confuse Americans about the state of the nation's abortion
laws. Nearly all anti-choice senators voted down Daschle's proposal, demonstrating their interest in prolonging the controversy
rather than passing a law. Senators Barbara Boxer and Dianne Feinstein then proposed a ban on post-viability abortions with a broader
health exception written to conform with *Roe v. Wade*. NARAL
supported that proposal actively, but it, too, was defeated.

In a particularly damaging blow to our cause, the American
Medical Association suddenly endorsed the abortion ban despite

its legislative committee's earlier opposition to the bill. Publicly, the motives for the endorsement were a mystery, but it was widely rumored that the AMA had reached an agreement with the Republican leadership of Congress. They would support the ban in exchange for higher Medicare reimbursement rates for physicians. They were willing to risk jail time for some of their members in exchange for higher fees. Booz Allen Hamilton, an outside auditing firm hired by the AMA, later helped produce a harsh report criticizing the organization for negotiating its endorsement without even consulting with the American College of Obstetrics and Gynecology, which strongly opposed the ban.

Not long after the AMA endorsement, the Senate voted on the ban. As the vote proceeded, I stood in the ornate reception room just steps from the Senate floor. Senators were streaming into the chamber to vote up or down, and we could hear each one announced. Some of the defections were especially painful, not simply because we were losing votes, but because some pro-choice senators were supporting a bill that put women's health at risk and compromised physicians' medical integrity.

"Mr. Daschle, aye," the clerk read. "Mr. Leahy, aye. Mr. Specter, aye."

My heart sank as each pro-choice ally's vote was read. Once they voted for the ban, I knew it would be nearly impossible to regain their support. I was frustrated and disturbed that women's health, lives, and rights were made pawns in a political game once again. But I was even more disappointed that some of our allies had felt it necessary to move to the other side. When the final tally was announced, the abortion ban passed by a margin of 64–36. A cheer erupted from a group of anti-choice activists across the room. Both politically and substantively, it was a painful and difficult defeat for women's rights and health as well as medical privacy.

But there was little time for wallowing in our loss. When President

Clinton vetoed the bill, the anti-choice leadership again post-poned the override vote so it would happen at the most politically charged moment, just prior to the 1998 congressional elections. If supporters of the ban could attract just three more votes, they could override the president's veto and the bill would become law. The import was clear: We were three votes away from the first fed-eral criminal ban on abortion in American history.

CHAPTER SEVENTEEN

I N THE MID-1990S, PROMINENT NATIONAL POLLS BEGAN TO show growing support for restrictions on abortion, a trend that Harrison Hickman's polls for NARAL confirmed. More important, even many people who believed abortion should be legal described themselves as "pro-life." Harrison scrutinized the numbers, analyzing the views of various demographic groups, searching for a coherent explanation for the slippage, but he found none. He then serendipitously stumbled onto a list of media markets in which the anti-abortion Arthur DeMoss Foundation was running an advertising campaign entitled, "Life, What a Beautiful Choice." The campaign seemed a direct response to the anti-choice movement's concern about the success of "Who Decides?" The advertisements' soft images of adorable babies did not mention abortion directly, but the reference was clear, as was the strategy to co-opt the word "choice." Harrison found that the most significant declines in support for the right to choose coincided precisely with the markets in which the DeMoss campaign was running. Those markets alone were responsible for 60 percent of the national decline.

While "Who Decides?" had changed the terms of the debate over a woman's right to choose, these new data compellingly illustrated the fact that public opinion is not static: It changes over time in response to different influences. The DeMoss ads were one such influence, and the distorted debate over the abortion ban was probably another. However, while these anti-choice advertisements were heavily funded, there was no similar effort on the pro-choice side. Moreover, the media's coverage of the issue naturally focused on controversy, producing a "he said, she said" dynamic in which stories typically gave equal time to pro- and anti-choice spokespeople rather than exploring the substance of the issue. After the 1989 and 1992 marches, for example, television networks allotted equal air time to the hundreds of thousands of pro-choice demonstrators and the modicum of anti-choice protestors despite the enormous disparity in the turnout of each group. The sheer scale of the marches and the widespread support they demonstrated for a woman's right to choose were not emphasized, leaving many pro-choice viewers with the inaccurate impression that Americans were evenly divided on the issue, when in reality a solid majority supported pro-choice policies. As a result, many pro-choice people were reluctant to discuss their pro-choice views.

Harrison called me to explain his findings and argue that NARAL should take dramatic action.

"We have to take our issue directly to the public," he said. "We are losing people in the middle. We cannot expect to sustain support if we are only able to speak to people in the center when events like Supreme Court nominations or major Court cases give us a forum. The effect is that we make our point once and are then silent. The anti-choice groups won't be silent. They have a continual conversation about the issue, including every week in Catholic, evangelical, and fundamentalist churches, and much of that conversation is independent of politics. Our presence must be ongoing or we will suffer a serious setback."

I agreed. Our advertising only appeared sporadically and around political events, whereas the DeMoss campaign was a sustained, large-scale investment. It was time for the next logical step in NARAL's long-standing campaign to move the right to choose into the mainstream. The essential question behind "Who Decides?"— whether women or government should make choices about pregnancy and childbearing—was highly effective, but it also engaged people intellectually rather than emotionally. We needed to speak to their hearts by defining choice itself as a fundamental American value, not just a policy issue, and there was no value more American than the freedom to make one's own decisions about the most personal and private aspects of life. Communicating this message would require a fundamental change in the scale of our work. Political advertisements tailored to respond to an immediate threat or influence a specific campaign would be insufficient. We were proposing a sustained and massive presence on the airwaves, easily costing millions of dollars.

The strategy, which we called "Choice for America," was controversial in several respects. While NARAL had worked for many years to position the right to choose as a mainstream ideal that should be proudly embraced, many in the pro-choice community were still uncomfortable with discussion of "values." Many donors were reluctant to support an ongoing television campaign because they were accustomed to funding shorter-term projects from which they could withdraw once their goals were achieved. Some foundations viewed advertising campaigns as invitations for funding recipients to continue requesting more support indefinitely. Others were skeptical of the idea that television advertising could change people's views on a policy issue.

Harrison and I believed pro-choice Americans, as well as those whose views were more mixed, were eager for someone to speak to their core values rather than simply shout slogans or discuss policy issues. We saw Choice for America as an evolution of NARAL's ongoing work to transform the national discussion about a woman's right to choose. With the endorsement of the NARAL foundation board of directors, we devised a comprehensive strategy that included television and radio advertising as well as grassroots organizing. In each targeted media market, we would hire paid organizers who would conduct full-scale grassroots campaigns to encourage people to speak about and act on their pro-choice beliefs.

Harrison and I flew to Monterey, California, to present the idea to the David and Lucille Packard Foundation, a longtime supporter of NARAL and other pro-choice organizations. We began with our principal rationale that a television campaign supported by grassroots organizing could broaden understanding of the values that underlie a pro-choice position, improve support for pro-choice policies, and mobilize those who were already pro-choice. We were prepared to subject that hypothesis to a rigorous test. We proposed that Packard fund a $1.5 million pilot project in two test markets—Austin, Texas, and Columbus, Ohio, geographic areas whose demographics closely matched the national political mainstream. In each market, we would conduct scientific polling both before and after the initial test to measure whether the campaign helped to change individuals' views. Those results would be compared with identical polling in a control market—Nashville, Tennessee—where we would not advertise. This would ensure confidence that any change in Austin and Columbus was due to our advertising campaign rather than external factors like political or news events.

Packard agreed to fund the pilot project. Our next task was to formulate and film an advertisement, which proved to be a challenge from the beginning. While NARAL had previously worked with political advertising firms, this campaign was fundamentally different. It required a carefully crafted, mainstream message that would reach a broad audience, modeled on product marketing rather than political advertising. NARAL asked several major advertising firms to submit proposals. The Choice for America campaign would have been a lucrative account for any major advertising agency, but none of them responded out of fear that they might offend their corporate clients by involving themselves with a controversial issue. Only one submitted a proposal: the Seattle office of the global advertising agency DDB. From the moment they began their presentation, I knew the other firms' refusal was serendipitous. DDB Seattle was an ideal match for our needs.

"We know this is contentious," the firm's head, Keith Reinhart, told us. "Maybe there will be fallout from our corporate clients. But we think it's too important. We want to do the work."

DDB produced a signature ad entitled "I Believe." With an original score drawing on themes from "America the Beautiful" playing in the background, value-laden images graced the screen: two women hiking, a woman walking out of a voting booth, another wearing a hospital gown, a family with children standing in front of their home, an elderly couple sitting on a farm in front of a flagpole, a boy running across a field. A woman narrator cast choice as a fundamental value:

> I believe there's a reason we are born with free will. And I have a strong will to decide what's best for my body, my mind, and my life. I believe in myself, in my intelligence, my integrity, my judgment. And I accept full responsibility for the decisions I make. I believe in my right to choose, without interrogations, without indignities, without violence. I believe that's one of the founding principles of our country. And I believe that right is being threatened. The greatest of human freedoms is choice, and I believe no one has the right to take that freedom away.

Once the advertisement had aired in Austin and Columbus for six weeks, we anxiously awaited Harrison's polling results. When they finally arrived, the results were even stronger than we had hoped. Before the advertisements, more people in Austin described themselves as "pro-life" than "pro-choice." Our campaign actually reversed the balance of opinion—with more people calling themselves pro-choice than pro-life—a substantial achievement for having been on the air for only six weeks. In Columbus, young women and politically moderate women—two target groups of the campaign—responded especially well to the advertising, with support for the pro-choice position climbing by six percentage points among women ages eighteen to thirty-nine and by eight points among women who described themselves as moderate. Based on the success of the pilot project, Packard granted NARAL $10 million for the first year of a five-year Choice for America campaign that ultimately reached more than 12 million women between the ages of twenty-five and forty-nine in twenty-three media markets around the country. This represented 24 percent of all women in that age group nationwide.

DDB produced a series of advertisements that explored various aspects of the issue, such as personal responsibility, strong families, and women's health, while continuing to emphasize choice as a fundamental American value. These ads became vehicles for demonstrating that when women can determine the circumstances of pregnancy, families are strengthened. One such ad, for example, showed a mother letting go of a bicycle as her daughter rode alone for the first time. As the girl pedaled off, the mother reflected on her daughter's growing independence, integrity, and ability to make responsible choices. In another ad, a woman discussed choice and personal responsibility as she sat in a doctor's office awaiting an examination. The final ad in the series culminated in a call to action:

images of children playing while an announcer asked viewers how they could tell future generations that their freedom had been lost.

In one of the most compelling Choice for America advertisements, a woman stood above a swimming pool at the edge of a high-rise board preparing to dive. The image cut to the heart of the issue: a strong, decisive woman fully in control of her life, taking risks and responsibility, preparing carefully for the critical moment. At the end of the advertisement, she executed a perfect dive in slow motion. The ad required us to cast a professional diver, but one after another, American divers declined to appear even though many told us they were pro-choice. One said she feared receiving death threats. Another said identifying with such a controversial issue might hurt her career. Eventually, a French diver agreed to appear in the ad.

The reaction was immediate and positive. When the advertising began airing in Michigan, state legislators were inspired to introduce the first pro-choice bill the state had considered in many years. It failed, but for one of the nation's most anti-choice states, even the attempt was remarkable. Pro-choice state legislators in states like Massachusetts and Maryland wrote to thank us for providing a meaningful and effective message that made their work easier. Teachers called our office to say they were showing the advertisements in their classes to provoke discussions. An Episcopal priest in Philadelphia called me to compliment the advertisements as well.

"I haven't preached a sermon on the right to choose in many years," he said. "But this weekend, it will be the topic of both of my sermons. These ads have done a very important service. They have given people the language to talk about their values in a positive way."

Focus groups we conducted to assess the impact of the advertising provided compelling evidence of the change as well. In a

Columbus group, an older woman told of being moved to tears because "my side of the story was finally being told." She described how the ad had provoked her to reveal to her husband for the first time that she had an illegal abortion nearly forty years before. "We have been married for more than thirty years," she said, "but this was the first time I could talk about it."

Most important, Choice for America succeeded in its central goal: reversing the slippage in support for the right to choose in the media markets where we conducted the campaign. The percentage of people identifying themselves as pro-choice rose by an average of twenty points. We had proved our hypothesis. An integrated media and organizing campaign affected attitudes, mobilized pro-choice Americans, and created a better understanding of what it meant to be pro-choice.

The grassroots component of Choice for America was equally successful. We launched the "Choice Action Network," an online group of activists who received regular e-mail updates on issues affecting a woman's right to choose. They included suggestions for convenient but effective means of becoming involved, such as sending e-mails to their state or federal representatives. CAN, as we called this group, has since swelled to more than 650,000 activists who have played an influential and decisive role in many policy debates. Choice for America organizers also held house parties and activist training sessions, and initiated other grassroots activities.

A young woman in Milwaukee, Janette James, later told NARAL that one such grassroots organizing meeting transformed not just how she viewed a woman's right to choose, but how she viewed herself. When she became pregnant after her contraception failed, Janette, then an eighteen-year-old college student, felt she was not prepared to fulfill the tremendous responsibility of raising a child. She decided to have an abortion, but for many years afterward, she felt as though she had done something wrong. Then her mother was invited to attend a Choice for America grassroots organizing session, and Janette joined her. When she heard choice described as a fundamental American value, she was inspired.

"At that moment, it was not just something bad I did," Janette, who later became board president of NARAL Wisconsin, told us. "It was a right I had. I felt there were millions of women out there who feel they've done something wrong. I wanted to protect this right because others may need it."

Janette's transformation from pro-choice individual to pro-choice activist was precisely what we had hoped Choice for America would achieve. Having traveled a similar journey that began as one silent woman who had chosen abortion, I related to her very personally. I also knew that she embodied the reaction of many more women whom I would never meet but who were nonetheless newly inspired.

"Janette," I once told her, "the fact that Choice for America reached you so personally makes the entire campaign worthwhile."

CHAPTER EIGHTEEN

IT WAS JANUARY, AND NARAL WAS CONSUMED WITH LAST-minute preparations for our annual gala commemorating the anniversary of *Roe v. Wade*. The year was 1998, *Roe*'s twenty-fifth anniversary, and Vice President Al Gore—who was widely expected to run for president in the 2000 elections—was our keynote speaker. The usually intricate arrangements for the event were complicated by the extensive security the vice president required. The ballroom at Washington's Mayflower hotel, where the luncheon was to be held, had been extensively swept for security purposes. We expected an unusually large number of journalists eager to cover Gore as he assumed an increasingly visible political role. His presence would excite interest in the event and elevate the right to choose to national prominence at a time when we needed it most.

The morning of the event, Stephanie Kushner, NARAL's fund-raising director, called just as I was rushing out the door on my way to the office.

"Have you read the paper this morning?" she asked.

"No, I haven't," I said. On the anniversary of *Roe v. Wade*, personal threats against me typically escalated, and those were the only times I permitted NARAL to assign security to me. As a result I had a driver and bodyguard that morning and had planned to read the newspaper in the car.

"Well, you'd better. We have a problem."

I reached for my copy of the *Washington Post*, opened it, and saw the banner headline across the top of page one: CLINTON ACCUSED OF URGING AIDE TO LIE; STARR PROBES WHETHER PRESIDENT TOLD WOMAN TO DENY ALLEGED AFFAIR.

The Clinton sex scandal was unfolding, and its potential impact was immediately clear. Events could spiral out of control, cascading toward the devastating conclusion that the first pro-choice president in the history of the country might be forced to resign. Even if he remained in office, Clinton could be seriously politically weakened.

NARAL faced an immediate problem. The press would cover our event in even greater numbers, but with a very different purpose in mind. The status and future of a woman's right to choose was no longer the story. Clinton's scandal raged through Washington like a prairie fire, and Gore's appearance gave reporters an opportunity to question him about it. The conjecture about resignation swept Washington instantly, and Gore was suddenly viewed as the man who might succeed Clinton in the short term, rather than after the election.

The White House strategy was to keep high-level officials out of the spotlight until they established a plan for handling the crisis. To his credit, Gore attended NARAL's event—sober in mood, to be sure, and with a cordon of staffers whose job it was to keep the press at bay. Gore delivered his speech, an eloquent defense of "a woman's right to make what for many feels like the most important decision of their lives in freedom, in safety, and without the coercion of government." It was, needless to say, an awkward event, one that foreshadowed the substantial political turmoil that would unfold over the next several months.

My own feelings about the allegations against Clinton were complicated. Clinton's conduct was a reckless and indefensible indulgence that jeopardized both his presidency and the millions of people—including women facing the loss of their right to choose—who depended on him. It was difficult to reconcile Clinton's public leadership of women's rights and his private treatment of the women closest to him. At the same time, however, Clinton's personal misconduct did not negate his contributions to protecting, defending, and advancing women's rights. Clinton was the first pro-choice president in history at a time when he was the only barrier standing between American women and an end to our right to choose. He never once wavered in his commitment no matter how grave his political crisis became. He continued to veto anti-choice measures, including the abortion ban, despite the scandal. And nothing about the situation justified impeachment, a grave step vastly out of proportion to the offense, however personally inexcusable it was. The right wing was dedicated to the personal destruction of President Clinton, but to paraphrase Richard Nixon, "He gave them a sword."

The press tried to repeat the Packwood episode, pushing me either to condemn Clinton—in which case they would have said women's-rights leaders were abandoning him—or to excuse his conduct, in which case they would have leveled the same charges of hypocrisy and double standards we faced with Packwood. I refused to take the bait and be drawn into the politics of personal destruction. NARAL's comment throughout the scandal was that if the allegations were true, Clinton's conduct was wrong, but our focus would remain on our mission to protect and defend a woman's right to choose.

I took no satisfaction when the press revealed that Congressman Henry Hyde—a leading anti-choice Republican spearheading the impeachment effort—had once had an affair as well. When I was asked what I thought of Hyde leading the impeachment effort, I replied that I respected his integrity and believed he could be fair. NARAL had fought Hyde year in and year out on the Hyde Amendment, which bans Medicaid funding for abortions, but no matter how strongly I disagreed with him, he was never less than straightforward. When my comments appeared, he sent me a letter of thanks. Even when we disagreed, he wrote, I had always spoken of him with respect.

NARAL faced too many challenges to be distracted by the political circus. With the nation's attention diverted, the anti-choice majority in Congress was likely to become even bolder in their attacks on women's rights. The veto override vote on the abortion ban loomed, and we had other legislative battles to fight as well.

One of those legislative battles was a long-standing one: obtaining coverage for prescription contraceptives in federal employees' health plans. It was a commonsense measure that would reduce the number of abortions. It was pro-family as well. Women who plan their pregnancies are more likely to obtain prenatal care and bear healthy children. Access to contraception is also an absolutely critical element of a pro-choice society—one that enables a woman to prevent a pregnancy she did not intend. Yet the anti-choice movement has endlessly opposed access to contraception and family planning, including for women who receive their health care from the government.

The most eloquent testimony on the importance of access to contraception came from women who told NARAL about the difficulties they faced obtaining birth control.

A woman from Michigan recalled how she researched her insurance plan: "When my husband and I were choosing insurance coverage, the Blue Cross/Blue Shield brochure stated that it covered all prescription drugs—no exemptions were indicated for birth control pills. We found out that they weren't covered when I went to get my prescription filled."

Another woman, this one from Florida, faced difficulty obtaining coverage of birth control pills even though she used them to treat a medical condition: "[I have an] irregular (and very painful) menstrual cycle without contraceptive pills, so I must pay or be miserable," she wrote. "[I have to] visit my doctor and hav[e] him write a letter AGAIN stating that the pills are for regulation of my menstrual cycle, rather than contraception. This is extremely aggravating, very time-consuming, and completely ridiculous."

NARAL had fought repeatedly but unsuccessfully to guarantee contraceptive coverage for federal employees. Our annual efforts had raised public consciousness on the issue, but it was another development that finally turned the tide. In early 1998, the Food and Drug Administration approved a new drug called Viagra to treat male impotence. Almost immediately, insurance companies began announcing that they would cover the medication. I was pleased they did. Sexual health is important, and it should be covered like other medical services. But the health insurance companies were employing a blatant double standard: A new drug enabling men to make their own sexual choices was covered instantly. Yet the majority of insurers still refused to cover the Pill—a decades-old drug that, for women, served the same purpose. Women were justifiably outraged, so we believed the political climate on contraceptive coverage for federal employees might finally have shifted in our favor.

Still, the fight would be decidedly uphill. Only 131 out of 435 members of the House—where the fight over contraceptive coverage was always the most contentious—were fully pro-choice. The picture in the Senate was only slightly better: thirty-three solidly pro-choice members, representing a third of the body. NARAL mobilized our grassroots network in states whose representatives in Congress were undecided on the issue. We hired a firm that called constituents of these representatives and offered to transfer their calls directly to the Capitol switchboard. This was grassroots politics at its best and most influential. Swing congressmen were deluged with calls from their constituents, and Congress ultimately voted—by a narrow margin—to require contraceptive coverage for federal employees.

It may have been a victory for just one group of women—those who work for the federal government—but it was an important symbol, and a concrete step forward. NARAL had long worked for a broader requirement that all insurance companies that cover prescription drugs also cover prescription contraceptives, but Congress was not moving forward on that legislation. We were, however, making progress in the states. Working with our affiliates, identifying supportive state legislators, and providing them with support—and, of course, mobilizing our grassroots network once again—we passed several laws. As of 1999, only one state had enacted a contraceptive coverage law. As of this writing, twenty-one have done so.

Despite progress, women face many barriers to obtaining contraception. Even many state contraceptive-coverage laws, for example, allow doctors, hospitals, and pharmacists to refuse to provide contraception if they object on moral or religious grounds. That requirement may sound innocuous, but it is especially burdensome for women who live in rural areas with few health care providers and pharmacies. Even in major urban areas, the growing trend of Catholic Church management of hospitals has eliminated access to family planning services for many women.

I remain astonished by the hypocrisy of those who say they oppose abortion but also oppose family planning. Even opponents of legal abortion—*especially* opponents of legal abortion—can and should support access to contraception. This is a simple choice between fewer abortions or more, and the anti-choice movement has repeatedly chosen more.

CHAPTER NINETEEN

E MILY LYONS, A NURSE AT THE NEW WOMAN, ALL WOMEN Health Care Clinic in Birmingham, Alabama, was accustomed to the anti-choice protestors who picketed the facility every day, waving graphic posters and shouting abusive insults. But on the morning of Thursday, January 29, 1998, a bomb exploded in the clinic, tearing out Emily's left eye, damaging her right eye, and filling her body with shrapnel, leaving Emily in critical condition. A security guard named Robert "Sandy" Sanderson was killed.

Unlike many previous attacks on women's health clinics, this bomb was not intended to shut down the building or intimidate its occupants. It was designed to kill

I did not know Emily personally, but I kept careful track of her progress. It appeared that she would survive, although she faced an agonizing recovery, and her body would never be the same. During her rehabilitation, Emily had to learn to walk and speak again as well as to see with her remaining eye. The impact of anti-choice violence was becoming devastatingly clear. Clinics were closing. Fewer doctors were willing to perform abortions. Today, nearly 90 percent of counties in the United States have no abortion providers at all, and fewer medical schools train obstetrics residents in how to perform the procedure.

Abortion is becoming less available even though it remains legal. Women who need abortions must often travel long distances, a practical impossibility for many who cannot afford to take time off work, arrange extended child care, and pay for travel. In one especially heartbreaking case, a young girl from a poor family in Mississippi—where there is only one abortion clinic in the entire state—was raped and impregnated. Her family drove the long distance to the clinic, where they learned that state law required their young daughter to submit to an intimidating lecture about the purported risks of abortion, then wait twenty-four hours to undergo the procedure. They could not afford either another long drive or a motel. The morning after the lecture, the clinic staff discovered the family in the parking lot, sleeping in their car in the sweltering summer heat.

While violent incidents like the Birmingham bombing were the extreme acts of a relatively small fringe, the entire anti-choice movement resorted to deceptive and intimidating tactics to prevent women from exercising the right to choose. One particularly intolerable tactic has been the proliferation of "Crisis Pregnancy Centers," a trend NARAL began to investigate in 1998. These are often propaganda mills operated by anti-choice organizations, carefully disguised as medical clinics—including staff wearing lab jackets like those worn by physicians. They lure women with promises of free pregnancy tests. Crisis Pregnancy Centers often receive state financial support, in many cases the proceeds of "Choose Life" license plates.

The propaganda consists of telling women they will have to wait thirty to forty-five minutes for the results of a pregnancy test, although the actual test requires only three to five minutes to complete. In the interim the women are bombarded by anti-choice rhetoric. NARAL compiled a compelling research report documenting many such stories. In one case, when a sixteen-year-old Texas girl told the center staff that she wanted an abortion, they presented her with a stuffed doll and a pair of scissors. "This is what your baby looks like now," she was told. "And we want you to start cutting her up because that's what will happen if you have an abortion." In Arizona, a sixteen-year-old girl who had been raped was shown a film that included brutal images of dismembered fetuses. "They just emotionally raped her," the girl's father explained. A California woman offered this account of a center she visited for a pregnancy test:

> When I arrived at the "clinic," a woman . . . took me in another room and asked me a series of questions. . . . [The woman] then looked at a chart on her desk and told me how pregnant I was. She stated, "Your baby will be born on September 17." This was before the pregnancy test was even done. . . . Next, she turned on the machine for a slide show. I asked [the woman] if I had to watch the slide show. She said yes, I had to watch it. She took my urine sample, and left the room, closing the door behind her. The slide show presented pictures of large bloody fetuses and told horror stories about women dying from abortions. It claimed that abortion was a leading cause of sterility, deformed children, and death. One slide was of a dead woman lying under a sheet. The voice reported that she had died during a legal abortion when the suction machine, which was hooked up wrong, blew pressure into her body, causing her uterus to explode . . .

NARAL's research identified an anti-choice activist who authored a manual for Crisis Pregnancy Centers and delivered a speech in which he frankly discussed their use of deception. "Obviously, we're fighting Satan. . . . A killer, who in this case is the girl who wants to kill her baby, has no right to information that will help her kill her baby. Therefore, when she calls and says, 'Do

you do abortions?' we do not tell her, 'No, we don't do abortions.' "
One center in Massachusetts calling itself "Problem Pregnancy"
opened an office on the same floor as a Planned Parenthood clinic
and posted a sign on its door reading PP, INC. Counselors from the
center walked the halls of the building harassing women who were
searching for Planned Parenthood. A court ultimately ruled that
the center's PP, INC. sign infringed on Planned Parenthood's service mark.

In an environment of such deception and intimidation, it was
critically important that we sustain President Clinton's veto of the
abortion ban. NARAL set up a war-room approach. This included
daily strategy meetings; updates on the latest developments; a review of press coverage; and a running tally of senators classified as
solid votes to override the veto, solid votes to sustain, those undecided, and those leaning in either direction. The vote chart was
updated daily with intelligence from our contacts on Capitol Hill,
where our relationships were extensive. If a senator began to lean
in one direction or the other, our network of staff contacts informed us, and we responded quickly with information relevant to
the particular senator's concerns. Allison Herwitt, NARAL's head
lobbyist, had spent years cultivating these contacts and nurturing
these relationships, and as a result of her work, our intelligence
was superb. I concentrated my lobbying on the senators who were
leaning and those who were still undecided, while tallying the
votes of our solid supporters. Senator Barbara Boxer of California, with whom we conferred almost daily, coordinated pro-choice
strategy on the Hill.

According to the old cliché, "All politics is local." In dealing
with an issue as controversial as the abortion ban, a corollary ap-
plies: All politics is personal. Before asking an elected official to
take a stand on a controversial issue, one must first have built a
long-standing relationship grounded in trust and mutual respect. I

have seen many activists attempt to pressure legislators by presenting demands and framing their position as the only one that is either logically or morally tenable. That approach seldom works. A successful advocate understands and respects an elected official's perspective, the political pressures to which he or she must respond, and the context in which he or she is operating. I often offered members of Congress who wrestled with a vote on reproductive rights the following advice: "You don't have to struggle so hard. It's really not your responsibility to make decisions for women. You must trust women to make the right choices. Your role is to protect our ability to do so."

After employing that respectful approach with lawmakers for many years, we were able to draw on a reservoir of trust and goodwill. Even in the heat of the debate, senators respected and listened to NARAL's perspective. We had also refined and clarified our message. Rather than focusing on medical technicalities or engaging in a statistical debate, we emphasized that the ban threatened women's health and asked the question that had always distilled the issue to its essence: Who decides? Should women and their physicians decide what medical procedure is safest and most appropriate for their unique circumstances, or should politicians do so for them?

This was a momentous vote, and we knew it would be a close one as well. As the vote began, I stood in the Senate Reception Room, greeting senators as they entered the chamber, thanking our supporters while watching the vote tally. By the time the vote began, there were no more minds to change, but it was important for me to be there nonetheless. My presence was a demonstration to our allies of NARAL's support in the face of a controversial stand. In the end, every senator who had opposed the bill also voted to sustain the veto.

Joy over our victory soon gave way to sorrow. On October 23, a sniper hid in the backyard of Dr. Barnett Slepian, an ob-gyn in the Buffalo area. Just after Dr. Slepian and his family returned from Friday night services at their synagogue, the sniper shot him in the back through his kitchen window. Dr. Slepian's son rushed into the kitchen to find his father soaked in blood. The family called for help, but it was too late. He died within hours.

In the aftermath of the murder, Dr. Slepian's friends and family revealed a portrait of a warm, quiet, and caring doctor who performed abortions because he believed they were an essential part of reproductive health care, but whose real joy was delivering babies. When women with wanted pregnancies were advised to terminate because of terrible birth defects or risks to themselves, Dr. Slepian encouraged them to get a second opinion, carefully and compassionately making sure they knew of every available option. He was a forceful advocate of birth control and education as means of reducing the need for abortion. He was also fearless: He had been warned repeatedly about a growing wave of violence against abortion providers—including the recent shootings of other doctors in Canada and upstate New York—but he refused to be intimidated. At the time of his death, he was the only abortion provider left in Buffalo.

Shortly after the murder, an extremist anti-abortion Web site that routinely posted pictures of abortion providers framed in "wanted" posters and dripping with blood showed Dr. Slepian's photo with a line through it brutally signifying that he was dead. The Web site's creator, Neil Horsley, was quoted in the New York Daily News as having no regret about Dr. Slepian's death: "I have been forced to accept the idea that thousands of babies are being killed each day. So I have been inured to that kind of tragedy." Horsley later launched a Web site on which he posted pictures of women patients as they entered abortion clinics.

The Friday following the Slepian tragedy, Emily Lyons joined

1. My three little daughters—Lisa (two and a half), Anya (seven months), Tasha (one and a half)—who have given my life joy and meaning, and whose needs were foremost in my mind as I faced one of the most difficult decisions of my life.

2. Tasha, Lisa, and Anya in Athens, Greece, where our family spent a challenging but adventurous year while my first husband completed research on his Ph.D.

3. The beginning of a new and hopeful chapter in our life as a family: my wedding in 1972 to Fred Michelman.

4. With Bill Clinton during his 1992 run for the presidency, the beginning of a close friendship and the first national campaign in which a presidential candidate embraced a woman's right to choose as a positive, winning political issue.

5. Preparing to speak at the 1992 March for Women's Lives in Washington, D.C. Crowd estimates showed we far exceeded our goal of five hundred thousand marchers supporting a woman's right to choose.

6. With Justice Harry Blackmun—author of the majority opinion in *Roe v. Wade*, the decision that transformed my life and those of so many other women—and his wife, at a NARAL tribute dinner after his retirement from the Supreme Court.

7. My address at the 1996 Democratic National Convention in Chicago was an indicator of NARAL's growing political influence—and the fact that the right to choose was positioned in the mainstream of political discourse.

8. As Secretary of Health and Human Services, Donna Shalala was a critical player in the Clinton administration's defense of a woman's right to choose. She joined NARAL at our 1998 gala event commemorating the twenty-fifth anniversary of *Roe v. Wade*.

9. Emily Lyons is an extraordinary woman who inspired me and many others with her determination after she was severely wounded in an abortion clinic bombing—which occurred during a harrowing period of violence by anti-choice extremists. She spoke at a NARAL event in New York in 1998.

10. Early in the 2000 presidential campaign, NARAL made the controversial but ultimately successful decision to endorse Al Gore for the Democratic nomination—thus ending a divisive and distracting debate about whether he was fully pro-choice.

11. After he left the presidency, NARAL honored President Clinton at a New York City luncheon for his courage and consistency in defending a woman's right to choose against an increasingly hostile anti-choice Congress.

12. I addressed the Democratic National Convention once more in 2000, when the race between Al Gore and George W. Bush presented both high stakes and a sharp choice on a woman's right to choose. Gore believed strongly in a woman's right to choose, while Bush had called openly for a ban on abortion.

13. Secretary of State Madeleine Albright is a personal inspiration and friend whose daughter, Katie Albright, served on NARAL's board of directors. They both attended a NARAL dinner in 2002.

14. In a sign both of NARAL's influence and the importance of a woman's right to choose, every major Democratic presidential candidate addressed a NARAL dinner in Washington in January 2003. After they spoke, I joined Senator John Kerry, Governor Howard Dean, Congressman Richard Gephart, Senator Joe Lieberman, Reverend Al Sharpton, and Senator John Edwards onstage to demonstrate our united commitment to defeating George W. Bush.

15. I campaigned hard for Senator John Kerry in 2004, including NARAL's endorsement of his campaign at this event in Washington.

16. Ed Harris and Amy Madigan were among the many celebrities who supported NARAL over the years. Both became good friends, and Amy served on NARAL's board.

17. Dagmar Dolby and Lisa Perry, NARAL Pro-Choice America Foundation board members, were contributors, friends, and two of the most passionate pro-choice activists I have ever known.

18. The people who matter most: When NARAL held a tribute for my retirement in 2004, my family was there. *Front row from left:* my grandchildren Anastasia, Nikolas, and Matthew. *Back row from left:* my daughters Anya, Lisa, and Tasha, as well as me and my husband Fred in Washington, D.C., January 2004.

19. Senator Hillary Clinton, who attended the NARAL tribute in Washington in 2004, is an inspiration to millions of women—and a highly effective pro-choice advocate.

20. Sharing a moment with Julian Bond, chair of the NAACP, one of the NARAL tribute's keynote speakers, January 2004.

21. With my colleagues at the pinnacle—and end—of my career with NARAL: leading more than one million pro-choice Americans at the 2004 March for Women's Lives in Washington. *Front row from left:* Kim Gandy, President, NOW; Anthony Romero, Executive Director, ACLU; Ellie Smeal, President, Feminist Majority; Kate Michelman, President, NARAL Pro-Choice America; Gloria Feldt, President, Planned Parenthood Federation of America; Secretary of State Madeleine Albright; Senator Barbara Boxer; Congresswoman Barbara Lee; Congresswoman Nancy Pelosi; and Congresswoman Eleanor Holmes Norton.

22. When I ascended the stage at the 2004 March for Women's Lives to bring my service at NARAL to a close, I reached for the hand of someone who reminds me why we must work so hard to protect the right to choose: my granddaughter Anastasia.

23. The future generation—our five grandchildren: Ben, Sam, Nikolas, Matthew, and Anastasia, at the beach on the Fourth of July, Stone Harbor, New Jersey, during a brief respite from my work in the 2004 presidential campaign.

NARAL in New York City to unveil a television spot she taped on our behalf criticizing Republican Senator Al D'Amato for voting against the Freedom of Access to Clinic Entrances Act, which enhanced security at women's health clinics. D'Amato was locked in a tight battle for reelection against Representative Chuck Schumer, the author of FACE and one of the most forceful pro-choice leaders in Congress. As Emily walked into the room where we were holding the press conference, I was overcome. She could barely walk or see, and much of her hair had been singed off. Months after the bombing, her body and legs were still laden with shrapnel that nine surgeries had been unable to remove completely. The relatively brief plane fight to New York had been an ordeal. I embraced her, searching for the words to express my thanks adequately. Emily showed not a trace of bitterness, nor was she intimidated. Instead, she was resolute and resilient. We wanted to capture that quality, and the raw dimensions of the tragedy, in our advertisement. It was straightforward—no photographic effects or slogans, simply Emily speaking into the camera and telling her story.

"When a bomb ripped through my clinic, I almost lost my life. I will never be the same. When Al D'Amato had a chance, he voted against protecting women's health clinics from anti choice violence. How could D'Amato vote against a law that protects women from tragedies like mine?"

On Election Day, the people of New York agreed. D'Amato, one of the Senate's longest-serving and most entrenched incumbents, was defeated and Schumer took his place. Many analysts said a woman's right to choose was one of the decisive issues in the race. Nationwide, Republicans attacked several pro-choice senators for voting against the abortion ban, but not one of them was defeated because of that issue. It was a satisfying end to what had otherwise been an enormously trying year.

CHAPTER TWENTY

A S THE 2000 PRESIDENTIAL ELECTION YEAR DAWNED, THE controversy over the abortion ban was a compelling reminder that without a pro-choice president, women would be hostage to the caprices of an anti-choice Congress. Had Clinton not been in office, the abortion ban as well as other measures he vetoed would have become law. If an anti-choice president was elected in 2000, all the progress we had made under Clinton would be at risk. More ominously, the Supreme Court remained closely divided over the fate of *Roe v. Wade*. With only one or two anti-choice justices on the Court, the case could be overturned or the right to choose eviscerated, exposing women to even more restrictions than the states had already passed. There had not been a vacancy on the Court since 1994, the longest period without an opening since James Monroe was president. By that historical trend, Clinton's successor was likely to appoint enough justices to determine the future of a woman's constitutional right to choose. The 2000 presidential election would be among the most important we had ever faced.

But it was also certain to be a highly charged campaign. The Republican contenders were staunchly anti-choice, but some of them—like Gary Bauer and Alan Keyes—were so outspoken and extreme that they made the leading candidates, like George W. Bush and Elizabeth Dole, seem moderate by comparison even though they shared nearly all the same views. As governor of Texas, Bush had signed more anti-choice laws than any other governor in the nation, making Texas one of the nation's most anti-choice states. He had endorsed a constitutional amendment to overturn *Roe v. Wade*, and during one campaign had promised "to do everything in my power to restrict abortions." Now that he was running for national office, however, he dismissed a woman's right to choose as "hypothetical" and unworthy of further comment. Bush's reassuring refrain—"America isn't ready for a ban on abortions"—was factually accurate, but also a political smoke screen. He apparently expected women not to worry as he promised his far-right base that he would use his presidential powers to take away one of women's most fundamental rights. America may not have been ready for a ban on abortion, but Bush certainly was. Meanwhile, Elizabeth Dole, considered Bush's most serious competition for the Republican nomination, favored a ban on abortion as well.

Many of the Republican candidates attempted to deflect the issue by saying a president was powerless to curtail the right to choose as long as *Roe v. Wade* remained in force. That, of course, was a lie: Congress and the states were already restricting women's rights in far-reaching ways. The Supreme Court may have upheld *Roe* in the broadest of terms, but under *Webster* and *Casey*, government could—and did—make abortion more difficult to obtain. The next logical step was the overturn of *Roe* itself, an event that would be all the more likely if one of these anti-choice candidates was elected. However, both the public and journalists were susceptible to the claim that, with *Roe* in place, the right to choose was irrelevant to this election. Despite several close calls, the Supreme Court had upheld *Roe* for more than thirty years, and eight years of a pro-choice president had provided a false sense of security about the right to choose even though states had severely restricted it over exactly that period. Our polling showed that most Americans were almost completely unaware of either the restrictions that had already been enacted or the threat posed by the 2000 election.

Bush successfully used his amiable personality to maintain a moderate image despite his hard-line anti-choice record. Because Dole was a woman, many voters and journalists assumed she was pro-choice, a misconception she did little to correct. If she succeeded in concealing her anti-choice views, she might be able to reassure the pro-choice Republican women whose votes NARAL needed to win the general election. At that point, either Bush or Dole seemed likely to be the Republican nominee. It was imperative that we educate voters about their anti-choice views and records before they were labeled as moderates for the duration of the campaign.

We were victims of our own success. In the decade leading up to the 2000 presidential campaign, NARAL had so successfully positioned a woman's right to choose as a positive political issue that it was difficult for anti-choice candidates to be elected if they openly declared that they wanted to ban abortion. Our polling in the early primary states confirmed that most voters did not know the Republican front-runners were anti-choice, nor were they aware of the immense powers the president wields over reproductive rights. Few even understood how close the Supreme Court was to overturning or undermining *Roe v. Wade*.

NARAL had to elevate the threat to the forefront of the presidential election. That required becoming involved in a presidential campaign earlier than we ever had, and with the unusual step of advertising in a Republican primary. Early in 1999, we began airing advertisements in New Hampshire and Iowa to expose Bush's and Dole's anti-choice views. We produced and widely disseminated extensive research materials on the powers of the presidency—from appointing lower-court judges, Cabinet officials, and Supreme Court justices to preparing the federal budget and issuing executive orders—and how they could be used to restrict a woman's right to choose.

We harbored no illusions about our ability to influence far-right Republican primary voters, but we did believe we could both persuade moderates and make it more difficult for Bush and Dole to hide their anti-choice views in the future. I began an intensive process of educating reporters about Bush's record in particular, meeting them one by one to expose the governor's anti-choice views and precisely what powers he would wield as president. Most reporters appeared to leave the meetings with a clearer understanding that Bush's views were far more extreme than he was pretending. But it also seemed that once they returned to Bush's campaign plane, the governor would charm them with such trifles as a playful nickname and these journalists would immediately revert to believing he was a moderate, harmless candidate.

The year also brought additional controversy within the pro-choice community. It began with a proposal by anti-choice Republican congressman Chris Smith of New Jersey, a moderate on economic issues but far out of the mainstream on women's rights. Smith moved to reinstate the global gag rule, which stripped foreign family-planning organizations of U.S. funds if they used their own money to provide abortion, discuss the option, or advocate changes in their countries' anti-abortion laws. President Clinton had repealed the gag rule in one of the executive orders he signed early in his administration. If it were reinstated, family-planning services for the world's neediest women, in the poorest of countries, would be dismantled.

Under normal circumstances, Smith's proposal would have faced an all-but-certain presidential veto, but an unrelated issue provided the opportunity he needed to force Congress to accept the gag rule. The United States was in deep arrears with our dues to the United Nations. The Clinton administration was working with Congress to repay the back dues when Smith persuaded the Republican leadership to blackmail the president. The House would only support the U.N. dues if Clinton agreed to the gag rule. The rule would be included in an omnibus appropriations bill funding not just the entire State Department but the entire federal government as well. If Clinton vetoed the omnibus bill, he would trigger a shutdown of the whole federal government.

That would have been a grave step, but signing the measure was problematic. Despite the many myths propagated about international family planning, the United States does not pay for abortions in other countries—federal law has prohibited that for many years—but we do fund family-planning services on which some of the world's poorest women depend. These services help prevent unintended pregnancies, promote prenatal, maternal, and childhood health, and limit the spread of AIDS and other sexually transmitted diseases. An estimated six hundred thousand women—99 percent of them in developing countries—die of pregnancy-related causes each year, and widely available family planning services could save many of them.

Congressman Smith's proposal placed women's lives at risk, and I had met many of them. My husband's academic specialty is French-African literature, and I had traveled with him to Senegal, Cameroon, and the Ivory Coast, among the poorest countries in the world. Poverty in these countries is pervasive. It can be felt the moment a visitor steps off the airplane. In Senegal, I visited local programs to learn more about African approaches to early child-hood development, and what I saw broke my heart. Services for women and children barely existed. Women had almost no control over how many children they bore and the circumstances under which they became pregnant. Far too many felt they were com-pletely without hope. Without access to effective contraception, many told me they used folk remedies, often dangerous ones, to prevent or terminate pregnancies. One woman in Senegal told me she inserted animal dung into her vagina to cause a miscarriage.

In these countries, social equality for women was but a vague hope. The cultural barriers against contraception were enormous, and Smith's proposal to reinstate the global gag rule threatened to sever a lifeline for those women courageous enough to take control of their reproductive lives. Their visits to family planning clinics were often their only access to medical care of any kind—the only place their vital signs were checked, the only place they could get an AIDS test, the only place they could get prenatal care if they chose to have children.

I knew countless women would die if the United States cur-tailed support for family planning in the developing world. Ac-cording to Population Action International, an estimated 125 million women around the world wanted to plan their families but lacked access to contraception. This policy would worsen their plight and make abortion more necessary, often in countries with highly restrictive abortion laws. Women would be driven to un-safe, clandestine abortions, which already kill nearly eighty thou-sand around the world every year.

During congressional debate Representative Jim Greenwood, a Republican from rural Pennsylvania and one of the most eloquent and effective pro-choice leaders on Capitol Hill, succinctly captured the threat. With the global gag rule in place, Greenwood warned, "women in places like India and Bangladesh and around the world will not get these [family-planning] services, and some of them will die. It is wrong, and it is un-American, and it should not stand."

When NARAL first learned about the Republican strategy to blackmail Clinton on the gag rule, we dismissed it. After all, Clinton had vetoed an identical measure the year before and there was no reason to believe he would accede to such blatant extortion now. Repealing the gag rule was one of the signature achievements of his administration; reinstating it would threaten poor women's lives. Clinton had repeatedly faced down threats from Republican Congresses on other issues and prevailed. Soon, though, rumors circulated that Clinton was seriously considering accepting the Republican demand. By the time White House Chief of Staff John Podesta called me and other pro-choice leaders to his office, the administration had already reached an agreement.

"This is what we must do," I remember Podesta saying. "I know you disagree and I know it's difficult. But you need to accept the fact that this is going to happen." Podesta said the gag rule would apply for only a year and promised that the White House would fight to repeal it when it expired. During the interim the White House had obtained some concessions to ease the impact of the measure.

The consequences of the gag rule would be devastating for women. I was deeply disappointed and angry, as were many other pro-choice leaders. Clinton was one of our closest allies, and the White House had not even notified pro-choice groups until the agreement had already been reached. Equally disturbing, the president was giving in to pure political blackmail. U.N. funding and international family planning were completely unrelated. By acceding to the threat, Clinton might embolden the anti-choice leadership in Congress to extort him on other issues. Because the Smith proposal would also write the gag rule into federal law, Clinton could not repeal it as easily as he had with his earlier executive order. While I understood the need to consider other priorities, I could not help but feel that when policymakers are faced with competing interests, the rights of those with the least power in our world—in this case, poor women—are often the easiest to abandon.

The outcry from pro-choice groups was immediate. Wendy Sherman, a top official at the State Department and close advisor to Secretary of State Madeleine Albright, met with the pro-choice groups in an attempt to quiet our criticism. The meeting was rancorous. The coalition groups were angry that Clinton was acceding to the calumny of anti-choice blackmail. Sherman resented the fact that we were criticizing the administration even though they had been a steadfast ally over the years.

"This is a betrayal," one of the pro-choice leaders said.

"Yours is not the only issue we have to consider," Sherman retorted.

For all intents and purposes, the battle was already lost, but I decided to call Secretary Albright regardless. We had been friends for many years, and I admired her greatly. Our friendship long preceded her public career. Albright was one of the first advocates for women that I had met when I moved to Washington. While a professor at Georgetown University, Albright often assembled a diverse group of women for potluck dinners at her home, where we would discuss women's issues. Her dedication to women's rights, especially in impoverished and intolerant societies, was genuine and profound. When Warren Christopher retired as secretary of state, I was a strong advocate for Albright's nomination to replace him. She was, and remains, a wise and wonderful mentor to me, and I regard her as one of the towering women in American history.

But each of us also had a responsibility to uphold. I was an advocate for women and reproductive rights, and she was the secretary of state and a spokesperson for the Clinton administration.

"Madeleine," I said quietly, "I have a feeling this is going to be a difficult conversation. It's especially hard for me to be on the opposite side of you on a women's-rights issue, but it's important that I talk with you about this."

I could sense impatience in her voice. Then, she began:

"The pressure we are getting from the women's groups is unfair. This administration has been consistently committed to women's rights. But we also have an obligation to foreign policy. We can't hold the entire United Nations and our whole foreign-aid budget hostage to this one issue. This wouldn't be happening if there were any other choice. I don't think the impact of this policy will be as dramatic as you believe. And either way, we aren't endorsing the policy. We are promising to try to repeal it."

"I don't question your commitment at all, Madeleine," I replied. "I want you to understand that. I disagree with you very strongly on this, but I do not for a moment doubt your commitment to women's rights. But we need you now. And I object to the way this was handled. It is unfair for your allies to learn about something like this after the agreement was already reached. Sometimes friends have to give each other bad news."

I also thought there *was* an alternative: to call the Republicans' bluff and let the matter be settled in the court of public opinion, where I was confident we could prevail. In order to prevent the world's poorest women from obtaining desperately needed family-planning services, the Republican leadership was willing to close down the U.S. Department of State and diminish our standing at the United Nations. I understood Albright's perspective, as well as the president's. They did what they believed they had to do. But so did I. I sent President Clinton a respectful but frank letter before he signed the bill.

> We are at a disappointing moment in our nation's history. Anti-choice Republicans have forced the greatest nation on earth to adopt a policy out of step with its people and their values. This policy threatens the health care, the fundamental right to reproductive services, and the very lives of millions of women around the world.
>
> The agreed upon restriction on U.S. funding for international family planning will have severe repercussions worldwide. NARAL calls on you to make a strong public commitment now to reverse the harm done by these restrictions.

Clinton signed the appropriations bill containing the gag rule. A year later, as promised, he signed another law repealing it, but that bill left room for the next president to reinstate it. We knew we would face this fight again, which made the presidential election even more important. The next president would hold the fate of a woman's freedom to choose—and the lives and health of millions of women not only in the United States but also across the world—in his or her hands.

CHAPTER TWENTY-ONE

NARAL'S EFFORTS TO COMMUNICATE THE ENORMOUS STAKES of the 2000 presidential election were complicated by Senator Bill Bradley's dark-horse campaign for the Democratic nomination. Initially, Bradley—an immensely respected former senator with a long record of commitment to social progress—energized the party's progressive base. NARAL did not plan to be involved in the primary because voters were fortunate to have two solidly pro-choice candidates from whom to choose. But as Bradley struggled for traction, he searched for issues that would distinguish him from Gore, and he believed that the right to choose could be one of them. As vice president, Gore was strongly and unquestionably pro-choice. But as a congressman and senator in the 1970s and 1980s, he had opposed Medicaid funding for abortion services. Bradley aired attack ads saying Gore had changed his position and was not reliably pro-choice.

Gore's position had indeed evolved, a fact I knew personally. In the late 1980s, I read with admiration about forums Gore and his wife, Tipper, held to discuss proposals to strengthen communities and families. I believed any discussion of that topic should include efforts both to improve the circumstances under which women bore children and to empower women to exercise control over their reproductive lives. I called Gore to suggest that he and I meet.

"Senator, these forums you and Tipper conduct are very important. I'd appreciate an opportunity to discuss how reproductive choice and the circumstances surrounding a woman's decision to have a child affect families and communities. And I hope we can discuss Medicaid funding as well."

We decided to meet privately, away from the bustle of congressional activity, in the Capitol Hill apartment of his father, the legendary Senator Al Gore Sr., whose courageous stand against the Vietnam War I had deeply admired when I was a young activist. I remember the apartment as comfortable, not lavish; a warm environment perfectly suited to our discussion. My goal was not so much to lobby him on a specific issue as to begin a thoughtful and comprehensive dialogue about how reproductive freedom and choice affects women and families as well as the health of entire communities. I was impressed with the depth of Gore's intelligence and his open-mindedness. He expressed his belief that public policy plays an important role in shaping the future of society and that it should account for the full range of influences on communities, including the circumstances under which children are born.

It was immediately clear that the widely held stereotypes about Gore—that he was stiff and stilted—were inaccurate. He was warm, thoughtful, and funny. We discussed how society could place greater value on childbearing by broadening education, expanding access to family planning, improving prenatal care, and supporting parents.

"The first critical decision a family makes is when and under what conditions a child is brought into the world," I said. "This decision indelibly shapes the course of a child's and family's life. I am disturbed that the right wing has co-opted the issue of family values. Their policies would force a woman to bear a child against her will and then deny her the support necessary to raise it. The right wing has little understanding or compassion for the reality of women's lives."

"I agree," Gore replied. "To me, 'family values' should mean enhancing the health and well-being of women and families."

When we discussed Medicaid funding, I argued that poor women should have access to the same health care as those who are more fortunate: "Medicaid reflects our government's commitment to provide health care to those who are poor in our society. I believe it is coercive and discriminatory to use that benefit as a weapon to deny poor women a particular health service. The policy takes aim at the most vulnerable and least politically powerful women in our society. I believe it is fundamentally unfair."

Gore listened carefully, then said, "I do not believe government should interfere in women's private reproductive choices. My position is that government should not be involved in this decision. Medicaid funding makes government a part of this decision."

"I think there is another way to look at this," I replied. "First, I believe that denying access to a particular service to women who depend on the government for health care is the height of government interference. And in this case, such a policy also discriminates against poor women. Second, our society does not allow citizens to withhold taxes for any government activity with which they disagree. Our government does many things I do not like, but I must still pay taxes to support them."

We continued to discuss Medicaid funding and other issues on several occasions. Over time, Gore decided to support Medicaid funding, and the fact that he had thoroughly explored both sides of the issue demonstrated his sincerity and seriousness. I also believe that his relationship with Tipper and his three daughters was an important influence on his views. Gore was deeply, completely committed to equality and opportunity for women, and I felt he understood that women could only be fully equal if they were able to control their reproductive lives. His evolution on the issue was sincere, reflective, and open-minded—precisely how politics should work.

However, as the Iowa caucuses and New Hampshire primary approached in early 2000, Bradley argued that Gore's evolution on Medicaid funding was a sign that his dedication to a woman's right to choose was politically motivated. In one advertisement, Bradley called himself "the only candidate who's always been pro-choice," a charge I felt was unfair. While I disagreed strongly with his earlier votes on Medicaid, Gore had generally supported legal abortion, and he was now fully pro-choice.

I appreciated the fact that Bradley had always been fully pro-choice, but I also believed policymakers whose records were mixed should be encouraged to change their views, not be condemned for doing so. One of my goals at NARAL was to work with policymakers to broaden their understanding of pro-choice values and encourage an evolution of their views. If they were punished politically for their earlier records, they would have no reason to reconsider positions with which NARAL or any other organization disagreed. Sadly, mine was a rapidly diminishing view in our ever-increasing "gotcha" approach to public service.

Most disturbing, Bradley was using a woman's right to choose to divide pro-choice voters at precisely the time we needed to unify against the threat of an anti-choice presidency. If Bradley succeeded in raising questions about Gore's commitment to reproductive rights, it would be difficult to mobilize pro-choice voters when, as every serious observer expected, the vice president won the Democratic nomination. Bush would have an ironclad defense against criticisms of his anti-choice position: He would simply be able to say Gore was not pro-choice either.

Meanwhile, I was spending enormous amounts of time responding to reporters' questions about Bradley's attacks on Gore's record.

With the media focused exclusively on the dispute over Gore's past views, it was increasingly difficult for NARAL to communicate Bush's current—and total—opposition to a woman's right to choose. I was forced to spend my time commenting on an intramural dispute between two pro-choice candidates rather than working to defeat the anti-choice one. When the Bradley campaign began distorting my statements about Gore's record to make it sound as though I questioned his commitment to reproductive rights as well, I believed we had to take decisive action. I felt the only way to stop attacks on the vice president's pro-choice record would be for NARAL to consider an extraordinary and controversial step: endorsing Al Gore.

NARAL had never endorsed a presidential candidate in a primary contest in which more than one pro-choice contender was running. Endorsing Vice President Gore would be unprecedented and controversial. Bradley supporters—of whom there were many among our staff, board, contributors, and affiliates—would see an endorsement as unwarranted interference in a primary and unfair criticism of their candidate. Under normal circumstances, we would have remained neutral in the primary because we viewed our role as supporting pro-choice candidates, not choosing among them. However, the stakes in this election were too high for NARAL to remain silent. The vice president would almost certainly be the nominee, and we could not allow choice to be neutralized as an issue in the all-important general election. Shortly before the critical New Hampshire primary, I asked our board to convene a special meeting to consider endorsing Gore. I laid out an extensive explanation of the situation and then summarized my case.

"A woman's right to choose is at risk in this election. Gore will almost certainly be the nominee, and we must clear up any doubt about his pro-choice views. In order to mobilize them against

Bush, voters must see Gore as a strongly committed pro-choice candidate. I realize endorsing Gore would be a highly unusual step, and I know some of you are Bradley supporters. I hope we can have a frank and open discussion today, because I know we are all committed to considering this decision very, very carefully.

"Both candidates are pro-choice," I continued, "but one of them is using the issue to divide voters when it is vitally important to unite them. NARAL's support is a widely respected seal of approval on the issue of a woman's right to choose. If we endorse Gore, his qualifications as a pro-choice candidate will be unquestionable, and we can focus on the real threat, George W. Bush."

The Board debated the issue for the entire day, and the discussion was intense, but serious, open, and respectful. We discussed how various constituencies—especially our donors and affiliates—would react if we supported Gore, as well as an endorsement's long-term impact on NARAL as an organization. At the outset, some members of the board were opposed to an endorsement, but after careful consideration, a consensus emerged: Endorsing Gore was the best option for preserving the right to choose as a viable issue in the general election. The vote was unanimous to endorse.

We decided to call Gore to inform him. I placed a speakerphone in the middle of the table and dialed the White House switchboard. Gore called back a few minutes later.

"Mr. Vice President," I said, "I'm calling to tell you that, after an all-day meeting of NARAL's board, we have decided to endorse you for president. The right to choose is on the line in this election, and we want you to have the full weight of pro-choice voters behind you."

"This means a great deal to me," he replied. "NARAL is very important and will be influential in helping me reach women voters. Thank you very much for your confidence."

Soon afterward, Gore returned from the campaign trail to attend a press conference announcing NARAL's endorsement. Press conferences are usually sober affairs, but this one had the excitement of a campaign rally. News networks carried the event live. The room was completely packed. Gore's statement, in which he promised to defend a woman's right to choose, energized the crowd. In my statement, I explained that while we respected Bradley's pro-choice record, we were troubled by his divisive tactics.

"We had to step forward and clarify the record," I said. "We reject attempts to use this as a wedge issue to divide pro-choice voters, and that is what the Bradley campaign has been doing."

I was confident the endorsement was necessary, but it was still difficult to deliver what I knew was a terrible blow to Bradley, who had been a thoughtful and committed pro-choice senator. During his years in the Senate, Bradley had taken politically controversial pro-choice positions on issues like parental involvement laws. His office door had always been open to NARAL, and he always listened respectfully. In 1991, when Clarence Thomas was nominated to the Supreme Court, Bradley—perhaps the Senate's most eloquent advocate of improving race relations—had been rumored to be undecided. I went to see him and made the case against Thomas's nomination.

"Senator, this could mean the end of a woman's right to choose. I respect your deep commitment to diversity, but this nominee does not share your views and values on a number of constitutional issues."

Bradley, a quiet and contemplative man, listened to my arguments attentively and replied simply. "Kate, thank you for coming in. I appreciate what you've said. I'm thinking carefully about this."

Bradley ultimately cast a principled vote against Thomas. It was difficult to endorse his opponent in the campaign Bradley hoped would be the pinnacle of his career, but far more than personal relationships were at stake. In politics, there are times when it is necessary to take positions that alienate friends, and this was such a situation.

The morning of the press conference announcing the Gore endorsement, NARAL placed a courtesy call to the Bradley campaign to inform them. Understandably, they were outraged. Anita Dunn, a high-ranking official in the Bradley campaign who was a personal friend of mine and a longtime NARAL consultant, faxed a letter abruptly terminating her relationship with us. In the press, Bradley dismissed NARAL as a "Washington-based interest group." I understood their frustration. They knew our endorsement would be devastating for their campaign at a time when it was already struggling.

"This," a member of Bradley's senior staff reportedly said upon learning of our endorsement, "is the nail in the coffin."

That prediction was accurate. Reports of our endorsement led the news that evening and the next morning. What little momentum Bradley had faded, and he soon ended his candidacy, setting the stage for a difficult and deeply contentious fall campaign between Al Gore and George W. Bush, two candidates whose views on a woman's freedom to choose could not possibly have been further apart.

CHAPTER TWENTY-TWO

OUR MESSAGE FOR THE PRESIDENTIAL CAMPAIGN WAS SIMple: Americans were voting for the future of the Supreme Court and the fate of *Roe v. Wade*. The next president would wield extraordinary power over a woman's right to choose. We knew most Americans found that argument compelling if they heard it, but they were also being inundated with messages on dozens of other issues. It was not enough to convince Americans that reproductive rights should be protected.

As the general election campaign took shape, the Supreme Court delivered a powerful reminder that the right to choose might be determined by the 2000 election. While the federal abortion ban received more publicity, more than thirty states, beginning with Ohio, had quietly enacted their own bans. Their laws were emblematic of a common anti-choice tactic. Because voters pay closer attention to developments in Washington, anti-choice politicians have been able to conduct a largely unnoticed campaign to restrict the right to choose at the state level. Legal challenges to the state abortion bans culminated in *Steinberg v. Carhart*, which tested the constitutionality of a Nebraska abortion ban similar to the federal proposal Clinton had vetoed. The Court had already diminished constitutional protection for reproductive rights in the *Webster* and *Casey* decisions in 1989 and 1992, but if *Steinberg* upheld an outright ban on previability abortions for the first time, the case would directly undermine the foundation of *Roe v. Wade*. Most legal experts believed the case would be decided by a narrow margin and that Justice O'Connor—the architect of *Casey's* "undue burden" standard—would probably cast the decisive vote. NARAL was confident that the law's lack of a health exception was a serious flaw, but the undue burden standard was so vague that we could not predict the outcome of the case.

On June 28, a NARAL staff attorney called from the Court. "We won! The law was overturned. That's the good news."

"That's wonderful!" I said, elated and relieved. "What was the vote?"

"That's the problem. The vote was only five to four, and the Court ruled on very narrow grounds."

O'Connor cast the decisive vote to overturn the Nebraska law, writing that it was unconstitutional because it did not contain an exception to protect women's health. Her objections were so detailed and precise that the opinion provided a guide for anti-choice legislators to draft a new law that they could claim addressed her concerns. The federal ban would almost certainly be reintroduced and the battle would begin anew.

Steinberg was a critical victory both legally and for women's health, but like other successes, this one provided false reassurance to pro-choice Americans: Most were unaware the case was even being argued, and when it was decided, the media emphasized that the Supreme Court overturned the abortion ban and upheld *Roe v. Wade*. Few people understood either the narrow grounds of the decision or the fact that the right to choose survived by just one vote. As a result, communicating our message in the presidential campaign was even more challenging.

Many Republican voters, even those who were pro-choice, were eager to elect a president of their own party and were therefore willing to believe that Bush's moderate rhetoric was sincere. We had to persuade them, as well as independents, that Bush would use his power as president to restrict a woman's right to choose just as he had as governor. Once we convinced them of that point, we needed to convince them that the rights to privacy and freedom of choice were so important—and revealed so much about Bush's view of women, as well as the role of government— that they should cast their ballots based on their pro-choice beliefs.

Bush, who tried repeatedly to avoid discussing reproductive rights, was clearly concerned that voters would discover the true depth of his anti-choice views. When he spoke to his far-right base, he clearly stated his intention to restrict abortion, but his tone with the general public was considerably more nuanced. He tried to sidestep questions about the Court by saying he would not employ a "litmus test" for judicial nominees, but promised to appoint "strict constructionists," a label that politicians commonly use as code for "judges who oppose *Roe v. Wade*." When asked to name the justices he most admired, his answer was revealing: Justices Scalia and Thomas, two of the Court's most outspoken opponents of *Roe*.

Our message about the Supreme Court was only one facet of NARAL's political strategy. We also conducted an extensive grassroots mobilization that built on our years of work to broaden and strengthen the pro-choice movement by bringing it into the political mainstream. We had carefully and methodically built a database identifying several million pro-choice individuals, including their names, addresses, telephone numbers, Congressional districts, and local voting precincts, allowing us to target our outreach with surgical precision.

NARAL concentrated our efforts in twenty states we believed

would make the difference in the presidential election, as well as in fifteen Senate races and ninety-one House campaigns. In many of the targeted races, we set up full-fledged independent campaigns that included paid organizers, advertising, and get-out-the-vote efforts. In some target states, NARAL's voter list accounted for nearly 10 percent of the expected voter turnout. The scope of the campaign was historic: We made 3.4 million telephone calls to pro-choice individuals, mailed 4.6 million pieces of literature, mobilized 2.1 million voters, and raised and spent $7.5 million for the campaign. The effort was monumental, and with polls continuing to show a tight race, we believed NARAL's efforts could be decisive.

As the campaign entered its final days that October, our polling showed that pro-choice voters were increasingly aware of the threat to *Roe v. Wade* and that the right to choose was becoming a more prominent force in the campaign. Then, during a meeting I held with journalists in Minneapolis, one of them made an observation that astonished me.

"The amazing thing," she said, "is that this state could end up voting Republican for president for the first time since the early seventies."

I was as stunned as I was disturbed. Minnesota, one of NARAL's targets, was a closely contested state, but it typically votes Democratic in presidential elections. A majority of Minnesota voters were pro-choice, and we were confident that we would win the state. The idea that Minnesota voters might prefer Bush for president was both troubling and difficult to believe.

"It's not that Bush is winning the popular vote," she said. "It's that Nader is draining support from Gore."

Ralph Nader, who repeatedly argued that there was no meaningful difference between Gore and Bush, was running for president as a candidate of the Green Party. NARAL's political team had periodically discussed whether we should oppose his candidacy directly or whether doing so would lend Nader more credibility. In the end, we decided not to engage in a debate with him. National polls rarely showed Nader exceeding 2 or 3 percent, and even that small number was probably inflated. Voters tend to be more enthusiastic about a protest campaign early in an election cycle, but by the fall, most decide to vote for a candidate with a realistic chance of success. Nader's candidacy seemed more like a nuisance than a real threat.

But, on closer examination, the national polls were misleading. In some states, including Minnesota, Nader's support registered 8 or 9 percent. The race was so close in those states that Nader might actually draw enough votes away from Gore to give Bush a victory. When a journalist in Seattle said Bush might win Washington State—another NARAL target—I knew the Nader threat was serious. I called Alice Germond, NARAL's executive vice president.

"Alice, we have a serious problem in a number of important states. Gore is down in the polls, Bush is up, and Nader is the reason. We can't ignore Nader any longer."

The situation demanded swift and decisive action, but the election was only three weeks away, and we had not budgeted resources for a campaign against Nader. I called our largest donors, explained the situation, and asked for contributions for an emergency advertising campaign. Stephanie Kushner, NARAL's director of fund-raising, sat with me in the car, dialing donors' numbers and handing me her cell phone as soon as I completed a conversation on mine. We quickly raised a substantial amount of funds for the effort. NARAL directed our media consultants to produce an advertisement immediately.

"The message needs to be very simple. A vote for Nader is a vote for Bush and a Supreme Court that will overturn *Roe v. Wade*," I said. "I don't want to attack Nader personally. That's not the way to persuade his supporters. We just need to inform them of the impact of their votes."

The advertisement was straightforward:

> If you're thinking of voting for Ralph Nader, please consider: This year a five to four Supreme Court decision narrowly protected *Roe v. Wade*. A single vote saved a woman's right to choose. As president, George Bush would reverse the Court . . . with anti-choice justices Scalia and Thomas in control. Bush's goal? Ending legal abortion. Voting for Ralph Nader helps elect George W. Bush. Before voting Nader . . . consider the risk. It's your choice.

NARAL's political team targeted seven states where Nader's support appeared sufficient to deny victory to Gore: Maine, Minnesota, New Mexico, Oregon, Vermont, Washington, and Wisconsin. Within twenty-four hours after the advertisement began to air, Nader's support began declining steadily in each of the seven states. The influence of the advertising itself was multiplied by the national media's intensive coverage of our anti-Nader campaign. Nader was also campaigning heavily in Florida, but polls showed Gore leading Bush in the state, and the cost of running our advertising there would have been prohibitive.

Nader lashed out in response to our campaign, insisting that NARAL was exaggerating the threat to the right to choose. Even if *Roe v. Wade* was overturned, he argued, that did not mean abortion would necessarily be banned; states would simply be allowed to do so. But that was precisely the point: Many states were poised to ban abortion the moment the Court empowered them to do so.

By saying there was no difference between Gore and Bush, Nader was dismissing a woman's right to choose—an issue on which they were absolute opposites—as trivial and unimportant. Nader had no realistic expectation of winning the election. He was risking the presidency of the United States simply to make a rhetorical point, and NARAL could no longer ignore the threat he posed. The campaign revealed a side of Nader that I remembered from the Bork battle of 1987, when he insisted on testifying before the Senate even though it was clear that doing so would undermine our cause.

Regardless of my frustration with Nader, I admired the zeal and passion of his supporters, one of whom I met after I made a speech in Oregon, where our advertisements were on the air.

"How can you do this?" he demanded. "Ralph Nader is trying to transform our democracy and realize its potential. You're only looking at this one issue."

"Fundamental freedoms and individual rights are what our democracy is about," I replied. "A woman's right to choose is a fundamental freedom. It is central to guaranteeing women equal rights. You cannot dismiss the lives and health of half the population as just one issue. If Ralph helps to elect Bush, many of our hard-won rights will be at risk. I admire your activism and your vision for the nation. But putting George W. Bush in the White House is not a strategy for success."

He was polite, but it was clear that nothing I could say would change his mind.

Meanwhile, I was concentrating on a new constituency of my own: Matthew, our daughter Lisa's nine-year-old son and a budding political activist. The campaign awakened Matthew's political conscience, and he quickly became one of Gore's greatest admirers. Matthew was especially interested in Gore's leadership on the environment and civil rights. We talked on the telephone often.

"Matthew," I would say, "Gore's going to be on C-SPAN tonight; I want you to watch and tell me what you think."

Once, I asked Matthew why he supported Gore.

"Because, Grandma Kate, he cares more about the things that are important to people's lives." He had distilled the difference between Gore and Bush to its essence better than any high-priced political consultant.

Matthew stayed with Fred and me on Election Day so he could share the excitement of both what I believed would be a victory and the busy activity leading up to it. Gathering intelligence about voter turnout around the country, shifting get-out-the-vote resources, and monitoring exit polls are all essential on the day of an election. I felt anxious but optimistic. I knew NARAL's mobilization was unsurpassed in our history. Our work to build a mainstream movement—the many years we had invested in positioning the right to choose as a positive political issue—was paying dividends, a fact the election results seemed to confirm. We won twelve of the fifteen Senate races we targeted, bringing the Senate to a 50/50 split between Democrats and Republicans, and effectively ending the six-year dominance of the anti-choice Republican leadership. Pro-choice candidates prevailed in sixty-seven of the House races NARAL targeted, recouping some of our losses in the 1994 elections. Perhaps most satisfying, exit polls showed that the Supreme Court was one of the five most important issues for Gore voters. Gore also prevailed in every state where our Nader advertisements had aired.

I was standing outside NARAL's glass-encased conference room where staff were gathered when I saw Gore's picture flash on the television screen with a graphic of my home state, Pennsylvania— one of our key targets—and a blue check mark. I grabbed Matthew's hand and rushed into the room. We seemed to be on the verge of victory. Although he did not carry his home state of Tennessee, one more large state would give Gore a majority in the electoral college. Florida, where we were unable to run the Nader ads, was our most serious concern. But soon, anchormen declared Gore to be the winner of Florida's electoral votes and the next president of the United States. Spontaneous cheers erupted. People embraced. After nearly two years of continuous and exhausting effort with so much at stake, it finally seemed that we had won.

And then—suddenly—it all began to unravel.

It was almost surreal, beginning with a spotty report by various news anchors stammering that they may have spoken too soon, that the exit polls in Florida were now too close to call. They reclassified the state as undecided. Gore had clearly won the national popular vote, but he needed Florida's electoral votes to prevail. A dreadful pall descended on the room. The polls were now closed. There was nothing to do but wait.

A couple of hours later, Florida's Republican secretary of state, Katherine Harris, declared a narrow victory for Bush. His margin was only a few hundred votes; Nader had received 97,000. The networks reported that Gore was placing a call to Bush to concede.

I was incredulous. While I have always maintained a healthy perspective about elections, this one was especially important. In what felt like an instant, a historic victory became a devastating defeat. Matthew was upset and bewildered.

"I don't understand," he said. "How can Gore win and then not win? How can he get more votes and not win?" I explained the electoral college. Matthew seemed to understand, but to his nine-year-old eyes, the situation seemed fundamentally unfair. Matters only became more confusing when the networks announced Gore had retracted his concession and the outcome of the election was once more in doubt.

I looked at Matthew. It was well past midnight, and he was exhausted.

"Fred, why don't you and Matthew go home," I suggested.

"Grandma Kate," Matthew insisted, "I want to see what's happening."

"I know, honey, but it may be a while before we know the outcome," I said. "You go to bed, and I promise I'll wake you up when we know something for sure. It may be a while before this is over."

There was no reason to wake Matthew up the rest of that night. Many long and uncertain days lay ahead.

CHAPTER TWENTY-THREE

C AMPAIGNS ARE AN EXTRAORDINARY, EMOTIONALLY INTENSE, physically draining experience. It is difficult enough to lose them, but to have worked so hard and to have come so close only to face weeks of uncertainty was especially agonizing. We were left with all the tension of the campaign, but we were powerless to affect the outcome. There were no more advertisements to air, voters to mobilize, speeches to give, or funds to raise. The entire outcome depended on the Florida recount. I called Vice President Gore to offer my support.

"Al, I want you to know I'm thinking about you and Tipper. I can only imagine how hard this is. You know we'll do anything you believe is helpful."

"I appreciate that," Gore replied. He sounded confident but cautious. "This is a matter of law now, and the law is on our side. If everyone's ballots are counted, we'll win. Our focus is on the legal strategy."

In early December, the U.S. Supreme Court issued its first opinion in the dispute, raising concerns about the recount procedures but remanding the case to Florida officials for further review. The tone of the opinion—authored by Antonin Scalia, Bush's model justice—was ominous, but at least the recount would continue. A few days later, our hopes soared when the Atlanta-based 11th Circuit Courts of Appeal, typically a conservative court, denied a Bush challenge to recounts in three Florida counties. That Friday, December 8, the Florida Supreme Court ordered a statewide recount of disputed ballots. Unless the U.S. Supreme Court interfered, Gore stood an excellent chance of victory.

That Saturday, Gore's campaign manager, Donna Brazile, spoke to a meeting of NARAL's affiliates in Washington. During her remarks, an aide passed her a note delivering devastating news: The U.S. Supreme Court had just announced it would hear arguments in the case, placing the recount at serious risk. Brazile handled the moment with grace and poise, sharing the news with the audience and turning to scripture for inspiration in a moment that was both personally and politically difficult. "May justice roll down like water, and righteousness like a mighty stream," she said.

When the affiliate conference concluded, I made a long-scheduled visit to Florida, where my parents had retired. It was difficult for me to leave Washington during the recount dispute, but my parents were coping with health problems and I had been unable to visit them during the campaign. I knew both of them had voted for Bush; the last Democrat they had supported for president was Kennedy in 1960, largely because he was Catholic. I believe my story had opened their eyes to the complexities of a woman's right to choose, but it was not enough to change their votes. Even though we disagreed about the election, they understood how much it meant to me. They were warm and sympathetic. I was still at my parents' home when Alice Germond called from Washington.

"The Supreme Court just stopped the recount. It's over."

I was devastated. By blocking the counting of votes that could have changed the outcome, the Supreme Court had anointed

George W. Bush president. The White House and House of Representatives would now be under anti-choice control, and Vice President-elect Richard Cheney, who shared Bush's anti-choice views, would be the tie-breaking vote in an evenly divided Senate. For the first time since *Roe v. Wade*, the entire elected national government was controlled by those who opposed reproductive freedom and choice. Opponents of abortion would be able to enact policies stretching *Roe* to the breaking point, and there was every reason to fear that with time, it could be overturned outright.

The next day, my office called to say I had been invited to join a gathering at the vice president's home following his concession speech, but it was too late to arrange a flight back to Washington. It was painful not to be able to be there. That night, my parents and I watched on television as Gore delivered one of the most poignant, eloquent, and historic concession speeches in American history. He promised to help Bush heal the nation's divisions and urged his supporters to accept an outcome we believed was fundamentally unfair. It was the finest moment of the campaign, which made it all the more painful. This was the Al Gore I knew— thoughtful, heartfelt, patriotic, and devoted to the greater good of America. It was sad that many Americans only came to appreciate those qualities when he conceded.

As soon as I returned to Washington, I called a staff meeting. I was deeply concerned about our professional family, which included many young, idealistic, energetic activists whose experience with electoral victories and defeats was not as long as mine. For many, it was their first campaign, and it was devastating.

"I've been through many campaigns. It's one thing to lose fairly. But to lose by having the Supreme Court deny a recount is especially frustrating. I'm devastated, and I know you are. But we have to keep the long view in mind. It's important to grieve, but then we have to fight back. We need to harness all the positive achievements of this campaign, all the activists we recruited, and transform that energy into a movement that defends and protects the right to choose."

Our team was dejected and angry, but also determined. We faced a serious challenge. Bush made that immediately clear by nominating the recently defeated Missouri Senator John Ashcroft to be the United States attorney general. Ashcroft, who supported a constitutional amendment overturning *Roe v. Wade,* was one of the most extreme right-wing politicians in the Senate. As the nation's highest-ranking law enforcement officer, he would wield enormous power over laws and policies governing women's lives. Among other powers, his Justice Department would evaluate judicial nominees, argue cases affecting reproductive rights in the courts, and decide how vigorously to enforce clinic-violence laws. The Justice Department would be the epicenter of the Bush administration's assault against a woman's right to choose. Pundits called the Ashcroft nomination a clever political stroke by Bush. It rewarded the right-wing of his political base, and senators could be depended upon to confirm a colleague regardless of his extreme views. Even some of NARAL's strongest pro-choice allies in Congress endorsed Ashcroft's nomination.

NARAL rejected the view that Ashcroft's confirmation was inevitable, nor did we accept that the Senate should automatically ratify whomever the president-elect chose. We hardly expected Bush to appoint a pro-choice attorney general, but Ashcroft was an ideologue elevated to an especially powerful position. The coalition of groups that had opposed the Bork nomination immediately reconstituted itself to oppose Ashcroft.

I was at my home in Pennsylvania for the holidays when I

heard the news that Bush had nominated Ashcroft. I returned to Washington immediately to mobilize NARAL's staff, board, members, affiliates, and grassroots supporters.

"I don't have any illusions about how difficult it will be to oppose Ashcroft," I said. "Everyone expects him to be confirmed, but I believe we can mount an effective opposition and possibly even defeat him. We need to bring the full force of our organization to bear on this. At the very least, we will send a message to this administration that we will not allow it to trample a woman's right to choose without a fight. Ideally, we will defeat the nomination. But short of defeating him, our goal is to get at least forty votes against Ashcroft. Forty votes would be an important statement that we are prepared to fight for our rights forcefully. We have a nationwide network of activists who stood with us during the presidential campaign. Let's give them something to take a stand on."

NARAL launched our "Stop Ashcroft!" campaign, publicized his extreme anti-choice record, and unleashed the full power of our grassroots network. We sent e-mails to our online activists asking them to contact their senators and urge an anti-Ashcroft vote. Our Web page featured a special "Web Action Center" that activists could use to send e-mails directly to their senators. We hired a firm to cull nearly 400,000 pro-choice voters in our database, inform them of the Ashcroft nomination, and connect them to their senators' offices.

Many political observers scoffed at the campaign, dismissing it as a hopeless cause and predicting that we would be fortunate to persuade fifteen senators to vote against the nomination. Initially, we counted only twelve reliable anti-Ashcroft votes in the Senate. The attitude of many senators was typified by Bob Torricelli of New Jersey, a strong pro-choice leader who was nonetheless quoted in the press as saying he would probably vote to confirm Ashcroft.

Shortly afterward, I saw Torricelli at a reception following Hillary Clinton's swearing in as a senator. I knew it might be my only chance to talk with him.

"I must tell you, Senator, we're both astonished and upset about your public statements of support for Ashcroft."

Torricelli tried to deflect the issue by saying senatorial decorum compelled him to speak fondly of a colleague. "Besides," he said, "as attorney general, he'll enforce existing law."

"Ashcroft is an extremist," I replied. "He's spent his entire career working to overturn laws that protect women. His values are antithetical to everything you stand for and have fought for. The fact that he is a colleague in the Senate is not enough to justify threatening the individual rights and liberties of Americans."

"Kate, the president has a right to name his own cabinet," he replied, offering the rationale that many senators espoused when we spoke with them about Ashcroft.

"Of course the president has a right to nominate whom he desires," I said. "But as a senator you have a responsibility to examine the nominee's fitness for the office. There is no question that, as attorney general, Ashcroft will pose a real threat to our rights and liberties."

NARAL's personal lobbying of senators and the outcry from our grassroots base made steady and deep inroads against Ashcroft. By the time the Senate Judiciary Committee voted on Ashcroft, several of its members had already indicated they planned to oppose him, leaving us only two short of the margin required to block his nomination. Two of the remaining undecided senators, Democrat Russ Feingold of Wisconsin and Republican Arlen Specter of Pennsylvania, were pro-choice. I had met with both, but as the committee meeting began, we did not know how either would vote. Feingold opened his statement with a litany of issues on which he disagreed with Ashcroft.

"He's going to vote with us!" I thought. If Feingold opposed Ashcroft, the committee would be tied, a serious blow to the nomination. But in a statement that seemed bizarre, Feingold listed all the reasons Ashcroft should not be attorney general, then concluded by saying the president nonetheless had the prerogative to appoint whomever he preferred. Both Feingold and Specter supported Ashcroft, allowing his nomination to pass the committee narrowly. NARAL placed advertisements in their hometown newspapers to inform their constituents about their votes. I heard afterward that Feingold was incensed.

However, the anti-Ashcroft coalition did succeed in reaching other senators. In a battle that skeptics said we should never have fought, NARAL alone generated more than 300,000 letters, telephone calls, e-mails, and other contacts to senators' offices urging them to oppose Ashcroft. When the final tally was announced, Ashcroft was confirmed—as we expected—but we also achieved a stunning number of votes against him: forty-two senators. The pundits were astounded, the pro-choice activists elated. Although exhausted and demoralized by the election results and the recount battle, we were reinvigorated. We had organized and mobilized effectively. Many more threats to a woman's right to choose awaited, but at least the administration knew pro-choice Americans would fight back!

The day of Bush's inauguration was a sad reminder of how much pro-choice Americans had lost in the 2000 election. Eight years earlier, Bill Clinton's inauguration was a day of celebration; today was a day for commiseration. Two days after Clinton took office, I was invited to the White House to watch him transform the lives and raise the hopes of millions of women by signing five executive orders that NARAL had helped to draft. On January 20, 2001, when Bush assumed the presidency, we were on the outside looking in—and deeply concerned about the future. Some pro-choice advocates still clung to the hope that Bush's rhetoric of moderation and compassion was sincere. His father had been a disappointment to the right wing, they reasoned, and maybe this new president would be as well. NARAL knew Bush's record in Texas too well to entertain that expectation seriously, and the Ashcroft nomination was clear evidence of his intent to restrict a woman's right to choose. Still, even I was surprised by the brazenness of his immediate attack on women's rights.

On January 22, 2001, the anniversary of *Roe v. Wade* and his second full day in office, Bush signed an executive order reinstating the global gag rule. "It is my conviction," the order read, "that taxpayer funds should not be used to pay for abortions or advocate or actively promote abortion, either here or abroad." That was a blatant distortion: Since 1973, it has been illegal for foreign groups to use U.S. funds to provide abortions. Bush was simply trying to harass and silence groups that used their own money to provide abortion services. The gag rule would have been unconstitutional had he imposed it in the United States.

Bush signed the order quietly, apparently hoping most voters would not notice. His staff insultingly tried to claim the timing of the order was coincidental and that it was unrelated to either the anniversary of *Roe* or the fact that thousands of anti-choice activists were holding a demonstration in Washington that day. With the stroke of a pen, Bush severely imperiled the lives and health of the world's most vulnerable women. The effect of the order was immediate. Family planning clinics in some of the world's poorest countries began to cease operations.

Other assaults on the right to choose ensued. Bush's first budget attempted to repeal the requirement that federal employees' health plans cover prescription contraception, an act so extreme he was repudiated by his own party. When a seat opened on a Food and

Drug Administration panel on women's health, Bush appointed an anti-choice obstetrician who suggested that his patients treat premenstrual syndrome with prayer and refused to insert the IUD as a form of birth control. The Bush administration pressured federal health agencies to post inaccurate information about abortion and birth control on their Web pages.

Early in his administration, Bush faced a decision about federal funding of embryonic stem-cell research, a new arena of science that held immense promise for treating a range of ailments, especially spinal cord injuries. Scientists first isolated stem cells in 1998. Harvested from excess embryos produced for fertility treatments— embryos that were no longer needed and would literally be thrown away—stem cells can grow into almost any kind of cells. Scientists hope they can be used to treat conditions—like Alzheimer's disease, Parkinson's disease, and spinal cord injuries—in which previously irreplaceable cells have been lost. Despite its promise, the research is opposed by the most extreme anti-choice policymakers, who regard the fertilized egg as fully human from the moment of conception. As president, Bush wielded the power to suspend or severely curtail federal funding for stem-cell research. During his campaign, he had promised the religious right that he would restrict this important medical research. In the first month of his administration, he followed through on his promise and ordered a review.

There were two compelling reasons for NARAL to engage in the debate: First, if Bush suspended or limited federal funding for stem-cell research, the consequences for millions of people struggling with terrible ailments would be enormous. Second, opposition to stem-cell research was part of a broader strategy to establish the embryo as a full person from the moment of fertilization—a crucial rationale for overturning Roe v. Wade. At the same time, we knew that NARAL and other pro-choice groups would only inflame the situation by playing a high-profile role in the debate. Our public involvement would raise the issue of abortion and distract from the powerful medical and scientific arguments for the research. NARAL believed science and health organizations should assume the leading role as advocates for stem-cell research and that we should conduct our work behind the scenes.

For the first time in eight years, there were no calls to friends in the White House, no strategy sessions with allies in the Cabinet or the White House staff. No longer was there a president to whom we could make our case. The same institution of government that had valued us as partners now regarded us as a political enemy. It was a living reminder of the impact of the 2000 election. The politics of abortion was halting scientific progress for millions of people and their loved ones who were suffering with devastating illnesses and injuries, and there was little we could do to affect the outcome.

What I did not yet know was that my family would soon be among them.

Chapter Twenty-four

THE CALL CAME EARLY ON A MAY AFTERNOON, AND FROM the moment I heard the voice on the other end of the line, I knew something terrible had happened. The caller was a friend of Tasha, our middle daughter, who was living in the Hudson Valley in New York pursuing her passion: a career as a thoroughbred horse trainer. Fred and I were planning to take Tasha to the south of France that summer and were excited about the prospect of introducing her to a part of that country that we especially loved.

Tasha's friend was distraught yet blunt.

"Tasha had an accident. She's paralyzed. She can't feel anything. You need to get up here right away."

I stood at my desk, feeling momentarily paralyzed, frozen by emotions ranging from panic to confusion. I was scared to death.

"Please tell me what happened?" I asked.

"Her horse spooked. He reared up and fell over backward on top of her. Her body was crushed," came the chilling reply.

Fred and I raced frantically to the airport. By the time we arrived in Westchester, New York, it was early evening and our daughter was already in surgery in a critical-care facility. Fred and I waited in a cold and bleak room for word about her condition. It was agonizing to feel so helpless as Tasha lay on a table fighting for her life. When the first reports came, they were grim. Sometime in the middle of the night, the surgeon emerged from the operating room. His face was drawn and his tone direct.

"Your daughter will probably never walk again. The accident crushed three of her vertebrae and punctured her lung and liver. We had to reconstruct her spinal column and remove the splintered vertebrae from her spinal cord. Her condition is serious."

I could not breathe. Fear and agony for my daughter were all I could feel. It was several hours before Tasha was wheeled into the intensive-care unit and a few more before we were allowed to see her. As I saw her lying on that tombstone of a hospital bed looking barely alive, I thought I would die. When she finally awoke, I was hovering over her. Tasha looked up into my eyes and must have read the grief and fear they held.

"Mom," she uttered weakly, "we're still going to France, aren't we?" It broke my heart.

There would be no trip to France, of course, but that was the least of the uncertainties we faced. It was unclear whether Tasha would ever regain feeling or function. Soon our entire family descended on the hospital.

"The first thirty-six hours are the best indicator we have," a doctor explained to us. "If she doesn't at least move a toe, she will probably never move again."

I stared at her feet constantly for the next day and a half, periodically uncovering her toes, desperate for any sign of movement. Tasha struggled through her pain and paralysis to move her toe, but thirty-six hours came and went, and she was unable to budge. The doctors were gentle and reassuring with her—"You never know," was their refrain, "anything can happen"—but candid and bleak with us. Hope was dimming by the hour. One doctor in particular radiated negativity. She seemed to seize on every opportunity to tell us how unlikely it was that Tasha would move again. I tried to ignore her comments until I could no longer endure the pessimism.

"Please don't tell me that again!" I said. "We have to believe it's possible!"

The hospital staff insisted that my daughter be placed in a rehabilitation facility in New York. I was equally adamant that she come to Washington to be near Fred and me, as well as her sisters. She was in excruciating and constant pain, physical, emotional, and mental. Training horses was her life and passion, and in her mind, her life was over. She needed her family.

As the discussion about her rehabilitation placement intensified, I called Christopher Reeve, whom I knew through his long-time support of NARAL, for advice. Chris had also been paralyzed in a horse accident and, more important, he had undertaken an inspiring quest for recovery. Initially, I spoke with a top official of the Christopher Reeve Foundation, Michael Manganiello, who guided me through the first dark hours. Eventually I spoke with Chris personally.

"Chris," I said after explaining the accident, "I don't know what to do. The doctors say to keep her here in New York, but every instinct I have as a mother says she should be with Fred and me and her sisters."

"You are absolutely right. You need to be near her," he said. "One of the most important keys to recovery is the emotional support of the family."

Reeve recommended a rehabilitation facility outside of Washington, with which he was associated. The ambulance ride was long and agonizing. With every bump in the road, Tasha groaned in pain. During our drive back, I received a call from a renowned neurosurgeon and expert in spinal cord injuries who was the uncle of one of Tasha's friends. I had asked him to review X-rays taken before and after her surgery.

"I have bad news for you. I've looked at her chart, I've viewed her X-rays, and I've had colleagues look at them, too. The surgery was not successful. She needs to have it redone right away."

I was devastated.

"She's just been through an excruciating ordeal," I said.

"I know," he replied patiently. "But if the surgery isn't redone now, it's going to cause her terrible problems later. I can recommend an excellent surgeon at Johns Hopkins Medical Center in Baltimore. She can have the operation there and then recover near you."

Late in the evening, we arrived at the hospital outside Washington, where Tasha's doctor drew a diagram of the spinal column and neurological system, detailed the damage, and carefully explained the reasons for Tasha's paralysis. The neurological damage was extensive, and it was not yet possible to know whether it was permanent. Within a week she endured another ten-hour surgery.

Meanwhile, our family faced several practical issues. Tasha was uninsured, unemployed, and had no financial resources. We would have to negotiate the Byzantine process of qualifying for worker's compensation, disability payments, and Medicaid. Finally, someone reminded me that I had friends who might be able to help. I placed a call to Senator Charles Schumer of New York, who assigned a caseworker on his staff to help Tasha qualify for a small disability stipend through Social Security. Senator Barbara Mikulski's office helped her obtain Medicaid coverage in Maryland. Capitol Hill caseworkers—tireless advocates who work in relative obscurity, helping people resolve challenges with the federal bureaucracy—are among the great unsung heroes in public service. They were phenomenal. Tasha's difficulties were an acute reminder to me of how many other uninsured people are forced into desperate situations for which there seem to be few solutions. We were fortunate that I knew people who were in a position to help us, but most are not so lucky.

Following her surgery, Tasha spent several months in the Kessler-Adventist Rehabilitation Hospital outside Washington. Each day, I worked at NARAL until early evening, then drove to the hospital to see Tasha, usually carrying containers stuffed with meals so she could at least warm her spirits with home-cooked food. Her rehabilitative therapy was painful, difficult, and slow, but she was totally focused on her recovery, honing in on each small advance with complete concentration. After one full day of working on nothing else, Tasha phoned me at the office, the exhaustion in her voice overtaken by excitement.

"Mom, I moved a toe!"

Eventually, she called with more good news.

"Mom, I moved my foot! The whole foot!"

Every incremental step brought more work. Therapists believe the best treatment for spinal cord injuries is careful and deliberate movement therapy to stimulate regeneration of nerves. Her progress was slow; some days brought intense pain but no movement. At first simply moving a toe exhausted all her energy. With time, she could lift one of her feet and move one leg slightly. She was never able to move the entire leg, but she set an ambitious goal nonetheless—to walk with braces and crutches by synchronizing the limited motion of both legs. Her courage was limitless and her determination boundless.

One day, I arrived at the hospital to see Tasha in the therapy room, being helped out of her wheelchair, propped on crutches, and placed between the parallel bars. Her legs were as tiny and fragile as toothpicks. With her weight supported by the crutches, her balance maintained by the parallel bars, and her mind keenly focused, she inched one leg in front of the other. It was what the doctors in New York had insisted would never occur: a step. The whole room erupted in applause, I burst into tears, and Tasha all but collapsed in exhaustion.

Not long after Tasha's accident, my husband began experiencing problems with balance and memory. His symptoms were typical of a variety of different degenerative neurological disorders, including Alzheimer's, and, as a result, several visits to specialists were required before the doctors diagnosed him with Parkinson's disease. Suddenly, in the context of Tasha's accident and Fred's illness, the debate over stem-cell research took on a new and profoundly personal dimension for me. This field of science holds enormous potential for treating both spinal cord injuries as well as diseases such as Parkinson's and Alzheimer's. It is especially promising for Tasha, who is still young enough that scientific progress could transform many years of her life. Through the use of stem cells, she might be able to regenerate nerve pathways and regain function or movement in her legs. Similarly, Fred might be able to regenerate nerve cells destroyed by Parkinson's disease.

I was watching people I loved suffer, while the cures or treatments they and millions of others needed were subjected to an abstract political debate that seemed to place little value on their lives. While I appreciated the ethical complexities of embryonic stem-cell research, the political dispute seemed far removed from the reality of pain and suffering my family was experiencing. Opponents of stem-cell research were so absolutist in their views that they seemed incapable of balancing the value of potential life with the moral responsibilities society has to fully existing human life. In their view, a frozen embryo destined for destruction held more inherent value than the constructive lives and health of people like Tasha and Fred.

I do not believe opponents of stem-cell research are insincere. Indeed, one of them—Senator Sam Brownback, a Kansas Republican and a staunch opponent of a woman's right to choose—approached me after I testified before the Judiciary Committee against John Ashcroft's nomination. Brownback said he was deeply moved by my personal story and wanted to have a conversation about the moral issues involved in the debate over abortion. My staff initially opposed the meeting. At best, they believed, it would be a poor expenditure of my time. Brownback's views on reproductive health and rights issues were extreme, and a meeting would not change either of our positions. Moreover, Brownback was leading the effort in Congress to ban human cloning, including a ban on therapeutic stem-cell research. But he persisted in his attempt to arrange a meeting, and I finally agreed. Brownback felt as sincerely and strongly about his views as I did about mine and I felt his views deserved as much respect as my own. I have always tried to make the nation's conversation about a woman's right to choose more civil and respectful, and this was an opportunity to advance that goal.

As we talked over lunch in the Senate cafeteria, Brownback was thoughtful and well-meaning. He explained that his opposition to abortion derived from his belief that an embryo was fully human and that it deserved the same legal rights and protections as those living outside the womb. I responded that while I respected his personal religious and philosophical views, they should not be imposed on all women through law. I also assured him that women understood that pregnancy embodied the potential for full human life. However, I explained, there were circumstances under which women were required to balance their responsibility to that developing life against other moral responsibilities, including, in my case, my obligation to my three living daughters. I said that I believed each reproductive choice involved moral and ethical responsibilities, the greatest of which was the decision to become a parent. The decision to bear a child and to assume responsibility for nurturing that life to its fullest potential is, without parallel, among life's most important choices, I argued, and one that women must make willingly. Only then can children and families have the greatest chance for success.

Our discussion then turned to Brownback's bill banning human cloning.

"Senator, you are sponsoring a bill that would ban human cloning—including therapeutic cloning that is performed only to produce cells for medical research," I said. "This research could lead to medical therapies that could give my own daughter hope that she will once again walk on her own; that she will recover her life."

The discussion was thoughtful and provocative. Neither of us changed our views or abandoned the values that underlay them, but we did reach across the political divide to make a personal connection. Brownback and I could not be further apart philosophically or politically, but we had a genuine exchange of ideas and perspectives—a rare occurrence in the acrimonious debate about abortion.

In August, in a nationally televised address, Bush announced a weak attempt at a compromise on stem-cell research. Rejecting the pleas of dozens of Nobel laureates and thousands of patients suffering from terrible illnesses and injuries, he dealt what amounted to a death blow to stem-cell research. Research on existing stem-cell lines could continue, but federal funding could not be used for research on newly harvested embryos. Bush claimed these current lines were ample, but scientists disagreed: There turned out to be far fewer viable stem cells than Bush asserted, and even those were inadequate. Without federal support, the research was essentially crippled.

The policy made no sense, and it could not withstand scrutiny as an ethical statement. If Bush actually believed a fertilized egg was a full human being, it was inconsistent to allow the research on current lines to continue. If his logic—that a fertilized egg was a human being—was followed to its logical conclusion, commonly used contraception techniques, like the IUD, that prevent the implantation of a fertilized egg should also have been banned, as should any infertility treatment that required excess embryos. Many anti-choice politicians, in fact, openly advocate precisely that, but the Bush policy attempted to placate his far-right base without offending mainstream Americans. He conceded just enough to the anti-choice movement to appease them, and restricted stem-cell research just enough to foreclose hope for people like Tasha and Fred. As occurs so often, the needs of individuals—real people with lives and hopes—seemed to have been forgotten amid a political dispute.

CHAPTER TWENTY-FIVE

F OR AN EARLIER GENERATION OF AMERICANS, "REMEMBER Pearl Harbor!" was the rallying cry born of an event which was to sear America's psyche. To another it was the memory of a dark, rain-soaked November afternoon when President Kennedy lay slain in Dallas. For a later generation, both black and white, it was the afternoon on which Dr. King was taken from us. Today's generation will never forget that crystal-clear blue September morning shattered by the explosions as 747s flew into the World Trade Center, the Pentagon, and a lonely field in Pennsylvania—9/11.

I was in Orlando, Florida, visiting my mother. We were adjusting to life without my father, who had died earlier that year. My relationship with my father was complicated, as many parent/child relationships are, but I loved and admired him greatly. He was one of the most powerful inspirations in my life.

My mother and I were at home when the phone rang that fall morning. My sister was on the line.

"Are you watching the news?"

"No. What's happening?"

"A plane crashed into the World Trade Center."

No one knew exactly what had happened, but it was clear from the beginning that we were witnessing a catastrophe. I turned on the television and watched in shock as the second plane struck and, in an instant, it was obvious that America was under attack. I felt physically rooted to the spot where I stood, as though I could not move. The horror for those at Ground Zero was unimaginable, and the agony of others watching on television, knowing people they loved were trapped in the buildings, must have been unbearable. The thought of it made my heart sick.

From such a distance, the tragedy seemed abstract, its enormity too much to comprehend. When news reports of the Pentagon attack, then of a plane down over Pennsylvania that was apparently headed toward Washington, the danger became real and personal. "Oh, my God," I thought. "Fred and Tasha."

Fred was in our apartment just three blocks from the Capitol, which might be one of the terrorist targets. He was in no condition physically to evacuate, nor was Tasha, who was still undergoing intensive rehabilitation in Maryland. I grabbed the phone and dialed their numbers, but all the circuits into Washington were dead.

I was equally anxious about our staff in Washington—our office was just a few blocks from the White House, another potential target—as well as the many people I knew in New York. NARAL's New York affiliate was located in Manhattan, and many of my personal friends lived there as well. I was finally able to reach NARAL's Washington office by telephone.

"This whole city is panicked," our receptionist told me. "The streets are jammed. No one knows what's going on. Nobody knows what to do."

We had no choice but to assume that Washington and New York were under full-scale assault and that more attacks were likely. I decided to close our office so NARAL's staff—some of whom were young parents—could join their families. I asked for the phone numbers of friends in New York and began the frustrating process of trying to obtain an open phone line to call them.

Eventually, I was able to reach Fred. He and Tasha were safe, but we were deeply shaken. While I was glad to be with my mother during the chaos, I also needed to return to my family and staff in Washington—but with the airports closed until further notice, simply traveling home would be a challenge. Later that day, I spoke with a colleague in Washington who mentioned that the parents of one of her staff were visiting Florida. They had decided to rent a car and drive home rather than wait for the airports to reopen. I met them near the highway and together we drove through the night.

At dawn's early light the next morning, we drove past the Pentagon on our way into Washington. I will never forget the experience. The crash site was still smoldering, and a blanket of smoke lingered above it. In the side of the building—a concrete structure so solid it was difficult to imagine anything damaging it—there was a gaping gash ringed in black. The traffic that clogs Washington's bridges even in the early-morning hours had vanished. There was absolutely no sign of life. The whole scene was utterly desolate and eerily calm, like a lunar landscape. It was deeply unsettling.

In the days that followed, I thought that, in some small way, some good might be recovered from the ashes of 9/11. The attacks forced us to think about what it meant to be Americans, shocking us into a new appreciation of freedom and tolerance. We were confronted with the specter of religious fanaticism taken to its extreme. Now that our shared ideals—like democracy and individual rights—were under such bold attack, perhaps Americans would come to value and appreciate our freedoms more deeply.

In the days after 9/11, our Choice for America ads were still being broadcast on television. It had not occurred to me to take them off the air. They were neither strident nor partisan. However, many Americans felt it was important to turn the country's attention toward issues that would unify the nation. When NARAL received a small number of complaints about the propriety of the ads, I immediately directed that they be removed from the airwaves. My personal instinct was that there was no better way to honor the ideals the terrorists had attacked than to continue an open and vigorous dialogue about important issues of personal liberty. However, the concerns we heard about the ads were understandable, and I respected them. I also suspended our fund-raising appeals, which did carry a sharper political message. It was not the time to ask for contributions. The time for reengaging in the debate about the right to choose would come, but this was a moment for Americans to unite.

There was reason for hope. Despite my early doubts about his leadership, I was heartened by President Bush's efforts to bring the country together. When the world learned the extent of the Taliban's oppression of women—from the ban on girls going to school to the prohibition against women laughing out loud—President Bush spoke out forcefully. However, any hope for a more civil political climate was short-lived. Some leaders of the far right seized the moment for partisan purposes. Two days after the attacks, I watched in shock as the news networks replayed comments that Jerry Falwell made on television as Pat Robertson nodded his approval:

> The abortionists have got to bear some burden for this because God will not be mocked. And when we destroy forty million little innocent babies, we make God mad. I really believe that the pagans, and the abortionists, and the feminists, and the

gays and the lesbians who are actively trying to make that an alternative lifestyle, the ACLU, People for the American Way, all of them who have tried to secularize America, I point the finger in their face and say: You helped this happen.

Rather than building on the country's unity by limiting his focus to the threat to national security, Bush continued to push an aggressive and divisive radical right domestic agenda. This included nominating extreme conservative judges who will impose their personal views, especially their opposition to reproductive rights, from the bench.

Supreme Court nominations tend to attract more press attention, but lower federal court judges are highly important as well. District judges are the first line of defense against laws that intrude on personal privacy and restrict individual rights. Because the Supreme Court hears so few cases, federal appellate courts are the courts of last resort for most women. When a state enacts a restriction on abortion, for example, district courts are the first place it is challenged, and appellate courts are usually the final forum in which that challenge is heard. A NARAL study from 2003 showed that judges appointed by anti-choice presidents were far more likely to uphold restrictions on a woman's right to choose. *Casey's* standard permitting restrictions on abortion provided they did not impose an "undue burden" on women gave lower court judges wide latitude to interpret the law. Once confirmed, these judges enjoy lifetime appointments, so it was especially important to ensure that only qualified, unbiased jurists who believe the Constitution protects individual rights were approved by the Senate.

From the earliest days of his administration, Bush explicitly recruited judges with a goal of influencing social policy. He summarily dismissed the American Bar Association from its traditional

nonpartisan role in evaluating judicial nominations under both
Republican and Democratic administrations alike. He replaced
the ABA with a highly partisan, far-right group called the Federal-
ist Society. We fully expected Bush to nominate conservative
judges, but many of those he appointed were so active and extreme
in their hostility to the constitutional right of privacy and choice
that we knew immediately we had to stand in opposition. Charles
Pickering of Mississippi played a key role in passing the original
plank in the Republican party platform in 1976 calling for the
overturn of *Roe v. Wade*. William Pryor, another nominee, called
Roe "the worst abomination in the history of constitutional law."
James Leon Holmes, a former president of Arkansas Right to
Life, had said a woman's proper role was to "subordinate herself to
her husband." Priscilla Owen, a justice on the Texas Supreme
Court, once wrote an anti-choice opinion so extreme that Alberto
Gonzales—who served on the Court with Owen and later became
U.S. attorney general—called it "an unconscionable act of judicial
activism."

No woman standing before any of these or other of Bush's appointees could expect a fair and objective hearing. Democrats had
regained the majority in the Senate after Jim Jeffords—a moderate
pro-choice Republican from Vermont—left the party because he
could no longer countenance Bush's far-right agenda. However,
the fact that Democrats were now in the majority did not guarantee that we could defeat the nominations. Fewer than forty senators were fully pro-choice, far fewer than a governing majority.
Furthermore, senators are inherently inclined to give the president
broad discretion in making appointments, and some initially felt
that appointments to the lower federal courts were not sufficiently
important to justify a full-fledged battle.

Pro-choice Majority Leader Tom Daschle was a strong ally on

judicial nominations. Daschle recognized both the gravity of the Senate's constitutional responsibilities and the extent of the threat presented by the most extreme of Bush's nominees. Daschle's leadership of the Democratic caucus was artful. While he would later be accused of being an obstructionist, the reality was that Democrats concentrated their opposition on only a fraction of Bush's extreme nominees.

We also found a strong and indispensable ally in an unlikely place: Harry Reid of Nevada, then the Senate Democratic whip. Reid opposes abortion for religious reasons, but unlike so many other anti-choice legislators, he is strongly committed to policies like family planning and sex education. He also understood the radical right's long-term strategy to use the courts to undermine women's rights and other areas of social progress. Behind Reid's gentle and humble demeanor lay an iron-willed determination and superb tactical skills. Reid agreed that many of the Bush nominees were far out of the mainstream on a range of issues, including civil rights. When I spoke with him, he outlined our political challenge clearly.

"As you know, there is a range of views in our caucus on choice, including my own, and we only have a two-seat majority. We can't assume that we'll hold the votes of every Democrat. But if we can present this matter in a larger context, if we can show how these nominees are part of a larger strategy that is at odds with our party's core values, we can present a more united front. It's especially important that you persuade the Democrats on the Judiciary Committee. We'll need every one of their votes to block nominations in committee. If committee members are split and the nominations reach the floor, it will be almost impossible to hold the caucus together."

As we did when Robert Bork was nominated in 1987, several

groups—including pro-choice, women's-rights, labor, and civil-rights organizations—coalesced to oppose Bush's most extreme nominees. In addition to regular strategy sessions with Daschle and Reid, the coalition lobbied members of the Judiciary Committee to seek their support in opposing the most extreme of Bush's nominees.

One such nominee was Charles Pickering of Mississippi. When I reviewed NARAL's research on Pickering's record it was clear that his nomination was the one on which we should make our first stand. He had been an ardent opponent of a woman's right to choose. It strained credulity to believe that he could now rule objectively on issues affecting women whose lives and health would depend on his decisions. In the end it was the overwhelming concern about his views on civil rights that derailed his nomination. Pickering's record was simply indefensible, and the Judiciary Committee defeated his nomination by a one-vote margin.

In the ensuing months, the coalition mounted determined opposition to a limited number of the most extreme nominees, succeeding in blocking each one. President Bush denounced those who opposed the nominees as "obstructionist," as though the Senate's only constitutional purpose was to march in lockstep and give unthinking approval to whomever he chose. In reality, the vast majority of Bush's nominees were confirmed, including many with demonstrably anti-choice records. NARAL opposed only the most extreme. Despite the narrow division in the Senate and the fact that he had been elected with a minority of the popular vote—Bush never showed any willingness to modify his approach or to match his uplifting rhetoric after 9/11. He was determined to use the courts to promote his far-right policy goals. The nominations were a political concession to his right-wing base. Bush was willing to send them to the Senate even if he knew they would lose.

These early nomination battles were a warning of the compelling importance of the upcoming 2002 midterm elections. Pro-choice leadership in the Senate was the only bulwark against Bush's efforts to scuttle the right to choose. If Democrats lost a single seat, anti-choice senators would recapture leadership of the Senate. Consequently, from the earliest days of the Bush administration, the 2002 Senate campaigns were our highest political priority. Several pro-choice senators faced difficult reelection efforts, including Jean Carnahan of Missouri, who was running to retain the seat once occupied by John Ashcroft. Georgia's Senator Max Cleland, who lost three limbs while serving in Vietnam but whom I have never seen without his famously beaming smile, was also pro-choice, a position that was often controversial in the South. "But then," he once remarked to me without a trace of complaint in his voice, "when's life ever been easy?" If anyone would know, he would.

NARAL also believed we had an opportunity to recapture two anti-choice seats in the Senate. In New Hampshire, popular pro-choice governor Jeanne Shaheen was running against anti-choice representative John Sununu for the seat once held by Senator Bob Smith, one of the most vocal anti-choice politicians in Washington. In Colorado, a pro-choice candidate named Tom Strickland was running a competitive campaign against anti-choice Republican senator Wayne Allard.

Each of the races was important, and I campaigned actively for every candidate, but there was one with whom I had a strong personal connection. Senator Paul Wellstone, an eloquent and tireless progressive leader, was standing for reelection in Minnesota. He first achieved fame when, as an unknown college professor in 1990, he ran a heartfelt grassroots campaign filled with wit and verve. He defeated an entrenched Republican incumbent. Regardless of controversy or political risk, Wellstone never wavered in his dedication to progressive values, including his unrelenting support for women's rights.

His campaign in 2002 was closely contested, but I was confident Wellstone would prevail. He possessed qualities that even the most sensitive polls do not always register. Paul's heart was far larger than his 5'5" frame. His ability to empathize with others, to walk in their shoes, was limitless, and I had experienced it personally. I often met Paul and his wife, Sheila, during walks around our Capitol Hill neighborhood. He never failed to ask about my life or to stop and talk about whatever business was before the Senate. After Tasha's accident, Paul was one of the first friends to call and offer support. Not long afterward, I saw Sheila and Paul. When he asked how Tasha was, I stood there and wept. Paul put his arms around me without saying a word. He was a small man but a strong hugger. I was confident he would continue to connect with voters just as he had connected with me and so many others.

Two weeks before Election Day, a mutual friend called.

"There's been a terrible accident. Paul and Sheila and their daughter were killed in a plane crash."

I felt like a bullet went through my heart. This tragedy cannot be happening, I thought. It was just too painful to bear. Between Tasha's accident, Fred's illness, my father's death, 9/11, and now Paul's accident, it seemed as though I was experiencing a season of heartaches. Paul was an icon to those of us who were privileged to know and be touched by him.

In addition to the grief, NARAL had to confront practical considerations. Without Paul on the ballot, his Senate seat would be at greater risk. As difficult as it was, Paul's friends had to do precisely what he would have demanded, carry on the fight—and do so quickly. When former vice president Walter Mondale agreed to run in Paul's place, I called Mondale's son and closest political advisor, Ted, to offer our support.

In Minnesota and the other battleground states, we worked to focus attention on Bush's anti-choice record and the threat that a Senate dominated by anti-choice leadership would pose to women, but 9/11 and national security eclipsed every other issue. The White House showed no shame in exploiting the 9/11 tragedy for political purposes, even running advertisements in Georgia questioning Cleland's patriotism. When Bush stood at the podium of the House of Representatives after that dark September morning less than a handful of months before, little did we think that his words, "You are either with us or against us," meant the upcoming midterms as well. On Election Day, there were glimmers of hope—Ted Mondale called to say turnout in Democratic precincts in Minnesota was high, and polls showed both Shaheen and Strickland in very tight races—but by evening, all was lost. Cleland was defeated, then Carnahan, Shaheen, and Strickland. In the most devastating blow, Mondale lost and Wellstone's seat fell to anti-choice hands. We lost every single campaign. It was one of the most devastating defeats in all my years as a political activist.

There were many reasons Democrats lost. Bush was able to nationalize the election by casting Democrats as weak on national security. The White House—led by the personal campaigning of the president—exploited 9/11 for political gain. Pro-choice voters cast their ballots on the basis of national security, not threats to the right to choose, and many pro-choice Democrats allowed themselves to be stigmatized as soft on defense. Some, like Cleland, waited too long before responding to Republican attacks, a fateful if understandable mistake. In politics, an opponent's attacks sometimes seem so absurd and shameful that it is difficult to accept that they might be believed. Moreover, the efforts of

NARAL and other progressive and pro-choice groups could have been better coordinated. We learned afterward, for example, that households in swing states commonly received multiple direct mail pieces from different groups on the same day. Voters were bombarded with advertising from every political angle. They were overwhelmed, and they simply began to ignore the flood of messages they were receiving.

Whatever the cause, the devastating fact was clear. The Senate, the only elected institution of national government that posed any defense against the anti-choice agenda, had fallen. Bush and his allies once more had the White House and both chambers of Congress under their control. And this time there was no doubt as to how far they were willing to go to restrict a woman's right to choose. From the moment of their victory, I knew the abortion ban that Clinton had vetoed was a fait accompli.

CHAPTER TWENTY-SIX

A S THE SENATE DEBATED THE ABORTION BAN OF 2003—THE latest attempt to resurrect the assault on choice—the discussion alternated between the bizarre and the insulting. Certain senators stood on the floor of the chamber railing against providers and exploiting diagrams of phantom abortion procedures as though they were medical professors. They discussed women's reproductive anatomy in intimate detail. Women themselves—many of whose pregnancies had gone tragically awry, whose health was at risk, who had actually undergone the procedures that were being condemned—were nowhere to be seen. It was as though women were disembodied objects reduced solely to our mechanical reproductive function rather than full human beings with lives, rights, and responsibilities.

I watched the debate with a mixture of frustration and determination. We knew the bill would pass. From a minority position in the Senate, our only hope for blocking it would have been a filibuster, a tactic requiring forty votes, and we simply could not muster that many votes on this issue. Pro-choice senators like Tom Daschle, Pat Leahy, and Arlen Specter had broken with us during the debacle over the issue in the 1990s, and it was highly unlikely that any of them would reverse their positions this time. My experience as an activist and lobbyist had taught me that politicians are seriously disinclined to change their votes, especially on a controversial issue.

While it was clear the abortion ban was unstoppable, we were determined to make a strong stand against it. As our opponents engaged in an inflammatory, one-sided public spectacle, NARAL could not silently sit by without offering a counter-balancing voice defining what was truly at stake. Moreover, we felt a tenable argument could be made to pro-choice senators who had previously supported the ban. Since the Senate's last vote, the Supreme Court had ruled in *Steinberg* that bans on abortion were unconstitutional unless they recognized the paramount importance of protecting women's health. The new bill, which contained no health exception at all, specifically and openly thumbed its nose at the Supreme Court, saying *Steinberg* was based on inaccurate information. The bill's authors did not seriously intend to enact a law that could be upheld by the courts. They wanted to inflame the debate, mobilize their grassroots base, and create another vehicle that the increasingly hostile judiciary could use to undermine or overrule *Roe v. Wade*. If they succeeded, the law would be the first-ever federal criminal ban on abortion; indeed, the first-ever federal ban on any medical procedure.

I made this case to Specter, taking care to acknowledge the difficulty of his position.

"I understand how hard it is to change positions, especially on an issue that is so controversial. But this bill is virtually identical to the state law the Court overturned in *Steinberg*. I believe you can make a strong case to your constituents that the bill is unconstitutional under precedent set since the last time you voted. Protecting women's health is very important, Senator, and this ban would set a devastating precedent that I hope you'll reconsider."

Specter was immovable, as were Daschle and Leahy. The bill was certain to pass, and all that was left was to make the most compelling case we could. Senator Barbara Boxer of California led the fight against the bill, and her statement on the Senate floor was extraordinary. Senators were "playing doctor," she said, noting that medical experts had repeatedly said "partial-birth abortion" was not a medical term. Doctors did not know exactly what it meant, so the only way they could be sure to avoid prosecution was not to perform any abortions at all. Boxer shared women's stories. She urged her colleagues not to imperil women's lives or health for political reasons. However, proponents of the ban were immune to opposing arguments. Predictably, the House passed the ban easily, and so did the Senate. It was delivered to President Bush, who was waiting eagerly to sign it.

On the day of the signing ceremony, I read the president's statement and felt the stinging condemnation of women that was implicit in his words. "For years," he began, "a terrible form of violence has been directed against children who are inches from birth, while the law looked the other way." This, I thought, is George W. Bush's view of Coreen Costello. In his mind, a woman he never met "directed a terrible form of violence" against a fetus she longed above all else to bring into the world.

When I finished reading Bush's statement, I knew that nothing I could say about the president could possibly be more revealing than his own words. That was precisely the statement we issued. "Today, we saw the real George Bush. If we could afford to, we would put that speech on television every day from now until the election." In a way, I was relieved that Bush had revealed his true beliefs so clearly that no reasonable person could say he was not intent on dismantling a woman's right to choose. We began airing a new television advertisement that showed the inside of a doctor's office while an unseen politician knocked on the door. The announcer warned that the government was now invading the doctor-patient relationship. President Bush had signed the first federal abortion ban in the nation's history.

When I watched the television news that night, the pictures of the signing ceremony were even more offensive than Bush's statement. As he signed the bill, Bush was surrounded by the most extreme anti-choice leaders in Congress—Rick Santorum, Tom DeLay, Henry Hyde, and others. They were smiling, gleeful, almost scornful. By the standards of their own rhetoric about abortion, I would have thought their demeanor would at least be sober. Instead, it was celebratory. Every last one of them was a man. As the president signed a law that threatened the health of thousands of women, one of the most image-conscious White Houses of modern times did not even have the common sense to include a token woman in the picture.

That night, I considered calling Coreen to tell her I was thinking about her, but decided not to. I did not want to intrude or make her feel like a pawn in a political game. I took some solace in knowing that she had been able to have another child because the procedure that best protected her health and fertility was available when she needed it.

The 2002 elections and their aftermath, especially the abortion ban, unleashed several political forces. On the one hand, even though the Republicans won the election solely on the issue of national security, it was clear that the Bush administration was determined to use its power to aggressively pursue legislation that would restrict women's access to reproductive-health services, including abortion. At the same time, as we predicted, the disturbing images of Bush signing the abortion ban surrounded by men made the anti-choice threat devastatingly and disturbingly real. From across the country, NARAL heard from pro-choice activists that they were deeply concerned and highly motivated. It was important that pro-choice Americans send an unmistakable message not only that we would oppose policies that endangered women's health and rights, but also that support for reproductive rights was broad, deep, and diverse. Pro-choice activists were also eager for a vehicle around which to organize and express their passion. It was time for an extraordinary step.

In early 2003, after a meeting of the pro-choice coalition, I pulled aside a colleague and friend, Eleanor Smeal of the Feminist Majority Foundation.

"Ellie," I said, "I think it's time for a march."

"I agree," she replied. "I'm hearing from all over the country that people want to *do* something. They don't want to just give money and write e-mails to their members of Congress. They want to act."

Both Ellie and I knew immediately the challenge such an event would face: The last pro-choice march, in 1992, had drawn 700,000 activists. It would be difficult to exceed that number this time, but it would be imperative that we do so. As with previous marches, if this one fell below our past marks, we would provoke stories speculating that the pro-choice movement was losing support or that the issue was no longer compelling. Another march could only succeed if it attracted a historic, almost unimaginable, number: one million people.

When I returned to the office, I made the case to NARAL's team.

"You know my views about marches," I said. "They are not to be undertaken lightly. They involve intense work. They're expensive. But it's time. We need to demonstrate that this country is pro-choice. This march will be a vehicle through which we can harness the energy of our activists and mobilize them. People need to see that they have the power to change the course the country is on, and a march could inspire them."

From my own memories of participating in historic marches,

such as the 1963 March on Washington and the anti-war demonstrations of the late 1960s and early 1970s, I also knew the power of the event could extend far beyond either the physical confines of the national mall or the day itself. For me, these marches were transforming experiences. After hearing Dr. King's stirring speech in 1963, I returned home even more committed to the cause of civil rights. Another march would be an opportunity to transform pro-choice individuals into pro-choice activists—and with the 2004 presidential election on the horizon, there was no better time to galvanize our movement.

The pro-choice coalition agreed. Unlike past marches, which were called unilaterally by the National Organization for Women, this event would be a true cooperative effort. This march would have to be the most diverse we had ever organized, reflecting the full breadth of concerns and priorities within our movement. Privately, we agreed not to publicize the goal of one million marchers; if we had, we would have provoked a constant stream of distracting headlines that measured our progress mathematically rather than focusing attention on the threats to a woman's right to choose.

Our projections showed that, in order to reach one million, one third of the marchers would have to be young women. These women, who had grown up with *Roe v. Wade* in force, and many of whom therefore took their rights for granted, presented both an urgent need and a difficult challenge. They were the future of our movement, and it was important to both cultivate the next generation of pro-choice leaders and demonstrate that young women cared deeply about the right to choose. Turnout from college campuses, we knew, would be vital, so our first task was to choose a date when students would be able to attend. The coalition scrutinized the spring break schedules of major universities along the eastern seaboard and as far west as Chicago—the section of the country within driving distance of Washington and therefore, we felt, the likeliest to produce significant numbers of marchers. After matching the schedules and consulting with the extensive bureaucracy of permitting offices in Washington, D.C., we settled on a date: April 25, 2004—barely a year away.

Each coalition group agreed to recruit 250,000 marchers. In order to ensure we did not simply target the same individuals, we began a complicated process of sharing lists and dividing the country into regions.

In addition to each organization's efforts to recruit our own marchers, we also sought to broaden and diversify the leadership of the march. The pro-choice movement has been criticized for being dominated by white women and for not fully reflecting the needs of women of color, a concern that was raised again as planning for the march took shape. Groups like the Black Women's Health Initiative were concerned that they had not been part of the process from the beginning, and focusing exclusively on the right to choose, they felt, was a narrow message that did not fully address the concerns of women of color.

I was concerned that the message of the march not be diluted so much that, in trying to say everything to everyone, it failed to communicate its message coherently. Massive protests against the World Bank and International Monetary Fund in the late 1990s had, I felt, fallen into exactly that trap. They had produced enormous numbers of marchers because they sought to embody every conceivable cause, but in doing so, they lost focus and failed to convey a clear message. Still, it was vital that women-of-color leaders bring substantial direction to the march and that we broaden the base of the pro-choice movement to include, and inspire, women of color. Moreover, we did want to communicate a broader message than simply the legality of abortion. Our belief was that a

woman's right to control her reproductive destiny was central to
her equality, health, and life. We settled on a theme broad enough
to welcome a diverse array of activists but specific enough to communicate a clear message. We called the event the "March for
Women's Lives." In the end, more than one thousand organizations, including many representing the needs of women of color,
cosponsored the march.

The preparations for the march were the most intense I had
ever undertaken, and they were a reminder that my job was completely all-consuming. I had happily devoted myself to NARAL
for nearly twenty years, but the circumstances of both my life and
my work had changed. Looking ahead, the most important and enduring challenge we faced was electing a pro-choice president in
2004; if Bush remained in office, a Supreme Court nomination
that might result in *Roe v. Wade* being overruled would be a near-
certainty. I also felt that my family—especially Fred and Tasha—
needed me more than ever. I could not give those demands the
attention they needed while still absorbed by the day-to-day—
often minute-to-minute—challenge of running a large national
organization. My family had supported the tireless effort I had put
into my work for all these years, and now it was their turn to be my
foremost priority. The March for Women's Lives, I announced,
would mark both the pinnacle and the conclusion of my time as
president of NARAL Pro-Choice America. It was time to focus
exclusively on the tasks that mattered most—electing a pro-
choice president and caring for my family.

The decision was bittersweet, but there was little time to reflect
on it. I spent the next several months traveling the country to recruit marchers. From a massive gathering of four thousand Jewish
women in Minneapolis to a private meeting of pro-choice activists
in Dagmar Dolby's living room in San Francisco, the energy was pal-

pable. My trips to college campuses were especially inspiring. When I visited the University of North Carolina, what was billed as a gathering of the campus pro-choice organization had blossomed into a massive rally. T-shirts, posters, and hats advertising the march were everywhere. When I was invited to speak at a "Master's Tea" at Yale—a routine gathering that normally attracts twenty or thirty students—dozens more attended. I participated in a bus tour of pro-choice leaders that traveled to campuses in several states.

NARAL's work was only one element of a broad nationwide effort. As we mobilized our activists, the other major sponsoring organizations—Planned Parenthood Federation of America, the Feminist Majority Foundation, the National Organization for Women, the Black Women's Health Initiative, the Latina Institute for Reproductive Health, and the American Civil Liberties Union—conducted equally aggressive efforts. We could sense mounting excitement among our grassroots base, but we did not depend on our instincts alone. NARAL and the other sponsoring groups also ran a massive and professionalized organizing campaign, carefully monitoring turnout in strategically targeted markets and shifting resources to those where we seemed to need more support. Every time we initiated contact with a potential marcher, we captured as much information as we could, including telephone numbers and addresses. We compiled an extensive list of activists who had committed to attend the march and then followed up with them repeatedly to confirm their participation and help with travel arrangements.

One of the most important catalysts for turnout at the march came from an unlikely source, John Ashcroft. Almost immediately after President Bush signed the abortion ban, its enforcement was enjoined as a number of pro-choice organizations challenged the law in federal court. As the case was tried, the arrogance of the administration's response was breathtaking. The Justice Department demanded that hospitals turn over the private medical records of women who had undergone abortions covered by the ban. To defend this request, the department offered the stunning assertion that women had no reasonable expectation that their medical records would be kept private. The hypocrisy of this demand was heightened by the fact that the White House was simultaneously resisting reporters' requests for President Bush's personnel file from his service in the National Guard, which contained the president's medical records. Those, the White House insisted, were private. Eventually, growing pressure forced them to disclose large portions of the file.

The public outcry against this invasion of women's privacy was immediate. Recruitment for the march, which was already brisk, escalated quickly. It was difficult to know whether we would hit our goal of one million marchers, but clues began to suggest that we might. The number of buses chartered to carry marchers into the city was at least double what it had been in any previous march. Entire trains were sold out along the eastern seaboard.

As we focused on mobilizing marchers nationwide, I was also working to persuade one particular pro-choice American to attend, Senator John Kerry, who by early 2004 had secured the Democratic presidential nomination. Bill Clinton's appearance at the 1992 march had been a pivotal statement that he was pro-choice and that he intended to make his commitment to women's fundamental rights an important message of his campaign. Kerry's record was unequivocally pro-choice, but he was neither promoting that fact nor calling voters' attention to President Bush's anti-choice record to the degree I felt was necessary to fuel the gender gap in the election. I went to visit one of his top campaign operatives, Steve Elmendorf.

"The senator's attendance at the march would be a powerful message to the women of this country and to people who are concerned about individual rights," I said. "He could march with his two daughters. When President Clinton joined our march in 1992, it sent an incredibly important message to women. He made a choice to be a part of the march, and his attendance made it clear that women's fundamental rights mattered to him. This can be a similar moment for Senator Kerry. A woman's right to choose is one of his most powerful political advantages, and the history of the last decade shows that the campaign must take full advantage of it. Most Americans agree with Senator Kerry's position on reproductive rights, but they have to see the extent of his commitment if we expect them to vote their pro-choice beliefs."

Elmendorf resisted the idea. He cited scheduling concerns, but I also heard that the campaign was concerned about something else: Kerry's first foray into public life had been as a leader of antiwar marches, and his campaign was concerned about resurrecting that image. I thought the concern was exactly wrong. Kerry's antiwar activism was an essential part of who he was, and even those who disagreed with his position admired his courage and integrity. Kerry needed to present himself as who he was, not who pollsters and image-makers believed the public wanted to see.

"Steve," I said as our meeting concluded, "I want you to know that while I cannot say for certain how many people are going to be at this march, the momentum and intensity are beyond anything I have ever seen. This is going to be a historic day. By attending, John Kerry would be sending a very important message to women and pro-choice people across the country that he can be counted on to stand with them against those who want to take away our rights."

Kerry decided against participating in the march, instead attending a press conference at which NARAL and Planned Parent-hood endorsed him. As the weekend of the march approached, Washington was absolutely flooded with enormous numbers of marchers, and their diversity was extraordinary.

The morning of April 25, I walked out of my apartment and saw streams of marchers headed toward the national mall several hours in advance of the event. As I drove down Massachusetts Avenue toward a kickoff breakfast, I looked out the window and saw two elderly women crossing the street holding handmade signs. SUPPORT A WOMAN'S RIGHT TO CHOOSE, one sign said. The other read, PRO-CHOICE, NOT PRO-ABORTION. I looked at their faces and wondered whether they or women they knew had endured the humiliation and danger of pre-*Roe* abortions, as I had. Another group crossing the same street were young parents and children. A few blocks down, I saw a crowd of marchers dressed in punk-rock gear, their hair spiked and brightly colored. The diversity of marchers was the first concrete sign that the day would succeed beyond our most ambitious expectations.

"I just have a good feeling," I said to our staff when I arrived at the kickoff breakfast. The march was to begin at the Washington Monument, pass the White House, and conclude at the Capitol, where an all-day rally complete with music, celebrities, and speak-ers would commence. I climbed up on the stage at the monument to take in the scene. The mall was an absolute sea of humanity. I looked back toward the Lincoln Memorial and tried to locate in my memory the spot on which I had stood in 1963, more than forty years earlier. I wondered how many of the young people there would return home reborn as activists, their lives having been transformed far beyond the inspiration of that single day. Looking out, and looking back, was the first opportunity I had in months to reflect on the fact that my service at NARAL was drawing to a close. I could not imagine a more fitting moment. I turned to Ellie Smeal.

"This is bigger than we even dared to hope it would be."

As we gathered at the point where the march would begin, I looked around and saw some of the most prominent women in the nation. Madeleine Albright stood on one side of me. Senator Barbara Boxer was close by, as was Gloria Steinem. My colleagues in the leadership of the pro-choice movement were all there. I was especially happy to know that behind us, in that ocean of marchers, were the people who mattered most to me. For this day, the conclusion and capstone of my career at NARAL, my entire family was there—Fred, our daughters, our grandchildren, and my sister. We linked arms, put one foot forward and, taking our place in a long and unbroken chain of history, marched.

Later in the day, I was in the holding area behind the main stage, preparing to give my brief speech, when a colleague ran up breathlessly.

"We've looked at aerial photographs. We've done a grid count. We've compared it against head counts we're collecting on the ground. We have a crowd estimate: 1.15 million!"

It was exhilarating to hear the news, but in our hearts, from all we had seen and felt that day, we already knew. It was one of the largest marches in the history of the country and a seminal moment in the history of the pro-choice movement. For each marcher physically there, we knew there were several more who supported our ideals but were unable to attend. From this day forward, it would be difficult to say either that Americans did not believe in the right to choose or that they did not care enough to stand up for their beliefs.

I held a prepared speech in my hands, but I suddenly wondered what I could possibly say that could match the inspiration of the sheer scale of the turnout. As I contemplated what to say when I addressed the march, someone mentioned that the program was running behind schedule and that Carole King, the singer who had performed at so many historic marches, was being cut. She understood completely, but I objected. I found the stage manager.

"Carole's coming on stage with me."

"Kate, there isn't time."

"Listen," I said, good-natured but determined, "this is the last speech I'm giving as head of this organization. Carole's coming with me."

As I heard my name announced, I realized the answer to my question: There was nothing I could say that was more inspiring than what the marchers had themselves achieved. What I really wanted was to give everyone in the crowd, all 1.15 million of them, a warm embrace. I turned to Anastasia, eight years old and our only granddaughter. As I looked at her, I saw the reason I was marching, the reason for twenty years at NARAL, the reason for a lifetime of activism: her freedom, her future, her life.

"This is our moment," I said, and grabbed her hand. With my other hand, I reached for Carole, and the three of us ascended the stage together. I took the microphone and said the only words that mattered to me, the only ones that could begin to convey my feelings for these Americans who had taken a personal and decisive stand for their values and beliefs.

"I love you all!"

I handed the microphone to Carole, and she began to sing—a cappella, alone at first, then quickly joined by the unified voices of 1.15 million people—"I Feel the Earth Move," her signature anthem of protest, one I had heard on this same spot, by this same singer, as a young marcher before. I stood on the stage and sang, swaying to the music with one arm wrapped around Anastasia and the other embracing Carole.

Tomorrow would bring new threats to a woman's right to choose, I knew. But I held this moment in my heart.

Today, I thought, we made the earth move.

AFTERWORD

IT HAS BEEN A JOURNEY OF MORE THAN THIRTY-SIX YEARS since I sat in a hospital conference room, interrogated by men who held my fate, my family, and my choice in their hands. After all these years, I can still feel the humiliation, the shame, and the anger as though those doctors were sitting in front of me now, demanding to know whether I was capable of dressing my children in the morning and being intimate with my husband at night. I have dedicated the years since to ensuring that no woman ever had to endure my pain—or the even greater horrors of back-alley abortion that so many other women of my generation were forced to experience.

I have traveled a great distance since those wrenching days in 1969, and America has as well. The choice denied me, that the hospital review board had the power to make, has now been recognized as every woman's constitutional right. The majority of Americans believe it should remain so.

Sadly, dark forces have gathered upon the political horizons. In the aftermath of the 2004 elections, opponents of legal abortion control the White House and Congress, and the Supreme Court may soon follow. This confluence of political events is unprecedented. The anti-choice movement's stars are aligned, and their goal achievable: bending the arc of history into a circle so that for many women the journey will return them back to that interrogation room, or the back alley, or the prospect of forced childbearing. The possibility of a return to the past is so unfathomable for most people, so distant, that we are reluctant to believe it. For millions of women across the country, that dark future is now.

In thirty states, women seeking abortions are legally required to sit through misleading, state-mandated lectures or tolerate waiting periods that bear a sinister kinship to the days of the hospital review board. Becky Bell died of an illegal abortion years after *Roe v. Wade* banished the back alley to a terrible chapter in America's past—or so we thought. Restrictions on abortion mount as more and more women's health and lives are endangered. The policies of the right wing are restricting sex education and contraception and, as a result, making abortion more necessary even as they make it less safe and available. The Supreme Court is already poised to eviscerate, and perhaps overturn, *Roe v. Wade*. Those who once took false comfort in the notion that the Supreme Court would forever protect the right to choose are now confronting the reality that President Bush has already placed two justices on the Court, and may have the opportunity to name more. The import of these appointments is clear: Although he will serve in office for only eight years, President Bush may succeed in restricting personal freedoms for generations.

Americans stand at the crossroads. We can surrender to the false sense of inevitability that surrounds the anti-choice grip on American politics and policy and remain silent as they complete the historical circle. Or, we can break this cycle and set America's story on a course of our own choosing; a path that reflects our values, that respects women, cherishes children, and places real meaning and real commitment behind those values advanced by *Roe v. Wade*.

In this effort, we face the determined opposition of right-wing ideologues and the institutions of government they control. In the aftermath of the 2004 elections, we face yet another challenge. Defeatism! It is a state of mind that began to surface even before the first ballot was cast.

After I retired from NARAL, the Democratic National Committee asked me to head an effort called "Save the Court"—a national campaign to call attention to the threat Bush's reelection would pose to the Supreme Court on a variety of important social and constitutional issues, including a woman's right to choose. I was gratified to be able to spend time on precisely what I had decided would be my priority in 2004—electing a pro-choice president. I saw the Save the Court initiative as a hopeful sign that Senator John Kerry's campaign and the Democratic Party understood the potential political power of a woman's right to choose.

Tragically, it was soon clear that the Kerry campaign did not see that potential. On the contrary, they seemed determined to treat a woman's right to choose as a liability, not an opportunity. On one occasion, Democratic Party organizers canceled my appearance to speak at a pro-Kerry rally in Madison, Wisconsin, a progressive college town. It was a gold mine of potential young activists, and the capital of a state that had elected a pro-choice governor and two pro-choice senators. The organizers felt my appearance as a pro-choice activist might offend Catholic voters. The political decision to de-emphasize a woman's right to choose was emblematic of the central strategic error of the Kerry campaign. Their tortuous efforts to offend no one also risked inspiring no one.

Kerry embodied the strategy personally. I knew him to be fully pro-choice, and as a senator his record on reproductive rights was nearly unblemished. Yet when he was asked about the right to choose on the campaign trail he inevitably hunkered down and assumed an apologetic position. Eager to offer solicitous words for all those who disagreed with him—"I am personally opposed to abortion," he said at every turn—he neglected to inspire those who were on his side and who, it is important to add, constituted a clear majority of the electorate.

In the second presidential debate, when a member of the audience expressed the view that abortion was murder, Kerry's response was lame and defensive. "I can't take what is an article of faith for me," he said of his personal view that abortion was wrong, "and legislate it for someone who doesn't share that article of faith . . . but I can counsel people. I can talk reasonably about life and responsibility . . ." Pro-choice Americans needed to hear that he would be a strong and forceful defender of personal liberties. A John Kerry with the courage to state his convictions would have looked that voter in the eyes and said, "I respect your position, but I believe women should make decisions about pregnancy and childbearing, not the government. I respect and trust women. I value their lives, their health, and their privacy. I believe they can make better decisions for themselves and their families than politicians can. And I believe that when women have more choices, children have better lives. That's why I'm pro-choice!"

I tried repeatedly to urge this strategy on the Kerry campaign, but he was surrounded by advisors who were convinced, in defiance of all available data, that his support of a woman's right to choose was a liability to him. Throughout the campaign Kerry hesitated to state his pro-choice values fully, despite years of battletested experience—from Governors Florio and Wilder in 1989 to President Clinton in 1992 and 1996 to Al Gore's victory in the popular vote in 2000—showing that embracing one's pro-choice beliefs could be a positive and winning political issue. The strategy we had spent so many years proving to be advantageous was being discarded in favor of one that clearly would not succeed, and I felt frustrated that I could not seem to persuade the Kerry campaign. On Election Day, it was no surprise that exit polls showed Bush capturing 38 percent of the pro-choice vote.

I was equally concerned about the spasm of self-doubt that seized Democrats upon Kerry's loss. In the weeks and months after his defeat, some Democrats seemed bent upon accepting the demonstrably false claim that he had lost the election because of "values" issues, which became in many circles a code phrase for the right to choose. Kerry himself was asked on one occasion what lessons the Democratic Party could learn from his defeat, and his response was not that we had to do more to inspire our own base, nor that we had to improve our credibility on national security, but rather that we had to be more accommodating of anti-choice Democrats. Democrats' tent has always been large enough to accommodate people with a wide range of views; the question here was whether the party's leaders would stand firm in their fundamental values. At times, that seemed questionable. An anti-choice former congressman ran for chair of the Democratic National Committee with the endorsement of several prominent party leaders. National party leaders began recruiting anti-choice candidates to run for the Senate and even forcing pro-choice candidates from the field.

The reality, backed by exit polling, was that Bush won a relatively narrow victory *despite* his position on abortion, not because of it. A clear majority of voters said on Election Day that they were pro-choice and that abortion should remain legal. That issue had simply never been elevated to a position of importance, and—given Kerry's mixed messages—pro-choice voters could be forgiven if they cast their ballots on the basis of other issues on which the difference between the candidates seemed clearer. National security overwhelmed this election, as it had in 2002. All the data, including highly detailed and sophisticated exit polling, indicated that, if anything, Kerry's mistake was not speaking more forcefully about his pro-choice values.

Democrats did not make the mistake of publicly questioning their core values on any other issue—not Social Security, not economic policy, not the environment. On those, they held fast after the election. Women's rights seem to occupy a uniquely fragile place as the first repository of political blame and the easiest ballast to cast overboard. Nor is this a mistake the anti-choice movement has made in past elections their party has lost. They built their base of political power by steady persistence and adherence to their beliefs, not abandoning their values at the first sign of political difficulty. So must we.

Two generations have grown up since *Roe*; although they have lived with the reproductive rights we won, they were not shaped by the struggle to win them. They do not know what life was like for women like them in the years before *Roe*. The understanding and passion for the first principles of reproductive freedom are not embedded in their instincts. As a result, a sense of not just support for, but active *commitment to*, the core principles of reproductive freedom is thin and fragile, and therefore especially vulnerable to deceitful and dishonest campaigns of the kind the Bush administration and its allies have waged on issues like the abortion ban.

Restoring respect for those first principles—for the value we place on privacy and fundamental rights, our respect for women, our devotion to children and families—is the defining challenge of our time. We do not need to move to the right or reposition ourselves in the center; we need to articulate our values in a manner that reminds Americans that we *are* in the center. To succeed, we must meet our opponents on precisely the ground on which they

wish to debate: values. Therein lies the heart of the matter. For today we must challenge voters to choose between two visions rooted
in fundamentally different values.

The anti-choice vision says that abortion should be a crime,
and that childbearing should be a dictate of the state. It says that
the very resources—such as comprehensive sex education and access to contraception—that make abortion less necessary should
also be less available. It says that women who do not want to continue unwanted pregnancies should be forced to bear children
against their will, a circumstance so fraught with peril for all involved that thinking and compassionate people should shudder at
the thought. And this vision is capped by a cruel irony: Once a
woman does decide to bear a child, it is as though they believe society's interest terminates rather than begins. For if the policies
and priorities of the Bush administration are to be taken as a guide,
they are largely unconcerned about prenatal care; America's child
care crisis is not in the orbit of their interests; the shameful preva-
lence of childhood poverty and hunger and a lack of sufficient educational opportunity are not problems they are willing to invest
serious resources to solve; our scandalous rates of infant mortality
and low-birthweight babies are not, for them, serious issues worthy
of real solutions.

Our vision, the pro-choice vision, is different. It says childbearing should be a cherished choice made by women on the basis
of complete information and full options. A choice supported and
nurtured and valued, not just with rhetoric, but with resources. It
says that society will stand with a woman no matter what choice
she makes, whether it is the choice not to become pregnant, the
choice to bear a healthy child, or the choice to terminate a pregnancy. It says we will protect, *without apology*, the right of every
woman to obtain a safe and legal abortion. Our vision recognizes,

too, that abortion is not a choice any woman sets out to make; that every woman would prefer to avoid this choice if she can. We recognize that preventing unwanted pregnancies demands a real national commitment to reproductive health, one that encompasses policies to increase access to contraception and comprehensive sex education rooted in both responsibility and reality.

This is a compelling vision, but it also requires difficult choices. Americans need to grow up about sex! That we should need to do so at all is ironic: Our society is saturated with sex. We watch it on television, hear about it on the radio, and see it on billboards. As my old friend and colleague James Wagoner says, we use sex to sell everything from laptops to Levi's. Yet when it comes to preparing young people to live healthy and responsible lives in this society, we are frozen by our discomfort. The choices here are evident. As long as we treat sex as a secret taboo rather than a natural part of human life, people will engage in sexual behavior without the knowledge they need to act responsibly.

The standing assumption of public policy is that sex is only appropriate within marriage and for procreation. That is the basis of the more than $1 billion we have spent on abstinence-only sex education programs that are unproven and dangerous. It is why, according to a study published by the National Assembly on School Based Health Care, 77 percent of school-based health clinics are prohibited by state or local laws from providing contraception. It is why anti-choice politicians so persistently attack the federal family planning services for low-income women that, according to the Planned Parenthood Federation of America, prevent 1.3 million unintended pregnancies and more than 630,000 abortions each year.

This—sex only within marriage and for procreation—is the assumption. The reality is starkly different: 90 percent of Ameri-

cans are not virgins on their wedding nights.* This fact will surprise no one, at least not nine out of every ten of us. It is our refusal to acknowledge it—our ardent yet blind desire to believe that
our children, our friends, even ourselves, are all somehow crowded
into that one in ten—that is the problem. In Americans' personal
lives, our cultural lives, even our commercial lives, sex is pervasive. But in our political lives, our leaders profess to be a nation of
pious Louis Renaults in Rick's Bar in *Casablanca*, shocked, *shocked*
that anyone has sex before marriage. So why are we shocked to discover that we have the highest rates of unintended pregnancy,
HIV, and many other sexually transmitted diseases in the Western
developed world?

Is our discomfort with sex worth these costs? Surely not. Are we
willing to talk about issues that make us squeamish if the benefit is
fewer unintended pregnancies, fewer abortions, and lower rates of
disease? I hope so. I can be as old-fashioned as the next person—
often, my daughters have reminded me, more so. The flagrant dis-
plays of gratuitous sexuality that pervade our culture make me
uncomfortable. I dislike turning on the television and seeing people who scarcely know each other tumbling into bed. I find the use
of sexuality to sell products, especially when it involves teenagers,
profoundly offensive. But we must be realistic. Sending adoles-
cents raging with hormones into this culture without understanding human development and knowing how to prevent pregnancy
and sexually transmitted diseases is like handing them keys to a car
without seat belts or driver's education.

We need a strategy of aggressive prevention, one that makes
contraception widely available to both adults and young people; a

*R. T. Michael et al., *Sex in America: A Definitive Survey* (Boston: Little Brown &
Co., 1994).

policy that encourages young people to respect themselves and each other and not casually give themselves away, but one that also equips them to deal responsibly with the choices they make. Americans like to talk about responsibility. Not having sex outside a committed relationship is one responsible choice. It is the first choice I would urge on anyone who asked me for advice. But I would follow that advice with this: If you *do* have sex—and most people do—responsibility equally demands that you prevent unintended pregnancy and sexually transmitted disease. And if we expect people to be responsible, we must ensure the means of exercising responsibility—such as prescription contraceptives that are covered by insurance plans—are available.

With equal vigor, we must also support the choice to have a child. No woman should have to forgo prenatal visits because she cannot afford them. We need a national strategy for affordable, quality child care. Our country must invest heavily and thoughtfully in child health, nutrition, and learning from the very earliest ages, continuing through adolescence. This is as central to being pro-choice as access to safe and legal abortion or the prevention of unwanted pregnancy.

Nor can our concern for women and children stop at our own borders. Untold numbers of women around the world today die in horrific conditions because they do not have access to the reproductive health care they need. Their families live in wrenching poverty. Their children do not have adequate medical care. Our country must bear some responsibility for this tragedy, both because we have terminated the resources these women desperately need and because we have not made their plight the priority it should be. We cannot value the lives and rights of women around the world any less than we do our own.

In a world that is truly and comprehensively pro-choice, pregnancy will far more often be a choice. When women make it, their children will be healthier and more secure and given a far better chance to thrive. Women and families will be more economically secure. In those cases—less often, we hope, but still inevitable—when women need abortions, they will be able to obtain them in safety and dignity. And all these values are connected to another: An America that is genuinely and deeply pro-choice will be one that reaffirms its most basic democratic ideals—that the private lives of citizens are not the province of the state, that there are parts of our lives and our souls and beliefs that government may not touch, that we respect the individual as unique and autonomous and free. This is the essence of the question that has, for so many years, defined this issue for me: Who decides?

That pro-choice Americans firmly believe women, and not politicians, should decide does not mean we should gloss over the moral complexities of abortion. Women understand that a fetus, however one's personal convictions regard it, is a potential life that embodies something unique and special. Politicians, including pro-choice politicians rushing to portray themselves as moderate, seem recently to have proclaimed the moral complexities of abortion as though they had stumbled upon an original discovery. I am not aware of any woman who has ever contemplated pregnancy or abortion without innately understanding and respecting the value of potential life. It is embedded deep within us, spiritually for some, instinctively for all; we need no press release or political platitude to remind us.

There is no reason pro-choice Americans should be uncomfortable embracing the moral complexities involved in abortion; indeed, the fact that these choices are so complex is perhaps the most compelling reason that women, not politicians, should make them. However, neither should we embrace an overwrought or apologetic rhetoric that serves the interests of our opponents. We need no tutoring from anti-choice politicians on the moral value of potential life; the value we place on it is precisely why we are pro-choice. We need make no apology for our firm belief that women, and not politicians, should make decisions about child-bearing, and that abortion should be safe and legal for women who need it. We do not need to be either pro-abortion or apologetic for abortion. We do not need to portray women as Hamlets eternally wringing their hands and torn asunder by the difficult choices they face. We need only to respect the complexity of the choice and women's fundamental right, women's *human* right, to make it.

Thirty-six years ago, I was one woman, standing alone in a society that placed no value on my dignity, my freedom, my children, my choice. Deep within me, with the instinctive insight every woman has for the needs of her children, I knew it was wrong, morally wrong, to bring another child into my fragile family. I decided; and I acted; and the choice was mine, and no one else's to make, and I have never, not for a single moment, doubted the wisdom and rightness of my decision. I remember still the humiliation I had to endure to exercise it: sitting in an interrogation room before a panel of men; going to meet the man who had just deserted my family, clutching a permission slip that granted him as much control over my life as a parent over a child. I remember the horrors others endured: the women who climbed on kitchen tables in back alleys to be humiliated and degraded; women rendered infertile by operations with filthy instruments; women who succumbed to septic shock and died, leaving children motherless and husbands without wives and parents without daughters and young lives stripped of the infinite promise they held, all because politicians believed with a morally superior certainty that they knew best. And along with these consequences we must contemplate another: the true meaning, the real impact, of genuinely unwanted birth—what it means not just for parents, but for children, too.

If we do not take this threat seriously, our society will regress. Anyone who doubts how far the anti-choice movement will go need look no farther than their shameful interference in the Terri Schiavo case. Even so, the prospect of losing our right to privacy and choice seems so distant it is difficult for many to believe. Yet here we are, and here we have been; yet still so many refuse to recognize the danger. Perhaps the greatest challenge of being a pro-choice activist today is this: How does one avoid being accused of crying wolf when the wolves are so obviously and persistently and dangerously real? The only answer I know is to inform people of the facts and urge them to defend their rights. The arc of history is bending into a circle, and at this moment, there may already be a young woman, alone, afraid, enduring the humiliation and the horror.

What do we owe to that woman?

What do we owe to ourselves and our families?

What do we owe to the values we cherish?

The answer is clear: We owe it to her to ensure she is not alone—that we will stand with her—that we will value and defend her freedom as ardently as we would protect our own. We owe it to her not to act as though we are powerless; not to hand to our opponents a victory they have not won; not to allow the time it takes to attend a march or cast a vote or write a letter to a senator to be more important than her liberty and life.

America stands at the brink; but we have not yet crossed it. Our freedom belongs to us; it is our right, and it is our responsibility to protect it; and we have the power to do so. Decades ago, when *Roe* was not yet imagined and abortion was in so many places illegal, a small but passionate movement of Americans decided to transform the world. They did. Today the movement they have bequeathed to the next generation of pro-choice activists is large and powerful and vast; the freedom they left us is in jeopardy; and to save it, we need only activate, with a sense of personal responsibility and dire urgency, the movement they built.

I opened this story by invoking the words of President Kennedy, who spoke of freedom in its "hour of maximum danger." I close by quoting him more fully: "In the long history of the world, only a few generations have been granted the role of defending freedom in its hour of maximum danger. I do not shrink from this responsibility—I welcome it."

This is our moment. This is our responsibility. If we shun it, a dreadful society so many other women and I once knew will return. If we embrace it, another society—a very different society—a society that values women and supports children and protects the fundamental freedoms that animate what America is about—awaits.

ABOUT THE AUTHOR

KATE MICHELMAN is one of the most influential women leaders in America today: a seasoned lobbyist, a skilled political strategist, and former president of NARAL Pro-Choice America, the leading advocate for women's reproductive rights. For more than two decades, she has been one of the nation's most respected pro-choice activists, and has been instrumental in establishing a woman's right to choose as both a fundamental freedom and a prominent political issue.

During her tenure as NARAL's president, Michelman advised former president Bill Clinton, and her counsel has been sought by many of the world's most powerful leaders in America, from senators to cabinet secretaries. Named one of America's 200 Women Legends and Leaders by *Vanity Fair*, one of the Capitol's most powerful women by *Washingtonian* magazine, and one of the top grassroots lobbyists by *The Hill*, Michelman is quoted and interviewed frequently by the media, including *Newsweek, USA Today*, the *New York Times*, the *Washington Post*, and others. She has also appeared on CNN, CBS News, ABC News, NBC News, BBC News, and has been heard on NPR.

Prior to joining NARAL in 1985, she was executive director of

Planned Parenthood in Harrisburg, Pennsylvania, where she expanded the range of reproductive health services in the area. She also trained medical students and residents in child development as a clinical adjunct professor in the Department of Psychiatry at Pennsylvania State University School of Medicine.

Today, with reproductive rights threatened at every level of government and *Roe v. Wade* hanging by the barest of majorities on the Supreme Court, Michelman is guiding the pro-choice movement through what may be its most perilous period in a generation, continuing her mission to create a society that respects women's lives, health, and freedom.

Michelman is the mother of three grown daughters. She and her husband have five grandchildren.